PENGUIN BOOKS

The Penguin Guide to Children's TV and Video

With more than twenty years' experience in television, Jack Livesley has been a teacher, TV producer, script writer, program host, and co-author of several books on the media. He lives in Etobicoke, Ontario.

Frank Trotz has worked as manager of children's programming at both the CBC and TVO. A co-founder of the Factory Theatre Lab in Toronto, he now teaches in Etobicoke. Mr Trotz lives in Kleinburg, Ontario.

One of Canada's best-loved performers for children, Fred Penner is also host of the CBC's "Fred Penner's Place."

THE PENGUIN GUIDE TO CHILDREN'S TV AND VIDEO

WITH REVIEWS OF 400 TV SHOWS AND VIDEOS

Jack Livesley
Frank Trotz

PENGUIN BOOKS

PENGUIN BOOKS
Published by the Penguin Group
Penguin Books Canada Ltd, 10 Alcorn Avenue, Toronto,
Ontario, Canada M4V 3B2
Penguin Books Ltd, 27 Wrights Lane, London W8 5TZ,
England
Viking Penguin, a division of Penguin Books USA Inc.,
375 Hudson Street, New York, New York 10014, U.S.A.
Penguin Books Australia Ltd, Ringwood, Victoria,
Australia
Penguin Books (NZ) Ltd, 182-190 Wairau Road,
Auckland 10, New Zealand

Penguin Books Ltd, Registered Offices:
Harmondsworth, Middlesex, England

First published 1993

1 3 5 7 9 10 8 6 4 2

Printed and bound in Canada on acid free paper ∞

Canadian Cataloguing in Publication Data

Livesley, Jack
The Penguin guide to children's tv and video

Includes bibliographical references and index.
ISBN 0-14-015884-7

1. Television programs for children – Canada.
2. Videocassettes for children – Canada.
3. Television programs for children – Canada – Reviews.
4. Videocassettes for children – Canada – Reviews.
I. Trotz, Frank   II. Title.

PN1992.8.C46L58 1992   791.45'75'0971   C92-095660-2

For
Susan, Frank's wife,
and Nancy, Jack's partner,
for their loving honesty and support
and for our prime child reviewers
and critics
Sarah
Anna
Jennifer

Contents

Foreword

In 1953, when I was six years old, we didn't have a television set. As I recall, not many people did . . . apart from our neighbours. I've lost count of the number of hours I spent next door nestled on the floor at the left-front corner of an old upright piano, between the support leg and the sound board, but it was here that the miracle of television was first etched into my impressionable mind. There was no analysis of how these images got there, only the idea that they existed for my pleasure. I laughed, cried and shivered with anxiety. . . . My emotions were entirely vulnerable.

I have nothing but pleasant memories from that time. I made TV friends, followed the exploits of my heroes and saw some wonderfully talented performers at their best. My parents resisted the pressure for a while, but when my father got tired of carrying me home after my daily vigil was over, we bought our own television for me to fall asleep in front of.

When children first see the moving images on a TV screen in their home, they often feel that what they are watching has been created just for them. In 1953 I certainly was not aware that I was sharing this existence with so many. For all I knew, this was a private showing, and what I took away was definitely a personal and permanent perception of a magic realm.

Not in my wildest dreams did I ever imagine that I would one day become one of the people in that little box. I had no aspirations of becoming a performer, much less a "television personality" offering songs and stories and feelings to new generations of North American children. In fact, I didn't decide to perform until I was in my early twenties, and my decision then had nothing to do with my early television experiences. However, to this day I draw upon the memorable moments TV gave me in my childhood.

In 1984 I received a phone call from the CBC asking if I would like to host a new children's series. How on earth, I wondered at the time, would I find the creativity within myself to produce something that would be of value to anyone else? Unless I found an approach that made sense to me, all the writers and special effects in the world couldn't save me.

At this point I had made four record albums and gone on several national tours, so my perspective and philosophy on children's entertainment was clear. I believe children are the most vulnerable segment of society, human sponges who observe and imitate on the way to putting together their own perspectives on life. If I was to become part of this delicate process, I knew I had better think my role through carefully.

For me, the logical approach to developing a new program was to start by going back to my own childhood and retrieving what I felt was valuable from my own early experience. Everyone has a memory of a childhood corner where they felt absolutely comfortable, in the backyard by a favourite tree, curled up in a favourite chair, or like me, sitting under an old upright piano. That is the feeling I wanted the audience to have watching my program, and so discussions with writers and producers led to the creation of "Fred Penner's Place," now eight years old and seen across North America.

I am constantly thinking and rethinking what I do on the show, and why I do it. From the correspondence and other feedback I receive, I can monitor the direct effects of my work, and that is what helps keep me focused and productive. It is most important that producers of television for children and their families do not underestimate the potential of their work to communicate an experience, nor underestimate the intelligence of the audience. The potential to negatively manipulate the medium — and the audience — is high, especially in the commercial market. I like to point out to my children how cartoon characters are often used to sell a product, and that just because the characters are interesting visually, it doesn't mean that the product is good.

Forty years have passed since my introduction to the world of television in 1953, and now my wife and I are faced with many of the concerns of parents in the 1990s — including the issue of our children and "the box." The growth of television is awesome and the choice of programs vast. In many ways we are victims of technology, and trying to keep up with the momentum of change can put incredible pressure on us all. But we should never forget that we are guides for our children, and what we do affects who they are. There is no question that television is a powerful influence — positive as well as negative — so we must be conscientious when making our viewing choices.

The Penguin Guide to Children's TV and Video is a wonderful starting point for making these choices. It doesn't offer you absolute solutions to all your concerns, but as the authors say of television, "It's all in how you use it, what you do with it and the place you allow it to have in your own little constellation."

Fred Penner

Introduction

Of all the inventions that mark great eras in communications history, television must surely rank as the greatest since the written word. The telegraph, telephone, motion picture, radio, or for that matter the post office, each radically changed the way men live. Television is changing the way we think. It instantly transmits a replica of real events in lifelike motion, sound and color. It is pure electronic magic, something strange in the world, and to thoughtful people rather frightening. Not since man first learned to put his ideas down in writing, thousands of years ago, has any new technique for transmitting ideas had such an impact on civilization.

Irving Settel and William Laas,
A Pictorial History of Television

Television is the single most powerful communication tool in our world. It has profound effects on all of us, adults and children alike, and many of us worry about those effects.

The litany is familiar: the violence, commercials, sexual and racial stereotypes, the catering to the lowest common denominator. As well, television is difficult to control. You may have much to say about your child's diet or reading, and many of your child's comings and

goings, even in what sports and lessons and activities
he or she will be involved. But television is always
there, and children love to watch it. It's not a walk or a
drive away. It's there on Saturday morning when you
want to sleep in and your child is up at 6:30 because it's
not a school day. It's there when you arrive home from
work or from collecting your child at the sitter's or the
day-care centre. It's there when you want to have a few
quiet moments to yourself before the second workday
of dinner, baths, readings and bedtimes begins. It may
seem easy just to turn if off, but is it really so easy? To
control quantity and quality is a challenge.

We, however, believe that television and video can
be a positive force in our lives and the lives of our children. This book attempts to give parents some knowledge and therefore some control of this magical
medium. Our positive outlook has grown from our
combined sixty-plus years of working in education and
media, mainly in teaching and television, from our
talks with many parents and from our experiences
with our own children.

For every horror story we can cite a healthy one. A
young woman we know was a dyslexic child. By grade
three her problem was diagnosed, but she did not really learn to read until she was ten. From the age of six
she was a heavy television viewer and constantly
shared with her parents the stories and information
she gleaned from TV. Her parents were readers and she
was read to from a very early age. Weekends were family viewing and reading times. It was the stories on television and the films *Mary Poppins* and *The Sound of
Music,* which she saw many times, that eventually led
her to want to pick up a book and read it on her own.

The film version of *Mary Poppins* especially captivated her, and she was given a highly illustrated storybook version. Because she knew the lyrics of the
songs and many of the lines of the film, which she had
memorized, all of this came together. Then she started

to collect more books and to ask for them as gifts. Reading became a pleasure, not the chore it had once been. When she was in grade nine, *The Scarlet Pimpernel* was serialized for television. Fascinated with the story, she got a copy of the book from the school library.

This girl had a very good remedial program in her schools, but it was television and film that stimulated her interest in reading.

A second story concerns advertising on television. Two eight-year-olds had watched a commercial for "Go-Go, My Walking Pup" many times over. In this commercial, a cute little girl walks her mechanical Go-Go as if it were a real live pup. One day, as the two eight-year-olds were walking through the toy section of a large department store, they spotted Go-Go. They ran over, but slowed down in surprise as they approached it, because it bore very little resemblance to the toy they had seen in the advertisement. They took it down and tried it out, and both of them burst into riotous laughter, because this dog was absolutely ridiculous to them. Following the incident the children invented a game in which they parodied the ad, one playing the dog, the other the master. Perhaps satire and ridicule are the best defence against overt consumerism. So much for the power of commercials.

In an adult class on children's literature, which of course included children's television, a parent related an interesting story about television and her eight-year-old child. It's not necessarily a typical experience, but we pass it on because it illustrates our ideas about television and children, and what many parents no doubt hope would be the response of their children to television.

Her son loves TV and watches all types of programs: "Looney Tunes," "Ninja Turtles," and documentaries, "Reading Rainbow" and PBS's "Nova." His viewing has never been restricted. He gained amazing insight from watching the documentary series "The Civil War." Television has triggered an interest in topics his parents thought he was too young to understand. An episode on "Reading Rainbow" about volcanoes stimulated frequent visits to the library and an interest in books on volcanoes that lasted for a whole year. After a "Muppets" episode about flying pigs in space, he spent months investigating books about the sun. Even the "Ninja Turtles" led to his wanting to know all about turtles. So, back to the library.

This process had started with "Sesame Street" when he was three years old. There was a fishing scene, and he wanted to find out all about the ocean, so the family went to the library to borrow books about the ocean. The important thing is that the parents watched a lot of programs with him. They never suggested that he had to turn the TV off, but they didn't leave him to watch it the whole time. They also read to him. Books were always there.

Today he watches about twenty hours of television a week. Some of the programs he watches are not the greatest, but his parents feel that, like them, he needs "veg time." There's a lot of stress at school, and many children have lessons after school. This boy is at the top of his class in terms of reading ability and comprehension, and all his report cards show that he has a good attention span.

We heard another story from a teacher at a Toronto inner-city elementary school. In the early 1980s the movie *Helter Skelter,* a frank exploration of the Charles Manson murders, was shown on prime-time TV. The next day many of the kids in her grade four class were "on-the-ceiling crazy." It turned out that about fifteen of twenty-five children in this class had watched the movie, simply because their parents were watching it. This teacher remembers feeling angry at the parents' naïvety, which in this case she felt had robbed the children of an innocence that was their right. It was one of the first times that such a violent movie had been shown in prime time. The film presented ideas and images that were much too violent and explicit for children to comprehend, and as a result they were left overtired, overstimulated and terribly confused.

The effect this kind of program can have on children is very clear. The sad thing is that this form of child abuse continues, but usually only in the privacy of the home. While we believe in the positive nature of the medium of television, we also believe that there are programs that are totally inappropriate for children's viewing and that parents have a responsibility to control what television programs their children watch.

Television is a powerful medium, important in the lives of our children. We need to learn why and how to respect it for what it can do, for the riches it can bring into their lives. But there are good and bad television programs, just as there are good and bad books. You can most often choose to keep the books that you don't want in your children's lives out their reach. You cannot do this so easily with television. We think, however, that if you learn how to promote and use the good and valuable elements of television, then the bad will take care of itself — with some help from you, of course.

You should not feel guilty about watching television, especially when you watch it with our family and talk about it with your children. You should not feel guilty about letting your children watch, and by and large choose what they watch — with, and sometimes without, your guidance. If you are a discriminating and critical reader, there will be books and magazines in your home, and most likely your children will become discriminating readers too. If you become a discriminating and critical viewer of television, there's a very good chance your children will do the same. Good reading and writing habits begin at home. So do good viewing habits. So does good conversation and critical thinking. As parents and grandparents, we should read with, watch with and talk with our children.

In this book we focus on the positive qualities of television because there is so little written about children's television other than about its mind-rotting effects on kids. In our chapter on Saturday morning television, we guide you through cartoonland, giving you a map of choices identifying some good programs for your children. Our prime-time chapter deals with some of the best in Canadian television for young people, such as CBC's "Northwood," Filmworks' production of *Where the Spirit Lives* and great movies like *The Challengers*. In our review of daytime programming, we make no bones about what's good and what's not so good, and how relatively little there is for children during these hours.

We look at how television is used in schools, in the hope that we open up for you an area where television can come together with your children in a beneficial, educational way, and we present some questions that you can ask of educators if this is not happening. A survey of video stores offers some guidance about what to look for and where to look for it. Finally, a glimpse into the future will give you a sense of the potential of television.

As well as the programs we review in the early chapters, more than 400 reviews of videos and television series are provided for your consultation and guidance.

Through all of this, our hope is that you may come to share our sense of wonder about this medium, its beauty and power and its possibilities for the future. By becoming familiar with much that is good, we hope that you will be better equipped to select good programs to share with your children.

THE
PENGUIN GUIDE
TO CHILDREN'S TV
AND VIDEO

Chapter 1

BEWILDERING CHOICES

What I really do is tell stories. I manipulate.
Let's get it right out. You know, we talk about
the negatives and positives of television. The
medium of television is manipulation. . . .
The only problem is, who's doing the manip-
ulation, and to what end?

Clive Endersby, writer

What do you think about when you walk into the living room and see your child sitting in front of the TV set? Probably many things, most of which make you feel guilty. Most parents likely worry about the kid sitting alone in front of the set again, when it's time to make dinner, but they rationalize that an hour won't hurt. And it will give parents the well-deserved quiet time they need in the kitchen. Then another voice chides them about the kind of parents they are, letting television take care of their kids. Can't they do any better than that? Why aren't the kids sitting with some books, or playing a game, or working on some craft idea?

Many of you won't know how much television your child watches, even though you know you should. On the other hand, you really do have to make that dinner. And the TV has two neat half-hour slots, just right for the time you need. As in so many other situations during the day, you're torn between what you

need to do and the needs of your child. And so you walk
away, with your thoughts, and leave the kid alone in
front of the TV set for the next hour, and you get your
quiet time making dinner. But you pay. You still feel a
bit more of a failure as a parent because you're letting
your kid sit alone in front of that set.

You decide to do some reading to find out whether
you are doing the right thing with TV or whether, if
you continue on the way you are, your child will
become a couch potato with severely limited reading
ability. Your reading confirms all your worst fears
about your child and television — it tells you about
kids' addiction to television, about how television
destroys traditional family activities, breaks down
familial communication and interaction and robs kids
of their play time, and about how media events pre-
empt family events.

But if family events are of so little value to family
members, and have so little meaning, perhaps it's not
television that's the problem, but other things that
have nothing at all to do with television. If there is so
little communication in a family that television can so
easily break it down, you'd better look at what's not
happening in your family for reasons other than the
fact that you have a television set. The fact that
almost fifty percent of today's households have more
than one television set does not in itself mean that a
pattern of isolation is being created in the family. If
there are five televisions in a household, and the five
family members each watch their own set much of the
time and have little to do with each other, then these
people evidently don't *want* to have much to do with
each other.

A teacher of an adult class in children's literature,
in which television was treated as a form of literature
(which it most surely is), discovered that one of his
students, a mother of two, has three television sets in
her home. However, while each family member has his

or her own TV set, they all sit down together at the beginning of the week with the new TV guide and make a family and individual selection of programs for the week. The children are not allowed to watch an unlimited amount of television, nor are they allowed to watch just anything that happens to be on. They discuss the amount of television that the children can watch, what special programs are on, what is appropriate or inappropriate for their age levels, what they will watch together and what they will watch alone. It's not the number of TV sets in the house that determines the quantity and quality of communication amongst family members.

A television set is a dumb electronic machine, just a piece of furniture that projects images and sound. Human beings program it, and human beings receive the programs. We have the ability and the intelligence to decide what we watch, when we watch and how much we watch. The television does not decide for us.

Is there something intrinsically wrong with a child sitting alone in front of a television set? If you believe there is, what picture does this question conjure up in your head? What program was your child watching? How long had he or she been watching alone? We have said nothing yet about the child's age, the kind of program that is on, the length of time he or she has been watching or the time of day. Any assumptions have been your own. Now ask yourself if there is anything intrinsically wrong with a child sitting alone reading a book.

Many parents will disapprove of a child's sitting alone in front of the TV, but will view the child's reading a book alone as a good thing. Why do we respond in this way? We have somehow reached a consensus that there is something intrinsically insidious about television, that it is to a large extent, especially for children, a negative influence. On the other hand, we recognize books and reading as inherently positive in their effect. But what if the kid watching television alone is watching "The Road to Avonlea," and this is the only TV he or she has watched all day? And what if the thirteen-year-old bookworm is reading a copy of *American Psycho* that was left out in the parents' bedroom? This is of course a loaded image, but it helps us focus on the fact that for many parents, television is itself bad, while books, for some reason, are always good.

Young people have a different perspective about these issues. It's important to listen to what they say about television, especially those who have done some thinking about it. Here are a couple of their comments:

> I can't remember life without television. I've been entertained, educated, amused, sickened and bored by it. It has enabled me to witness great historical events, and other events I'd rather not see. With the flick of a switch the world was at my fingertips, the great, the glorious, and the stupid. But the choice is mine. I can easily turn it off.
>
> Sandra, age 18

> Too much TV makes you stupid. Too little TV makes you ignorant.
>
> James, age 11

Parenting is one of the toughest jobs in the world, and this part of parenting, handling television, makes it even more difficult, because while there are 100 books that say sit down and watch TV with your kids, there are 101 more that say don't let them watch it at all. Such is the bewildering world of television, and the choices that parents have to make every day. But the reality is that, although we could talk to parents till sign-off on a twenty-four-hour station about how they should be handling the TV issue with their children, most parents simply do not have the time for the problem.

As we've already noted, the authors of this book have a combined experience working in television and education of over sixty years, the greater part of this involved in television. We would not have stayed in the business this long if we had believed all the negative statements made about it. We want to give parents a sense of the creative power of television — yes, its *creative* power — and its importance in the lives of children, as well as a sense of the beauty and value of this medium at its best.

Television is a vital part of our culture. It's a fact. We can criticize it *ad nauseam* but it's not going to go away. We have to learn to live with it, but we will not be able to do this unless we change our negative attitudes to television and begin to see it for what it is — a powerful communication tool that can indeed overwhelm if it is allowed to, but, if used for the things that it does best, can be a wonderful part of our lives.

Let's examine some of the negative statements that are commonly made about television by people who don't understand the medium. Probably the most simplistic allegation made about television is that watching it is an antisocial experience. Certainly, if parents allow children to do nothing but sit in front of a television set in their spare time, they probably will become antisocial and withdrawn. But consider the bookish youngster who does nothing but sit in a corner with a book, ignoring everything else around. As any husband or wife knows, a book — or a morning newspaper — can certainly also be a deterrent to conversation. Reading is, by its very nature, a solitary, antisocial occupation. That doesn't mean it's necessarily bad.

Consider the young person who is completely deprived of television. As teachers, we have met parents who brag that, "Of course we don't let George or Mary watch TV." In such families one of two things usually happens. Either George and Mary spend a lot of time at their friends' homes so they can catch up on programs (some of which wise parents might be concerned about or want to discuss with their children), so that they can talk about them with their friends. Or George and Mary find themselves left out of school-yard conversation about the latest series or fad.

Whether we like it or not, television is part of our culture and our time. It's part of our social structure, good or bad, brings world events and commentary into our homes, delivers cultural information and cartoons, and makes us part of the consumer society.

When people brag about not watching or even owning a television set, perhaps we should ask them whether or not they own a bookcase. When they indignantly reply that of course they do, we might point out that just as there are good and bad books, the choice being theirs, so there are good and bad television programs.

But, critics complain, television is the direct antithesis of reading. If by this broad generality they are talking about eye movement, concentration, ability to go back and forth, reread or re-examine a story and so forth, the statement has some validity. But again what is usually implied is that all TV is bad and all reading is good. And of course this is not true. Certainly, reading requires skills, both physical and mental, but so does *real* watching of television. The active viewer uses imagination and thought processes in a creative and constructive way.

Television is a different activity from reading. So is going to the theatre or to a movie, or taking a walk, or having an argument. Swimming is different from skating. None of this means that one activity is "better" than another. They're simply different.

Today's young people are bombarded by stimuli and choice through an ever-widening variety of media.

One medium does not necessarily replace or supersede another. All are useful and valuable in an education/learning environment. Their value depends upon their use.

Critics have also claimed that TV destroys language growth. The language of television is said to have debased the language being taught in the classroom or books. The English language is a wonderfully flexible and adaptable medium. It expands and changes with time, social change and the impact of other cultures and tongues. If language becomes corrupted, television is not the only culprit. One need only peruse any daily paper to find examples of grammatical howlers, misused syntax and other solecisms. From our experience in the classroom, we know that educators' language is, to say the least, not always exemplary. Children's language development depends on all of their environmental influences: visual, verbal and aural. The major influence and example should be their parents.

Television is criticized as a passive activity that discourages creative play. For example, Betty D. Boegehold, in *Getting Ready to Read,* writes: "For the viewer, television is a world of silent passiveness. The action takes place on the screen. The child can't explore or interact with the screen. . . ." We don't believe this. These television-as-villain statements always assume that if children were not watching TV, they would be doing something "useful" or "creative" such as reading, writing, painting, doing the chores, being with the family or whatever. On the contrary, they might be doing something far worse, or just hanging around the corner store or the shopping mall. As for passivity, a 1988 U.S. Department of Education study suggested that there was very little evidence that TV in itself made children cognitively passive. "Creative play" is a term that needs some examination. To our minds, all the play time of very young

children is creative, in that it develops imagination
and/or physical prowess.

Good TV programs encourage creative activities. At
a parents' night a concerned mother told us about
watching her six-year-old son, ill and home from
school, glued to morning television. She was worried
that he was just wasting his time. That afternoon,
however, she saw him working away on the simple costumes and creations he had seen on one of the morning
shows. Programs such as "Mr. Dressup," "Polka Dot
Door," "Join In," "Under the Umbrella Tree" and "Fred
Penner's Place" all promote participatory activities.
Watching and listening (useful skills to develop) come
first, and then participation.

A grade nine English class gave us one of the best
examples we've found of the use, and complementary
nature, of different media. The class was studying the
novel *To Kill a Mockingbird*. Since there is a wonderful film adaptation of the book, teachers will often use
the film version along with the novel. However, what
was unique about this teacher's use of the film was
that he made it the basis of a comparative study of
what the novel does best and what film does best. In
this case, with a VCR, it was not just the film but the
film on video. This teacher is an expert with a VCR,
and all of the functions of the machine that can make
video a text in the classroom.

The students had read the novel. After their first
reading, and an analysis of the theme of racial prejudice and various other elements of the novel, the
teacher began a comparative examination of the film
and the novel. They were now reading the television
screen in much the same way as they had been
reading the novel in print. Scenes were examined with
the Stop–Start–Freeze Frame–Slow Motion functions
of the VCR. Facial expressions, camera angles, block-
ing of characters, set — all were examined with the
same attention as were the original scenes in print.

The teacher describes with much pleasure the growing facility of these grade nine kids with the techniques of film and video, and their obvious pride as they learned to use terms such as "long shot," "framing" and all the vocabulary that is needed in order to discuss a film.

The main questions throughout this video section of the novel study were: How does this scene work in print? How does it work in film? And, why are they different? It took some time for the class to become accustomed to this approach, but once the pattern clicked, they took off into discussions of both the novel and the film that were intelligent, exciting and a lot of fun. One of the students commented early in this activity: "Why don't we just watch the film? It's faster and we can get this over quick." This remark was used as a starting point for a discussion of the fact that print and film are different media, and it's not the time difference that's important. Each functions in a way that is unique to that medium. As the study of the novel and the film continued, the unique qualities of each medium became apparent.

Another example of the educational and entertaining use of prime-time television in the classroom demonstrates the medium as an art form. "Northwood" is a series shown on CBC for older teenagers in order to tap into the "Degrassi High" audience that has grown a bit older. "Degrassi High" is the very popular Canadian-made drama for teens. "Northwood" is grittier, and the situations are rather more adult, involving more of the lives of teenagers outside of the school scene than was the case in "Degrassi." The opening of "Northwood" is interesting. After showing all six episodes of the first series, the teacher asked the class to do an analysis of the opening, which is the same for each program. The exercise was to fill in the following chart for each shot:

Content	Technique (camera, sound, direction)

The viewing technique was Stop–Freeze–Discuss– Replay as necessary. What became obvious to the students very quickly, after about the fifth shot, was that the opening introduced, in a very fast collage of sight and sound and movement, all of the characters and all of the relationships that would be elaborated in the series. It's beautifully done, with interesting camera work and some great shots, and in just a few seconds we are given a preview of the series and a statement of what it's about, its mood and its style. What an interesting use of television, and what a strong statement about the beauty of the form! And it's not just a good teacher who makes this happen. It's a good program made by a team of artists and technicians.

Nearly every commercial promotes the idea that there's no problem that cannot be solved simply by buying the right product. Dramas, too, in which all problems must be solved in under an hour, tend to offer easy solutions. This leads some people to say that television fosters deceptive thinking. But isn't this also true in many children's stories? Just as parents are involved in children's reading, so they should be involved in their television viewing to discuss the solutions and possible alternatives to problems that arise. Let's face it, most kids aren't fooled by simplistic solutions, even though they enjoy them, as we all do when the villains in a mystery novel are caught, or criminals are foiled in a TV crime show.

So much is made of the number of hours kids spend watching television. The assumption is that if they watch too much television they won't read, they won't be literate. But what does it mean to be literate today? Let's think of the child of the nineties. It is no longer enough just to be able to read and write. Children must learn to see, absorb and react critically and creatively. Bombarded as they are by sound, picture and print, they must find their own standard of literacy for this new world, which is very different from the world in which we, their parents, grew up.

What does it mean when a five-year-old child cannot yet read, but can use the remote which he or she has just learned to "read" to control the television? What does it mean when (despite copyright laws) kids have their own library of favourite videos that they've taped themselves?

Children today are very different from the way we were. We must realize that the vocabulary that we use about television may not even apply to them. Books about television with titles like *The Plug-In Drug, Unplugging the Plug-In Drug, Amusing Ourselves to Death* and *Four Arguments for the Elimination of Television* blame television for the rise of everything from the crime rate to inflation, and the lowering of everything from morals to the value of the dollar. But these books are quickly becoming obsolete, because they come from another age, which was rooted in another medium.

No other medium has been examined in the way that television has, or been condemned so vociferously for what it does. What about the telephone, which is now used to sell everything from magazines to sex? Pick up any local tabloid, which is accessible to any child, and is seen everywhere, and you'll see that at least half of it is advertising, and a large part of it is advertising table dancing and different forms of sexual fantasy.

How many hours between the ages of four and eighteen do your children spend in schools? How much of this time is spent in the presence of truly creative, inspiring teachers? How often, in these hours, are the needs of children met? How much time is spent unproductively? No wonder children prefer to watch television!

But what of the judgement of the children? How do
we allow them the room to make their own decisions?
Are they just empty vessels with no values at all, upon
whom the power of the screen can write whatever the
TV and film moguls propose? Is television really an
all-powerful medium with the capability to corrupt
minds, to form lasting values? Should we follow the
advice of Gerry Mander, author of *Four Arguments for
the Elimination of Television,* and just eliminate it
altogether?

We've heard it said that if a dozen readers read a
passage from the same book, they would come away
with a dozen different images of the scene, but that
television stifles the imagination, a director doing all
the imagining for them. It's true that a director will
interpret a scene in a certain way, and different directors and camera people will give us different inter-
pretations. But to suggest that TV somehow
suppresses imagination is overstating the case. The
strength of television is that it can bring a world, or
many worlds, to a child or adult to interpret any way
they want. The imagination is simply brought into
play in a different way when one watches rather than
reads. Just as two people might look at Picasso's *Guer-
nica* and focus on different aspects of the painting,
deriving different meanings and experiencing different emotions, so film and TV viewers see and interpret
dramatic passages, or even commercials, quite differ-
ently, depending on many criteria, including age,
socioeconomic background, character and likes and
dislikes of each viewer.

TV can be used for good or for ill, depending on the
interaction between the screen and the audience.
Each brings to this exchange a certain content and
story, certain values. And each is changed by the
other. It's here, in the convergence of program and
audience, of sender and receiver, that we must begin
to look for the power of this medium. All viewers,

young and old, bring something of themselves to the experience. With children, this something includes the values their parents impart to them. We cannot abdicate this very important parental role of nurturing in our children a set of values and an acceptable way of handling the world and of living in it.

You probably choose the books your children read when they are young, in order to help them to develop good taste and a love for reading and the world of literature. As they grow, you allow your children to make more and more of their own choices. The same should be true with television. It's all in how you use it, what you do with it and the place you allow it to have in your own little constellation.

Chapter 2

THE SATURDAY MORNING MINEFIELD

All shows should be entertaining. They
should be fun. Kids need to relax too.
    Heather Conkie, writer / producer / actress

Saturday morning, and you're just waking up. You
know it's Saturday because of those sounds pulsating from the television set down the hall. Wonder what
that old cat and mouse are doing today? Then, shaken
fully awake, you realize it's no longer the old cat and
mouse. It's noisy. It's flashy. Multi-coloured lasers are
blasting. It may be a program, it may be a commercial.
You can't tell.

Saturday morning is a logical starting place to write
about children's television, because whenever we
mention children's television to parents, the usual
expectation is that we are going to talk about Saturday morning cartoons. This is the largest block of television during the week expressly devoted to children
— six consecutive hours.

If you were to peruse a current copy of the TV guide
to find out what the television viewing possibilities are
for a child on Saturday morning, you'd discover, if you
took the time to count them, that, in an area with over
twenty-five channels (including cable and pay-TV) Saturday morning, from 6:00 a.m. to noon, offers approximately 300 program slots, and that of these, the total
number of programs for children is approximately 110.

The recommended programs we list below are all those we consider worth viewing by kids. We don't mean educational, we mean good fun and entertainment, and, as a bonus, sometimes edifying. This means that about thirty out of 300 — ten percent of this morning fare — are worth watching. We'll take a look at these and some other not-so-good programs, and discuss the perils of this "minefield."

Before we go into this, though, here's an example of our selection for one Saturday morning time slot. We cannot take into account all the local stations across the country, but this selection from the Toronto area is probably typical. You'll have to make your own choices based on your local listings.

Sample 9:00 a.m. Schedule from TV Guide

Channel	Network/ Location	Program
3	Barrie, Ont.	"Renovation Zone"
4	CBS	"Garfield and Friends"
5	CBC	**"Sesame Street"**
6,7,41	Global	"Wild West C.O.W.-Boys of Moo Mesa"
9	CTV	"Raw Toonage"
13	Kitchener	"Brownstone Kids"
11	Hamilton	"Gardener's Journal"
12	Peterborough	"Visions of India"
13	La Chaine Française	"Magicien d'Oz"
17	PBS	"Streamside"
19	TVO	"Sewing with Nancy"
25	CBC (French)	"Vazimolo"
29	Buffalo	"Tom and Jerry Kids"
47	Toronto (Multicultural)	"Vivere al 100 Percento"

57	CITY TV	"De Caras Lindas"
	TSN	"World Class Wrestling Power Hour (continued)"
	A&E	"Time Machine"
	Vision TV	"Gurjat Darshan"
	YTV	**"My Little Pony"**
	Family Channel	**"Donald Duck Presents"**

The programs we've selected from this time slot are highlighted in bold print. We have tried to choose programs based on high production values and interesting and entertaining content. If most of our selections are network programs or series, this does not mean that we wish to demean local programming, which has its own value in each community. What's striking is that, even in this time slot supposedly geared for children, we can recommend only three of the more than twenty programs.

So here we go with the top thirty. Not all of them are "tops." Some of them do not have very good production values, but they happen to be the best in their time slot, especially when they're scheduled opposite a program such as "World Class Wrestling."

6:00 a.m.	"Polka Dot Door"
6:30	"Kidstreet"
	"Wonder Why?"
	"Under the Umbrella Tree"
	"The Littlest Hobo"
	"Fables of the Green Forest"
	"Size Small"
7:00	"The Little Mermaid"
	"Magic Library"
	"Free to Fly"
7:30	"Captain Planet"
	"Babar"
	"Care Bears"

	"Sharon, Lois & Bram"
	"OWL TV"
8:00	"Street Cents"
	"Dog City"
	"Winnie the Pooh"
	"Polka Dot Door"
8:30	"Welcome to Pooh Corner"
	"Today's Special"
	"Bobby's World"
9:00	"Sesame Street"
	"My Little Pony"
	"Donald Duck"
9:30	"Discover Your World"
10:00	"Fred Penner's Place"
	"Wonder Why?"
	"Maya the Bee"
10:30	"Street Cents"
	"The Littlest Hobo"
11:00	"Star Trek"
	"Babar"
11:30	"Take Off"

Much of the Saturday morning children's fare appears on networks that have a reputation for broadcasting good children's programs. First, TVOntario, the provincial educational television network of Ontario. While its mandate is to serve Ontario, many of its programs are seen in other provinces of Canada through other provincial educational networks. In fact, many of TVO's programs are seen around the world. Here's Saturday morning on TVO:

6:00 a.m.	"Polka Dot Door"
6:30	"Fables of the Green Forest"
7:00	"Magic Library," "Free to Fly"
7:30	"Sharon, Lois & Bram"
8:00	"Polka Dot Door"
8:30	"Today's Special"

At 9:00 a.m. TVOntario begins its adult programming.

Here we have some first-rate, award-winning
shows. "Polka Dot Door" continues to maintain its
high reputation, even though many adults groan at its
slow pace and seeming lack of energy and excitement.
This show, hosted by two young people and the now
famous Polkaroo, focuses on games, stories and activities for very young children. Its success lies in the fact
that it is precisely targeted at its audience of two- to
four-year-olds. It is not meant for adults. Many adults
look down on "Mister Rogers' Neighborhood," which is
also slow, and sometimes seems to wander at a snail's
pace. But not for its audience. Not for the two-, three-
and four-year-olds watching intently as Mister Rogers
talks directly to *them* about issues that concern them.
"Polka Dot Door" exemplifies an admirable kind of
television that is not seen very much any more: a soft,
gentle, loving kind of television for children that lives
very much in their world. Other producers of children's television could learn something by swinging
open the "Polka Dot Door" and taking a walk through
"Mister Rogers' Neighborhood."

TVOntario's "Today's Special," made for the pre-
school audience, is one of the most innovative and creative children's series ever produced in Canada, and
perhaps in the world. It certainly is one of the highest
quality children's programs ever to come from TVO.
Its format is well paced for children. The combination
of story, song, dance and magnificent puppet characters playing alongside real people is quite beautiful.
It deals magnificently with issues of importance to
young children, like moving house or a death in the
family. It introduces children to Canadian artists
such as Oscar Peterson and Karen Kain. However,
despite its superb quality and the strong positive
response to it from both children and adults, only
seventy-five of these programs were made before the

series was brought to an abrupt end. Nonetheless its
impact, even through repeats, is still very strong.
Why were only seventy-five programs made? Why
was this series not sold for syndication, and many
more programs produced? It seems to indicate a lack
of care about children's programming on the part of
one of Canada's prime producers of television for
children.

TVOntario falls somewhat short of what it could be
for children because of the priority it now gives to
adult programming. The Youth Programming department, which serves children between grade seven and
the end of high school, has been severely reduced, and
the new programs coming from it correspondingly cut
back. As well, the budget of the Children's department
has been flatlined for the past six years, despite many
award-winning educational series. It's no wonder that
there are so few new, original programs for children
from TVO, and that there must be so many repeats.

As an aside to this discussion of Saturday morning
TV, we must point out that TVOntario does provide a
full morning of children's programming on Sunday
from 6:00 a.m. to noon — a morning when many of the
other networks do not offer a great deal for children.
While much of this is repeats, it still represents a substantial block of good programming. We will say more
about some of these programs later.

Speaking of repeat programs, we don't mean to
argue that programs should not be repeated. We know
that children enjoy repetition of stories that are read
to them, as well as those that they see on the television screen. We also recognize that repeats are an eco-
nomic necessity for broadcasters. However, we believe
that programs should be repeated as part of a creative
process of developing a good schedule for children, not
simply used as an excuse for "bottom-line" budgeting.
This is one of the major problems of broadcasters, both
public and private. Children's programming is given

such low priority and such minimal funding that
many repeats are absolutely necessary.

The CBC now has a self-mandated policy of no
advertising to children under the age of twelve. This
policy of commercial-free children's television is
highly laudable, especially in the face of the barrage
of ads aimed at kids on most other networks. CBC's
programs for children run from 8:30 to 11:00 a.m. Its
Saturday morning roster is:

8:30	"Under the Umbrella Tree"
9:00	"Sesame Street"
10:00	"Fred Penner's Place"
10:30	"Street Cents"

Four good programs. "Under the Umbrella Tree,"
one of our favourite children's programs, is a series
about a neighbourhood group of friends, dealing with
many fun and serious issues that pre-school children
come upon. Beautiful puppets and good scripts, with
a lovely, engaging host. But CBC's Saturday morning
line-up has been cut back from three hours to two and
one-half hours, and "Under the Umbrella Tree" is into
its third and fourth rerun, with no more episodes in
production except for four specials being made with
Disney. "Sesame Street" is a rerun of one of the
weekday programs. "Fred Penner's Place" is one of the
best programs of its type for children. "Street Cents"
is excellent — a consumer show for kids, with a lot of
good humour and good tips about handling money and
related consumer issues. In 1991, it won the Children's Broadcast Institute Award of Excellence for the
ten- to twelve-year-old information series.

Think about the huge number of children watching
television on Saturday mornings (more than 3 million
at 9:30 a.m.), especially during the many cold months
of fall, winter and early spring. The problem is
that the admirable no-commercials policy of the CBC

makes it impossible for CBC Children's television to produce many new programs. Without the commercial revenue, it cannot develop and maintain a strong schedule of kids' programs on Saturday morning (and cannot even think about developing Sunday morning), as counter-programming to all the competing children's television. The programs on most other channels are sandwiched between a thousand zazzy commercials pushing everything from Frosted Flakes to the latest in war toys. While revenue from adult programming goes back into new adult programming, CBC's Children's programming department lacks the funding for the development of new materials.

It says a great deal about broadcasters' concerns about children and television when the largest of them cannot come up with a better Saturday schedule than the one above. We don't quite understand how it is that the CBC doesn't have the courage to introduce a very strong Saturday morning block, from 6:00 to noon, that would be a model of what children's television can be. The problem is, as it always has been, that programming for children is put at the bottom of the list in terms of priority and budget, and those who run children's programming constantly struggle to do as much as they can with very limited budgets, and even less support.

On to the CTV, another of our large Canadian broadcasters. Here are its Saturday morning offerings:

6:30	"Wonder Why"
7:00	"The Campbells"
7:30	"OWL TV"
8:00	"Winnie the Pooh"
8:30	"The Little Mermaid"
9:00	"Raw Toonage"
9:30	"Darkwing Duck"
10:00	"Goof Troop"
10:30	"The Littlest Hobo"

11:00   "My Secret Identity"
11:30   "Tarzan"

"The Little Mermaid," the new series, is a delightful offering for children. It is equal to the movie, with
fine animation, good songs, excellent stories about
issues that young children are dealing with. We wish
there were more programming like this — good animation for children. "Wonder Why?" and "OWL TV"
are two very good science information shows for children.

One of the best of CTV's Saturday morning line-up
is "OWL TV," the popular magazine-format science
show, featuring Dr. Zed. This award-winning series
features bright, articulate kids, excellent studio
experiments and on-location footage. OWL also produces "FROG," which we review in the final section of
this book. We should mention here that OWL, along
with its magazines for children, *Owl, Chickadee* and
Treehouse, also sponsors an internship program each
year for young producers and writers who show
promise in the area of children's television.

CTV's other programs, however, range from mediocre to outdated.

Global's Saturday morning children's line-up is
usually something like this:

6:30 a.m.   "Kidstreet"
7:00   "Ovide & Gang"
7:30   "Care Bears"
8:00   "Dog City"
8:30   "Plucky Duck"
9:00   "Wild West C.O.W.-Boys of Moo
             Mesa"
9:30   "The Addams Family"
10:00   "Teenage Mutant Ninja Turtles"
11:00   "Back to the Future"
11:30   "Dennis the Menace"

"Dog City" is one of the most creative of the new series for children, in its combination of Henson puppets and animation. Perhaps "Care Bears" is another program of some value in this morning that consists mainly of vacuity. At least in "Care Bears" there's a fairly good story and something more than empty packages. We say this even though for many "Care Bears" is saccharin sweet and piously moralistic. The rest is a collection of mainly inane material that ranges from the extremely repetitive "Ninja Turtles" to the very poorly written "Back to the Future" and the emptiness of "Dennis the Menace."

On Global it's often not clear whether one is watching a program or a commercial, because the commercials are, for the most part, better produced than the programs. We'll have more to say about this matter later.

Another Canadian network that deserves more than a cursory glance is YTV (Youth Television). YTV, as its name and logo suggest, targets youth and families. In its first few years it has developed several good series of music and talk shows for young adults. The unique, now defunct, "StreetNOISE" and the pop music feature "Rock'n Talk" have been very successful, as is "Hit List," with Tarzan Dan. There are also plenty of old favourite reruns such as "Little House on the Prairie," "Lassie" and "Get Smart," along with other imported comedy and adventure shows for family viewing. YTV does an excellent job of featuring young people as hosts, interviewers and program-break announcers, and does its best to work with community groups and its constituents to bring quality material to the screen.

But the network is one of the youngest and the bills must be paid. Perhaps this is the reason for the thinness of its Saturday morning line-up, which looks like this:

6:00 a.m.   "Waterville Gang"
6:30   "Size Small"
7:00   "Brownstone Kids"
7:30   "The Little Mermaid"
8:00   "Muppet Babies"
8:30   "Casper and Friends"
9:00   "My Little Pony"
9:30   "Super Mario Brothers"
10:00   "Teenage Mutant Ninja Turtles"
10:30   "Samurai Pizza Cats"
11:00   "Ghostbusters"
11:30   "Capt'N"

YTV is not so young any more that it could not provide some alternatives to the programs broadcast on many of the other networks. YTV is expressly for children, and as such, it has an opportunity, and even more, a responsibility to be something distinctly different. With its present Saturday morning line-up, it is not. As we have watched YTV over the years since its birth, it has changed, and it has improved the quality of its programming. We urge it to go further, and to take on this challenge of providing a different, new and unique kind of television for children on Saturday morning.

As for "Teenage Mutant Ninja Turtles," it's one program we still object to violently for a number of reasons. We concede that every kid is watching "TMNT"; it's a fine example of how peer pressure helps a series like this. Kids watch it because all their friends are watching and no one wants to be left out. Don't watch it and you'll be left out of a lot of school-yard talk and many "TMNT" games (all warlike).

Here's an experiment you might want to try in order to find out how the program works. Since most of your children are watching this series, the first opportunity you get, *listen* to the program without watching. What a revelation! It sounds like a video arcade, with its

barrage of stereotypical video game war sounds: ping,
pang, zap. Thirty seconds of these kinds of sounds
punctuated by the odd silly line such as "Gotcha now,
pizza face." The plot of these shows is the same every
week. And if you listen instead of watch, you get a good
sense of what this is all about — nothing. Perhaps it
would be better if this series had stuck more closely to
the original comic books — dark, violent, archetypal
good versus evil, a primordial story structure. At least
children would have some ideas to grapple with
instead of the emptiness here. And what we find most
disheartening with YTV and 'TMNT" is that this is the
centre, the focal point, of its morning for children.

Perhaps a viewing of one or two of these kinds of
programs now and then won't do any harm. But the
constant barrage of "WHAM," "BANG," "BLOW-UP"
and "DESTROY," combined with the snap, crackle and
zoom, zoom of flashing cereal and toy commercials is
mind-numbing after a while. Networks, and sponsors,
might be encouraged to vary their Saturday series as
some of them try to do during the week. It may not be
such a bad idea after all to recycle some of the old
shows about Casper, cats and birds.

And now the Family Channel, "TV the whole family
can enjoy together." In the words of the vice president
of programming: "One of the things that we hear from
parents all the time is that they do not feel that they
have to be in the room with their children to watch our
channel because they are confident that there will be
nothing coming up on the screen that their children
will have questions about or problems about, and will
need the parent to explain 'Mommy what does this
mean?' "

This is the main goal of the Family Channel, to
provide the kind of television that parents do not have
to worry about. The Family Channel is unabashedly
escapist and has very strict rules about violence and
language. The constant invitation on air to "Enjoy the

warmth and wonder of Disney" underscores the intent. The target audience for this network is children and the family. The channel is available from most cable companies across Canada for a monthly fee. Its licence, as set out by the CRTC, requires that twenty-five percent of its content be Canadian and fifteen percent international, with the remaining sixty percent coming from Disney Studios. The channel is commercial free, using its commercial time to promote its own schedule. As a pay channel, its licence does not permit production of its own new materials. It can, however, enter into partnerships with other Canadian broadcasters and producers for the development of new programs and series. All of this determines the kind of material that is presented on Saturday mornings.

A review of this channel's programs and promotional material very quickly confirms its commitment to being "safe" for children. The content of its programs for children on Saturday mornings (as at other times in the schedule) is far less violent and intense than much of the rocket-riding, bomb-blasting and dino-dancing found on other channels. Here's the typical Saturday morning schedule for the Family Channel:

6:00 a.m.	"Bumpety Boo"
6:30	"Mousercise"
7:00	"Sharky & George"
7:30	"Dumbo's Circus"
8:00	"Good Morning Mickey"
8:30	"Welcome to Pooh Corner"
9:00	"Donald Duck"
9:30	"Young Robin Hood"
10:00	"Maya the Bee"
10:30	"Bear, the Tiger & the Others"
11:00	"Babar"
11:30	"Take Off"

The segment from 6:00 to 10:00 is listed as "Kidstuff." The majority of it is from Disney, with some international exceptions such as "Maya the Bee." Most of the morning is cartoonland, except for the highly innovative series "Take Off," which combines drama, art work, music, children's humour, science, storytelling and more. This Canadian series explores ideas, and its aim is to encourage children to think laterally and to help them retain their natural curiosity. We're glad to see this series, and hope that Family will present more of this and less of Disney. But as we've said, there is much less zapping and bashing and destruction of people and objects than on most other channels.

Some of the content is drawn from other eras. "Good Morning Mickey" is a collection of old Disney cartoons. It contains some of the best scripts and the highest-quality animation of the whole morning. But here we move in to the problem with the Family Channel. While its prime target audience is children, the programs that it offers on Saturday morning are, for the most part, simplistic for the young people of 1990s. The animation in most of the programs is poor to downright bad. We applaud the effort that the Family Channel makes to avoid violence and bad language. However, as a result the scripts are often boring and vacuous. "Mousercise," a twenty-minute workout for children, is derived from an adult program and we wonder why it is necessary, and whether the exercises have been researched to ensure they are particularly suitable for children. "Dumbo's Circus" contains people in dreadful costumes performing to an inane script. So it's back to "Good Morning Mickey" for quality viewing. These old cartoons put all the rest of the programs in such bad relief that one wonders if the programmers feel that children are incapable of judging quality. "Winnie the Pooh" is a bastardized Americanization of the well known Pooh stories. In this series the characters are made to look slightly stupid rather than delightfully ingenuous. "Maya the Bee" has an intelligent feel to it, and a lovely mood created by crickets in concert. At 12:00 we have "The Best of the Mickey Mouse Club," a paean to its name-sake, and a startling example of a statement made by a television executive in charge of children's pro-gramming, that it is too risky to try new material for children, that derivative materials they know is what sells. And here, with the Family Channel, the deriva-tive material comes mainly from Disney. Where is the Canadian programming? Where is the programming that uses the best of the techniques and talents of tele-vision? Where is the programming that is made for children of the 1990s, who are very different from the kids for whom the Mickey Mouse Club and the Mickey Mouse cartoons were made?

In fact, to call the Family Channel a Canadian channel is somewhat misleading. The largest body of material comes from Disney. And we are exhorted repeatedly to "Enjoy the warmth and wonder of Disney." One wonders, after viewing a morning of this broadcaster's programming for children, whether it is in fact a loss leader for Disney. There seems to be no other reason for its existence, based on the programs it broadcasts, and the power of its Disney message.

If you've spent the money to subscribe to this channel, it most definitely needs your phone calls and letters to help it get on the right track for your chil-dren. Do what we did. Tape an entire Saturday morning's programs, then sit and skim through them, looking at enough of each program to get a sense of its quality in both content and production. And just as important, look at the material *between* programs, and listen carefully to the messages you are being given. Ask yourself if this is the kind of programming, albeit less violent than other channels, that you want your children to be watching.

While we're speaking about messages between programs, and underwriting and paying for children's programming, we must say a few words about the usual way of paying for television — commercials. One cannot look at the programs on most channels on Saturday morning without being struck by the fact that commercials are very carefully designed for this time. This is another aspect of the Saturday morning minefield that parents have to deal with — the number of commercials that your children are confronted with, and the power of these commercials. Like television itself, they are not going to go away, having become an essential part of television all over the "free market" world. A television commercial may be defined as a time slot used to promote a product, service or idea. Certainly these commercials promote products. Service? Sometimes. Ideas? Only as far as commercials do — that life will only be complete if the viewer buys (or persuades his or her parents to buy) the latest toy, video game, or delicious, active, almost heroic breakfast cereal.

These commercials last from fifteen to thirty seconds, and rely on movement, rapid cuts from one shot to another, vivid colours, "hypersound" and usually a direct voice-over appeal to the viewer. They are divided roughly into three types: those depicting children (with the occasional adult); those with children and animated characters; and those that are completely animated. There are usually five commercial slots set into and between programs, each featuring four or five different ads. The completely animated commercials, and even those that combine animation with human actors, often duplicate the tone and rhythm of the cartoons they interrupt. They are designed to harmonize with the viewing pattern already set, and so keep children from changing channels or turning down the sound.

As we all know, repetition is an important device in

television commercial-land. This is especially true in the realm of Saturday morning TV. Here the same ads, especially for toys and cereals, appear four to eight times between 7:00 a.m. and noon. As the morning progresses, ads for more sophisticated toys and video games begin to appear.

What product, services and ideas are promoted for young viewers? There's a bunch of eight- and nine-year-olds jumping and skipping with wonderful "Jumpit" and "Skipit" gear, ropes with counters so that you can keep score. These are two fifteen-second spots run together several times during the morning with a voice-over stressing that these mechanical counting wonders are of course "sold separately." This phrase and the ever-popular "batteries not included" are two of the most-repeated lines of dialogue all morning.

We can't have breakfast now without lots of animated adventure. Snap, Crackle and Pop are all over the house stirring up trouble, along with taste satisfaction and fun. As for good guys versus villains, to tie in with the adventure stories we're watching, the Shreddies twins, Freddie and Eddie, are involved in a thirty-second 1930s-style street crime adventure solved, nonviolently almost, because of the good taste of the cereal. Think of it: a couple of wheat flakes as heroes. In other episodes of this "series," the two heroes are involved in an attack by pirates and thwart train robbers on the Great Plains. All of these nefarious criminal types are overcome by being shot literally in the mouth with Shreddies, after which they all settle down amicably to a bowl of the stuff and become, of course, very nice guys.

And then there's Kool-Aid, with animated sharks and kids and fifteen seconds of quick-moving fun, followed by fifteen more seconds of promotion for "Dancing Man," who is available on an order form "from selected stores," batteries not included. This is

usually followed by two fifteen-second commercials
from a cool, jive-talking cheetah for Chee•tos, "those
crunchy potato chips."

Frosted Flakes has Tony the Tiger. We can meet
Tony at "certain selected stores" and take his picture.
If we buy two boxes of Frosted Flakes we may even get
a pair of sunglasses. There is also a seaside version in
which Tony windsurfs with his young friends. "Tony
brings out the tiger in you," says the voice-over. "And
you," grins Tony into the camera.

And now for a real "BAM BAM" ad, there's one for
Cheerios. The new Apple Cinnamon thirty-seconds
features several children rushing around and encountering exploding apples and burning hair (this no
doubt says something about the taste and bite of the
new Cheerios). Finally, one young girl, admiring a
picture in a gallery, is attacked by an apple that wraps
her in a red flaming cinnamon rope, and she is
delighted! All this is done to a happy, heavy song beat.

Two excited children (the girl is the calmer of the
two and seems to be laughing at the experience) are
haunted by the "new" Count Chocula and marshmal-
low bats and ghosts. There are lots of ghostly sounds
and weird creatures appearing and disappearing. It's
all enjoyable, not scary, and makes beautiful fun of
films like *Ghostbusters*.

As the morning wears on, we begin to get more of
the prime-time type of commercial. "Leggo my eggo"
features a silly routine between a father and son about
who is going to grab a waffle out of the toaster first.
While they bicker, Mom comes along and takes the
waffle. The point is that someone always has to win,
and in the 1990s it's Mom. And what about sharing?
No way! "Leggo my Eggo!"

A well-produced rock video clone, with a twelve-
year-old host, promotes a warlike Nintendo game
called "Mario." And one of the most sinister ads
we've ever seen was shown one morning during the

cartoonland stretch after 9:00 a.m. on YTV. It is a promotion by SEGA for a portable colour home video game system — the average zap 'em, blast 'em out of the air war game, but what concerns us is the style of the ad. The screen is narrowed to three-quarter size so we appear to be peeping Toms, looking in on a young boy who is playing the game. In secret? In his room? (There is a bed in the scene.) Worst of all is the way this handsome boy leers at us through the slit in the screen, clearly satisfied with owning this obviously expensive toy (no prices mentioned) — and having destroyed his enemy.

All these ads are interspersed among the programs we've discussed above. So what do we do about the ads? Ignore them, condemn them, order them off the air? Not at all. We are saying *be aware*. Be aware of what is being sold, and how it is being promoted and presented, and the fact that the way in which it is presented forms an almost seamless web between programs, so that often it's difficult to tell which is the program and which is the commercial. Know the techniques, and discuss them with your children. Find out some of the effects of these commercials. When you go to a toy store with your children, examine some of the items that are advertised on Saturday mornings to see if they are quite the same as those shown on television. Often the size turns out to be a surprise. Even though advertisers must show a real hand in commercials to give an idea of true size, the hand is often shown so briefly, the life-size comparisons so powerful, that children have no idea of the real size of a toy. Notice the variety of cereals in the supermarket and be aware of what your children ask for, and why. But have fun with commercials. Watch them with the sound off to see what difference it makes. Do they need the sound *and* the picture? Turn away from them and just listen. How does the sound work? Some gentle fun, talking about and playing with what kids are

watching can help develop discerning viewers, even at
very young ages. Media literacy, just like all language
and communications learning, begins at home.

What can you do about the fact that such a relatively small proportion of programs are passable children's fare on Saturday morning? First of all, be
reassured: not one of these shows will destroy your
child's mind, though a lot of them together can make
for a pretty dozy kid. So *look at the programs*. Tape
several channels from 6:00 a.m. to noon. Friends can
help by each taping one channel, then you can share
the tapes. You might even want to compile your
viewing notes and have a neighbourhood gabfest
about these programs and what you all think of them.
As your video review of Saturday morning fare, watch
the first three minutes of each program. You'll find it'll
pay off. At least you'll know what your child is watching, and you can ask a few intelligent questions about
the programs. Even more important, you'll get a sense
of what you want your child to watch, what is perhaps
questionable and what you definitely do *not* want in
your house on Saturday mornings.

Perhaps you can construct a Saturday morning TV
map with your children. Colour code the programs.
Talk about what you think is good and what's not so
good, and why. *And listen*. Kids listen when they are
spoken to with respect and when they feel that they
are being listened to and their opinions valued. Have
some valuable fun negotiating your way through this
Saturday morning TV miasma, come up with an
agreed-upon selection and your own map or chart of
programs, and then decide how much is enough.

Another way of managing the problem is to
approach Saturday morning television in the same
way you handle the children's allowance money.
Decide for your children how much time they are
allowed to watch TV on Saturday morning. If it is
thirty minutes, sixty minutes or ninety minutes, the

agreed-upon time can be spent in whatever way the
child chooses; but the amount of time is what you consider to be appropriate for your child, and only you can
determine this. For some, any television on Saturday
morning is too much. For others, thirty minutes is
okay, while others would agree to their children's
watching ninety minutes or more.

Next, *talk*. There is no other way to negotiate this
Saturday morning minefield other than through a lot
of talk. And the only way to be informed is to sit with
your children and do some watching with them. The entire schedule is not bad. Triviality can be fun in small
amounts, and you can have fun together. Television is
in many ways, including the simple fun and entertainment programs, an exciting medium. This Saturday
morning television experience can be exciting as well,
if you choose to make it so for your children.

And now a few observations for the producers of the
Saturday morning television fare for children, beginning with several statements from other specialists
who are concerned about issues surrounding children
and television. Margaret Loesch, president of Fox
Children's Network, commenting on making programs around concepts that children are already
familiar with, such as popular feature films like *Back
to the Future,* claims that "It's virtually impossible to
sell new ideas." For Peggy Charron, founder of Action
For Children's Television, "The problem with all that
stuff is it's concept design, not program design. I don't
think there are any writers on these concept shows
like 'Hammer.' There's no real imagination behind any
of them."

Concept design versus program design. Animated
versions of Wayne Gretzky and Michael Jordan?
Impossible to sell new ideas for children's programs?
Certainly, these shows are anything but wonderful.
No really original writing, no imagination. No female
heroes because boys will not watch cartoons about

females. It seems to be a very cynical business.

So TVOntario does a morning of repeats. CBC has
cut its Saturday morning schedule to two and a half
hours, much of it repeat programming. Saturday
morning from 6:00 a.m. to noon attracts the highest
number of child viewers of any time during the week.
But when the ratings begin to slide, rather than take
up the challenge to create good, exciting new programs for children, broadcasters back out. What Saturday morning needs is a big dose of wonder, awe,
mystery and intelligence, to excite children, instead of
relying on the "marquee value" of big names rehashed
in animation. CBS's Judy Price, vice president of
children's programs: "We don't set out to make it [Sat-
urday morning] a sixth day at school." Saturday
morning does not need to be a sixth day of school, but
it does need to use the best qualities of television to
build an exciting time for children that is fun, interesting, imaginative and sometimes even educational.

It seems that in the grand scheme of Saturday
morning television planning, not much attention is
paid to the world of the child, the mind of the child,
the joys of the child. Why is there so little in the way
of program design? Diana Huss Green, editor of
Parents' Choice Magazine, believes "the networks
have got to try harder" to raise the quality of programming for children. Perhaps here in Canada it is
once more a problem of too much American programming, too many American business interests. A look
at the number of slots of Canadian programming on
Saturday morning in our area is very telling: out of a
total of 300, only 22 are Canadian. These numbers are
approximate, since program slots change. But the
comparison is startling.

So we return to the CBC's honourable advertising
policy with regard to children's programming. The
commendable intent is to maintain the purity of children's programming. However, if the CBC has very

little or nothing to maintain the purity of, the policy becomes an empty gesture. What is wrong with corporate underwriting for the children's programming schedule, or for individual programs? The main argument concerns control, with broadcasters frightened of corporate attempts to enter into the realm of creative decision-making. It seems to us that this argument would be more fruitful if it led to better children's programs, and more children's programs. We have seen one large corporation give $800,000 to a private production company for a series designed to focus on environmental issues for children. Surely there is more of this kind of money, and surely broadcasters are strong enough to maintain their integrity in the face of corporate pressure.

We have seen very little in the Saturday morning schedule, and that includes a survey of all channels, that gives us hope that broadcasters are willing to take risks to create or acquire good programming for children. However, this minefield does offer a few programs worth looking for, and some of the programs we've recommended. There are still exciting possibilities for creating new and stimulating material for children, to make Saturday morning television viewing a truly exhilarating and entertaining experience for children.

Chapter 3

PRIME TIME: GOOD TIMES, SOMETIMES

I think one thing that is important to do, whether it's as a parent or as a creator of children's television, or both, is to try and simply equip children with a sense of what's real and what isn't, what's being done as entertainment, and what's being done as reality.
Andrew Cochran, executive producer

Prime time: the time of the evening, after dinner, when most of us want to slow down, put our feet up and watch some television. A break from the day. Perhaps an hour, maybe two; then, sometimes, three, and if you watch the news, four. It's the time of the evening when the younger children should be in bed, but many are not; and the older ones have to do their homework before they get to the set. It's the time when there is so much on so many different channels that you either have several TVs, or your family has mastered the art of negotiation to the point where everyone is satisfied some of the time. It's the time when television viewing must be most closely supervised, because many children don't go to bed until nine or ten o'clock, and much of the programming is not for them. It's the time of the evening around which much of the TV boardroom wheeling and dealing is done, because this is prime time: prime for the business of television, prime for the ratings, prime for the advertisers.

Prime-time television includes such well-known shows as "Rescue 911," "The Simpsons," "L.A. Law," "America's Most Wanted," "Fresh Prince of Bel Air," "America's Funniest Home Videos" and "America's Funniest People." (The last two we'll say no more about because we don't want to give them any free publicity.) One of the main reasons for our spotlighting prime-time television is that this is where the largest portion of TV production money is spent, because this is where advertisers want their names to be seen — because this is when most people across this continent are watching television. Sad to say, the main reason the highest-quality television programs (in terms of dollars put into production) are seen between the hours of 7:00 p.m. and 11:00 p.m. is that this is when the largest audience can be delivered to the largest number of advertisers. It's pure business. This does not mean that the programs, or some of them at least, aren't good. It simply explains why prime time contains both the best and some of the most insipid, insidious programs. Prime-time television encompasses both the most wonderful and the most revolting examples of television fare. For this reason we think that a good look at what happens during these prime-time hours should be helpful for parents.

Our focus in this book is on the positive qualities of television, so we want to draw your attention to what we consider to be worthwhile on television for young people. We decided to start by looking only at Canadian material, television we consider to be interesting and entertaining for young people. The results of our review are fascinating. We think that a look at Canadian prime-time television is very important here, because some parents and their children are probably unaware that there is a substantial body of excellent Canadian programming.

"Degrassi High" is one of the prime-time series we'll

discuss later. Linda Schuyler, who, with her partner
Kit Hood, runs the production company Playing With
Time, which produced the "Degrassi" series, told us:
"We didn't become prime time until we moved into
'Degrassi Junior High.' Our company had grown
enough so we could produce volume. We hadn't been
in a position to feed serious television before. We were
just doing six half hours per year. Also, we were able
to up our budgets, because we had brought in an
American partner, and so we were able to light well,
hire the crews we needed and get the quality that you
have to have in order to stand up in prime time. Our
earlier shows didn't have the production values of
prime time. Those were 100 percent Canadian
financed, either through private investment or pre-
sales through distributors. You want style, and our
prime-time stuff has got to look good enough stylisti-
cally to stand up to all the other stuff that comes on.
You have to have the budget for that, so it looks good
and sounds good." This is the challenge of creating
television for prime time, whether for adults or for
children.

It's true that most prime-time programs are American, and that many young people watch these more
than they watch the programs we'll discuss here. One
reason for this is that the American programs, which
have more advertising and publicity clout, and therefore more production money, get most of the attention
in our American-sourced television publications. And
too few parents are aware of the existence and value
of our own programs, with a few exceptions like "The
Road to Avonlea" and "Degrassi High."

We focus on Canadian creations because if someone
doesn't there may not be any in a few years, and we
want to encourage the production of more high-quality
Canadian programs. We need to blow our own trum-
pets here, to overcome our native shyness. This
chapter will tell you why you should be encouraging

your children to watch these programs — not simply
because they're Canadian, but because they're good
television.

We don't mean to suggest that because we live in
Canada, our children should be watching only Canadian-made television. Quality television from all over
the world is important for young people in helping
them to develop a global worldview. Still, there is most
definitely a kind of television that is recognizably
Canadian, often rooted in the land, somewhat slower-
paced and gentler in tone and approach than much
American TV. Once this would have meant inferior
stories, scripts and production values. This is no
longer true. "The Road to Avonlea" and many other
Canadian productions have thrust us into the arena
of world-class television. Nonetheless, we think that
there remains a distinctive quality to Canadian
productions.

First, let's look at the CBC/Soapbox Productions
series "Northwood," specifically an episode called
"This Old Man." This episode is early in the series,
which ran its third season in 1992/93. Brian, a
sixteen-year-old, works in a restaurant to pay the bills
his alcoholic father most often fails to pay. The old
man is supposed to have taken a job on a fishing boat.
Brian, meanwhile, is being besieged by phone calls
from the landlord of the houseboat on which they live,
who threatens to evict them the next day for nonpay-
ment of rent. Brian is broke, but his friend Kirk suggests to their high-school friends that they "borrow"
the prom ticket money and loan it to Brian. Next,
Brian receives word that the boat on which his father
was working has gone down in a storm. Everyone on
board is presumed drowned. Brian's friend Jennifer
convinces him to pay the rent anyway, since he will
receive enough insurance money to repay the loan.
After Brian pays the rent, he and Jennifer come upon
Brian's father — dead drunk. He had missed the boat

and gone drinking instead. Brian is torn between rage and joyful relief.

"Northwood," directed at an older teen audience than the earlier series "Degrassi High," which ended in 1991, focuses on the lives of teenagers and the real problems they face, mainly outside school and within their respective families. It's a very honest and courageous attempt to create a real world for its audience, to tell stories about topical issues of importance to young people without becoming preachy or didactic. It's not the fairytale teenage world of "Beverly Hills, 90210," nor does it contain a lot of violence or car chases. Instead, the relationships established as the series moves along are the focus. Each episode centres around one of the characters. This, along with the beautiful Vancouver setting, makes "Northwood" a fine Canadian series that takes on serious emotional and social issues such as family breakup, drug abuse and date rape in strong, entertaining, dramatic form.

There is more prime-time Canadian programming well worth viewing by young people. The series that everyone has come to know and love, "Degrassi High," also deals with issues important to young people. It's the latest part of a long series, which began with "Kids of Degrassi," and has produced a total of ninety-six episodes over the last eleven years. It has built a very large following. In its final few years, between 850,000 and 1 million Canadians watched "Degrassi" every Monday night. Linda Schuyler, describing her experience of the series, comments: "What fascinates me, as I look back, is that we have documented the growth of these Canadian kids from about nine years old up to about nineteen." This is the main accomplishment of the "Degrassi" saga.

As the series ended in February 1991, its producers were in the process of developing several projects that are outgrowths of "Degrassi High." The first, "Degrassi Talks," is a powerful documentary series about issues of current importance to teenagers, six half hours on topics such as sexuality, physical and sexual abuse, alcohol, drugs and depression. "We travelled right across the country, talking to Canadian kids about a lot of the issues that we had been dealing with in the dramatic series," says Linda Schuyler. "But we had kids talking to kids, and we've had kids on street corners in Edmonton and Whitehorse and Peggy's Cove, asking kids what they do when they're depressed, what do they think of masturbation, what're their views on homosexuality, would they have an abortion. And we have got kids talking to kids in a way that they would never talk to us." This documentary style communicates very well with its target audience.

Playing With Time seems to have found a very creative way of using the documentary genre to reach young people. Schuyler's description of the process gives you an idea of how this unique company produces its material. "We've turned the Degrassi performers into documentarians, and they're the ones who've been going out there with the Super VHS cameras, and they get all these kids to sign release forms. They're on their own. We meet in the office in the morning, we give them their challenge and their list of questions and their videotape for the day. They go out and they come back. What's really exciting is to come back to your hotel room and screen this footage. Here we all are, us seasoned veterans and these sixteen- and seventeen-year-olds, screening this footage and commenting back and forth on content and style."

When this series went to air in the spring of 1992, it received very strong critical acclaim, as well as praise from the audience for which it was made. Its impact has been very strong. This is prime-time television turned into educational television at its very best. Parents should watch the series both with their children and by themselves, to get a good sense of the world in which their teenagers live. It is available in video stores and in libraries.

Another video for parents to watch, either alone or with their teenagers, is "School's Out," the finale of "Degrassi High." Teenagers we have talked to describe this movie as one of the most authentic they have seen. They say this is just the way kids talk and act. "School's Out" brings to the screen some of the most difficult problems that teenagers face in their changing lives. (For more about this one, see the review section.) In terms of quality television for young people, Playing With Time has become one of Canada's most important production houses.

Filmworks in Toronto is another important production company. Again, young people have been the primary focus of its productions, but it targets all audience levels. "Where the Spirit Lives" was produced as a movie, which won a Festival Award on its theatrical release during the Festival of Festivals in Toronto in the fall of 1989, and later picked up three Gemini awards, including one for best TV movie. It is the story of young native children taken from their parents and carried off by plane to a religious residential school in 1937. This is a powerful drama about one of the most controversial episodes in the history of Canada and its native peoples, a solid portrayal of courageous Blackfoot children living through a sordid piece of history that Canada would rather forget — the federally approved forced removal of native children from their homes to English-language residential schools in an effort to assimilate them into white society. In the process, the nominally Christian schools cut off all contact with the children's families, language and culture. Later aired as a series of thirty-minute programs, this is high-quality television, with superior production values and story line, that is educational but in no way didactic.

"African Journey" is another series produced by
Filmworks. This story of a young man from Sudbury,
whose father works in the diamond mines of South
Africa, is fine viewing for young people and adults. It
addresses the black/white situation in South Africa,
and the problems of a young man coming to terms with
his identity. Luke Novak arrives from Canada to visit
his father, and immediately learns that his father is
trapped in the mine, along with the father of a black
boy, Timba. Luke becomes involved with Timba's
family, who live in a small native village. Past and
present come together in the story of the friendships
that develop.

"The Road to Avonlea" has become famous throughout Canada and around the world. This program
demonstrates how television, rather than fragment-
ing the family, can bring it together in the way families used to watch television. Sunday evenings have
commonly turned into a kind of "Avonlea" ritual.
Dinner is timed to allow for dessert in front of the television, and the family gathers to enjoy a beautiful
program together. The stories are excellent, with
beautifully crafted scripts, the directing superb, and
the acting fine and powerful. At one point in the
series, in a two-part story shown on successive
Sundays, the mood of the series swung into a darker
vein, with the story of a boy and his villainous father.
During a fight on top of a lighthouse the father falls
to his death. Some viewers objected strongly to the
violence and the blackness of the story. Several seven-
year-old "Avonlea" devotees reported that they hated
these episodes and assumed that the scripts were not
by the usual writer. They felt that "Avonlea" was
about people learning to be kind to each other, not
about people cheating and robbing and fighting. Such
insights show the value of discussing with children
what they see, especially in prime time, in order to
help them understand it.

These two "Avonlea" episodes were apparently an attempt to make the series "grittier," a term that has come to mean the introduction of violence and a rough edge. Perhaps the producers felt that this would attract a larger audience of boys. We hope that this exercise will not be repeated in the series. It is so full of fine stories of a gentle quality, and this style should not be changed, especially if it is in order to attract a larger audience of boys by injecting more violence and physical tension into the stories. It would certainly not be a very encouraging comment on boys. Producers and writers need to find a different way of attracting a young male audience, other than simply injecting more violence. One idea might be to create stronger positive male role models in the series. In the midst of all the violent tension in our world, "The Road to Avonlea" is the kind of series that families need to bring them together in an environment of joy and optimism. This series is an example of how magnificent the medium of television can be. It is prime-time television at its best. "Avonlea" began its fourth season in 1993.

Most people know about "Mr. Dressup" and "The Polka Dot Door" and "Degrassi High." Not everyone is familiar with movies such as *The Last Winter* and *The Challengers*, and movies now made into series such as "Where the Spirit Lives." This is material that stands up well against all other programs — good stories well told on film and brought into your living rooms in prime time.

The Last Winter is a first feature film for producer/writer/director Aaron Kim-Stanley. Many people know William Kurelek's book *A Prairie Boy's Winter*. It's everything Canadian — Canadian children in the season that exemplifies Canada, winter. Watching *The Last Winter* is like reading *A Prairie Boy's Winter*, and very much like looking at Kurelek's paintings. There is a vividness and naïvety that is

most engaging. *The Last Winter* is a Canadian beauty.
This film was made for family viewing and works very
well for children aged seven and up. It was shown in
prime time in the CBC Sunday night movie slot,
which, by the way, given the right movie, can be great
children's viewing. When the movies are about children, they are generally excellent. The showing of *The
Last Winter* made for a rich evening of television, since
it followed that evening's episode of "The Road to
Avonlea."

In a film for children, look for a story suitable to the
ages of your children. *The Last Winter* is a touching,
universal tale of fathers, sons and grandfathers, of
family, of country and city, and of magic, the magic of
Canadian winter. Ten-year-old Will, the central character, is played with fine understatement by Joshua
Murray. He has grown up on a prairie farm with his
family — a brother, a younger sister, his parents and
his grandfather. Will's father has been interviewed for
a new job in the city, and the story follows the process
of his getting the job, taking the family to look for a
new house, and Will's response to leaving the farm.
Much of the tale is built around the play of the children and the passage of the seasons, through which is
woven the tender story of Will's relationship with his
grandfather. *The Last Winter* will suit children aged
seven and up, but has something for all age groups.

This film has its problems: there is a mix of reality
and dream sequences near the end that may confuse
some children. However, this doesn't diminish the
essential beauty and truth of the film. It is the kind of
prime-time fare you should watch for, around which
you might create a special evening. Such an evening,
with a carefully organized TV dinner, can do a lot to
enhance your children's television viewing in a creative way.

An exercise you might try with a film like this, especially when it is available on video, is to quickly check

the introduction. You can tell a lot about the quality of
a film, its story and suitability for various age levels by
looking carefully at the first five minutes. In the opening of *The Last Winter*, the beauty of the world of childhood is set out immediately. The children are stretched
out in a meadow, luxuriating as only children can in the
warmth of the sun, talking about the universe. What
they're really doing is catching gophers. Finally one is
trapped, and the chase is on. Next we follow Will
through his nightmares about gophers, his talks with
Gramps (lovingly played by Gerrard Parkes) and his
overhearing the conversation between his mother and
father about moving to the city.

Co-produced by Lauron Productions of Toronto with
CBC Children's Television, *The Challengers* is a two-
hour special that has potential as a series. It is
another excellent program for families to view
together, and especially suitable for eight- to twelve-
year-olds. The film deals, in an entertaining and fascinating way, and without falling into the usual
clichés and stereotypes, with the problems of identity
and growing up. Mackie, played in a most natural and
engaging manner by Gema Zamprogna, is a ten-year-
old only child whose father, with whom she is very
close, dies suddenly. She and her mother are forced to
make a new start. They move from the city to rent a
home in a small town, from which her mother must
each day make the long drive to her job in the city.
Mackie is lonely and misses the city. Since she loves
music and excels at the keyboard, she tries to join a
group called The Challengers, three typical pre-ado-
lescent boys who want nothing to do with girls, and
certainly don't want one in their band. So Mackie
poses as a boy, calling herself Mack, and becomes one
of the gang. At the same time she meets and befriends
Jennifer.

Her impersonation is known only to old Zack, their
landlord, and her efforts to keep her secret and her

best friend, and take part in the upcoming concert at the recreation centre, both in the band, and in the dance routine with Jennifer, lead to some delightful moments. The plot twists and turns wonderfully, especially in such scenes as the fathers-and-sons fishing trip, during which Mackie must maintain her male identity in particularly difficult circumstances.

The relationships among the youngsters and between the kids and grown-ups are well developed. The adult characters, including even the minor ones, are very believable, especially Mackie's mother, played by Gwynyth Walsh, and Zack, played by Eric Christmas, who acts almost as a chorus to the action.

The music the kids are rehearsing for the concert helps tie various plot lines together and provides a fitting climax. The songs, the rehearsals and the various performances are the kind of television that seven- to twelve-year-olds love to watch, and will watch over and over again. We know kids who have watched it many times over.

The pace of the show is just right for young viewers, and the foreshadowing of possible plots and incidents for future episodes is deftly handled. There's much for parents and kids to discuss after viewing this show. Is it more fun to be a boy or a girl? Is one tougher than the other? How do lonely children and single parents cope in new surroundings?

The basic premise of disguise, the plot, the relationships and the themes of the film are all established in the first few minutes. The following exercise reveals quite a lot about how television works. You'll need a pen and paper, and your watch. First, just watch the tape and time the entire opening, which in this case is seven minutes. Then rewind and start writing down the sequence of images and elements of sound for this opening. For example, our notes included the following:

1. Mother walking worriedly down school hall.
2. Stage rehearsal — torch song.
3. Singer: boy or girl?
4. Shot from back of auditorium: parents and teachers.
5. Worried mother talks to teacher.

and further on in the scene

14. Mother/daughter behind opaque glass door: hug, muffled sob.
15. Funeral.
16. TV/video: freeze on Mackie's father in full frame.

The introduction goes on to establish their move from city to small town, with a scene of The Challengers, and finally to mother and daughter sitting contemplating their new lives. All of this is established brilliantly in the first seven minutes, with very few lines of dialogue. Everything is revealed through sound and picture. This gives a sense of how a good filmmaker works, and it's a good exercise for a quick evaluation of a new video.

A film that will interest slightly older children is *Glory Enough for All*, the story of Frederick Banting and the discovery of insulin. *Glory* is a powerful piece of television about something children study in school. Make sure you know about movies like this. Often we miss such films because they are not part of a series. We are all used to watching series because they're on at the same time each week and we know what to expect. If your children are selecting something from the TV guide, they are not likely to choose something like *Glory Enough for All* because it doesn't sound exciting. So it's important that you point the way to this kind of program.

As for the prime-time offerings of Canada's main broadcaster for young people, YTV, president and

chief executive officer Kevin Shea comments that from
3:30 p.m. to 9:00 p.m., "We are what would be termed
a youth service, in that we are programming to kids
below the age of seventeen. From 9:00 p.m. until midnight it's more programming for the whole family."
Says Shea, "We want kids to see our channel as their
channel." YTV has put many Canadian children on
the air, and children have begun to identify with the
network, using it as a source of information and entertainment. It's very important to have this kind of
service for young people, because in the television
world, young people are the most commercially
abused and the most under-served. YTV is addressing
an audience that has a great need, in today's social
context, for television that is made specifically for
them, both for information and for entertainment. As
YTV's program director told us, "Kids have as much
right to entertainment programming as adults have,
at their own choice of time."

The teen audience is the most difficult audience to
capture. Producers of television for young people will
tell you how they tear their hair out trying to create
something that will grab and hold this audience.
These are kids "raised to graze," says executive producer of "StreetNOISE" Dale Taylor. This series,
unfortunately cancelled in 1991, stands as an example
of the adventurous, experimental kind of programming that YTV is capable of, and we hope the YTV
people will be doing much more of this kind of risk-
taking in the future. (In fact, it is now in repeat broadcast, and selected tapes have been made available to
schools.) In "StreetNOISE," YTV tried to create a
program that would "outzap the zappers," a sort of
street video for kids. A fast-moving, quick-cutting
montage of images, sounds and effects, questions and
on-camera reactions from kids, literally on the street,
it was not every parent's cup of tea. At first glance —
and a first glance is all the viewer got — "Street-

NOISE" may have seemed superficial, loud and trite to some adults, but it dealt with questions of importance to young people, and accepted their answers without embellishment or prompting. It approached issues in a way that addressed the visual and auditory world of the teenager, and took that world very seriously. Every show had one segment dealing with an extremely serious issue. A sequence on drinking and driving was narrated by a young woman, a twentyish victim of a fatal alcohol-related accident that killed her parents and crippled her. The interview was interspersed with comments from teenagers about their own drinking and driving. Because of this personalized treatment, these few minutes sent a powerful message to young people in a better way than many we have seen.

The producers called "StreetNOISE" "info-tainment programming" for teens, providing a fast-paced half hour of opinions, concerns and attitudes. It was a unique explosion of ideas from around the world, driven by music and sensational visuals. "StreetNOISE" should be the flagship program of YTV. It was a venture into an exciting, experimental form of television. Producers should be applauded for having the courage to create shows like this.

Another example of this kind of program for teens from YTV is "Borderline High," which sought to encourage kids to stay in school. Hosted by Canada's own Alanis, who still attends high school while building her singing career, this hour-long special aimed to address kids who might choose not to complete their education. The well-crafted production, directed by one of Canada's best young directors, Richard Mortimer, stands as a model of what YTV is attempting to do. Looking at YTV, we do not see a number of series, but rather a collection of individual specials like "Borderline," each with its focus on something important to the youth audience.

"It is our intention to continue creating topical, informative and entertaining television for Canadian kids, youth and their families," states YTV. The YTV base inventory of programs that are now considered staple perennials are: "Canada Day/Concerts," "Youth Talk," "Rock'n Talk," "Canada's Best," "Awards" and "Hit List."

Three of these, "Youth Talk," "Canada's Best" and "Awards," are good examples of how YTV attempts to meet its stated intent. "Youth Talk" is a live ninety-minute national phone-in special that encourages young viewers to discuss issues of national importance. The YTV Achievement Awards recognize the outstanding accomplishments and contributions made to society by young aspiring Canadians in various fields of endeavour including artistic, environmental, entrepreneurial and social. "Canada's Best," a six-part series, which began in February 1992, featured many well-known Canadians including Maureen Forrester, Karen Kain, Alex Bauman, Glass Tiger, Robert Bateman and Rick Hansen. Even the most respected and internationally recognized Canadians endured uncertain early days and each offers advice to those who are starting out by reflecting back on their own personal and professional journeys. The 1993 series features people like astronaut Roberta Bondar and Canadian artist Ken Kirkby. The series follows some of the past YTV Achievement Award winners and couples them with nationally recognized people in the same field. The young achievers express their thoughts, dreams and frustrations as they pursue what is most important to them. "Canada's Best" also chronicles their lives since receiving their awards. We were most impressed by a program of "Canada's Best" that featured a young person who had saved several lives in a bus accident. The segment was very moving, and honoured a most deserving young person. In this age of predominantly poor press for youth, young people — indeed all of us, young and old alike — need to be reminded of the presence of positive, creative, courageous youngsters.

YTV's Children's Animation Workshop is another example of this network's commitment to children's creativity. In conjunction with the Academy of Canadian Cinema and Film, "Animation '91" featured the animated works of eight kids, who wrote, produced and directed their own short films under the teaching of renowned Canadian animator Aiko Suzuki. The program is a fine celebration both of these eight young people and of the National Film Board's Fiftieth Anniversary, featuring the work of Norman McLaren. The combination of McLaren's most famous animated works, his development of the art of animation, and the work of the eight young people, with their commentary on their work, is superb. This is the kind of television that moves out of the mundane realm of the sitcom and the soap, onto a level that makes excellent use of the medium. It brings fine works of animated art, and the workshops of young people, into our living rooms, where our children can watch this most entertaining program of shorts. Perhaps they will be inspired to develop their own efforts, in whatever direction, to higher levels of accomplishment.

This is the direction in which YTV is moving with great strength. However, young people will not gravitate to this kind of television as quickly as they do to "The Simpsons." Why, one might ask, would kids of eight to twelve be drawn to tune in to "Animation '91," if they happened to see the title in the TV guide? This is true of many of YTV's programs; they need both parents and teachers to bring them to the attention of kids. Teachers can be especially effective here, because such programs are most suitable for classroom use — in film production, guidance and family studies and health courses. In this, YTV is taking over a youth focus that should have been the domain of

public TV networks such as TVOntario. While TVO
has virtually given up the children's and youth
markets, it's encouraging to see a network like YTV
offering programs of value to young people.

In addition to those mentioned above, here is a list
of proposed programs from YTV:

"Costa Rica Cloud Forest:" 60 min.
Highlights the achievements made by five high-
school students from across Canada who travel
down to Costa Rica where they join an international team dedicated to helping save some of the
last untouched cloud forests in Costa Rica. The
students chosen represent the top five high
schools in Canada who have raised funds for the
development of this important nature reserve.

"Crystal Clear:" Christmas '92, 60 min.
The story of two ten-year-olds, Jean Marc, a fran-
cophone boy, and Terry, an anglophone girl, who
discover a way to save winter from evil aliens and
to communicate with each other in a unique way.
The pair learn about all they have in common and
why winter can be so much fun. Set during the
Bal de Neige (Winterlude).

"Canadian Improv Games:" 90 min.
Focusing on a friendly team improvisational competition for students from high schools across
Canada, this show highlights the final round and
sees the winner crowned.

"Kids' Help Phone '92:" 75 min.
In a most interesting fundraising project, YTV is
producing a special program from a series of live
concerts for children at Canada's Wonderland.
Hosted by YTV's PJs (Program Jockeys) and a
fine group of puppets, the Grogs, the program will

be released at all Jumbo Video stores and at
Canada's Wonderland. The goal is to sell 10,000
copies of the tape in order to raise $50,000 for the
Kids' Help Phone. The program was scheduled to
be broadcast in January 1993, after the initial
fundraising effort was completed.

"Live Unity in Toronto:" 90-minute special
A recording of the 1992 multicultural celebration
of the spirit of world unity that featured Cana-
dian and international musicians such as Dizzy
Gillespie, Buffy Sainte Marie, Seals & Crofts,
Red Grammar and Lisa Lougheed.

There is more. Suffice it to say that YTV is trying to
use television in a courageous way, to develop the kind
of programming that will be most valuable to young
people and at the same time to build a network that
will be lively and entertaining. There are strong indi-
cations that YTV is moving in the direction of socially
relevant, interactive television, in which its audience
will become as integral a part of the operation of the
station as the people who work there to produce the
programs. Indeed, with an experiment like YTV's
"The Write Stuff," the script for which was selected
from scripts written for the project by teens from
across Canada, YTV has already entered the realm of
allowing kids to script and produce their own programs. We want to encourage this move in the direction of exciting and creative uses of the medium.
    The problem for YTV, however, is that its program-
ming does not fit with the regular, popular network
fare. Young people do not gravitate naturally to programs with titles like "The Write Stuff." As we said
above, it needs the help of parents and teachers to
bring this kind of programming to the young audience.
We don't pretend to have the answer to the question
of how YTV should capture its audience. Perhaps one

solution would be to eliminate over time the rest of its prime-time schedule, which through the week features "The Muppets," "The Edison Twins," "Paul Daniels' Magic Show," "Smith & Smith," "Deek Wilson," "Leave It to Beaver," "Home and Away," "Zorro," "Fame," "Ronnie," "Wonderstruck," "The Littlest Hobo," "Black Stallion," "Wildside," "White Shadow," "Vidkids," "Doghouse," "Spatz," "Wide World" and "You Can't Do That on Television."

In the context of the programs we discussed above, this list is a real disappointment, since it mainly comprises poor-quality Canadian shows (except for CBC's "Wonderstruck," now defunct) and has-beens such as "Zorro." We hope that YTV is looking for better fare for its viewers and will replace all of this with more relevant, up-to-date programs that might just grab its young audience.

But we must put this criticism into the context of YTV's age as a broadcaster — it has been on the air only since 1988. As well, it has to fill twenty hours of airtime each day, which is a great deal for a young broadcasting company whose mandate is to serve children. The goal in creating YTV, as chief executive officer Kevin Shea states, was "to have a Canadian children's service before an American service came into Canada." Merv Stone, vice president of programming and acquisitions, gave us what we consider to be one of the best statements about children's television we've heard: "With children's television there comes a point where it's beyond the dollar. The very philosophy of children's programming is beyond the dollar. When you're dealing with kids' programming, whether the child is three years old or thirteen, there's a certain amount of responsibility on the part of the broadcaster. This is something we take very, very seriously."

We hope that in the years to come YTV will live up to this statement, and replace much of its obsolete content with higher-quality television for young people. It has the opportunity to deliver excellent television to its audience, but there is a tremendous responsibility in this opportunity.

Another example of responsible children's programming is "Kidzone," out of Vancouver's Knowledge Network, at the time of writing scheduled for weeknight broadcast at 7:00 p.m. in Vancouver. "Kidzone" is a magazine-format show for eleven- to fourteen-year-olds, with plenty of music and movement, and packed with information for young people presented in an entertaining manner. There are contests, book reviews and street raps with pertinent questions for kids. There are also well-dramatized environmental items and good consumer tips. The young hosts are lively and energetic, and have great fun introducing the fascinating educational items in each episode. "Kidzone" is a good combination of education and entertainment, which makes it ideal for broadcast to young people in the early prime-time slot.

If you check the TV guide, you'll see that there is not a lot of television programming specifically aimed at kids in that early prime-time slot. The reason for this is that children's programming doesn't generate the kind of advertising revenue that adult programs do. This makes it virtually impossible for the series "Street Cents," made by the CBC for the same audience as "Kidzone," to be broadcast in the evening, in the prime-time slot that it and children deserve. Instead, it is relegated to the Saturday morning slot opposite those seductive cartoons. "Street Cents" is a good example of a fine but poorly scheduled program that should be shown at a time that is appropriate for its audience, which, in our estimation, is 7:00 p.m.

Canadian television for young people may be coming into its own, but the sad reality is that few children watch it. No matter how much you would like your children to be watching what *you* consider to be the best programs, they are still likely to be watching what we found the students in a typical grade seven class were watching. If you have a child around this age, you should know what these programs are about in order to decide for yourself whether they are appropriate for your child. Here are some of their selections: "In Living Color," "Get a Life," "Growing Pains," "Who's the Boss?" "The Simpsons," "Unsolved Mysteries of America," "Fresh Prince of Bel Air," "Family Matters," "Married . . . With Children," "Saturday Night Live," "Arsenio Hall," "Beverly Hills, 90210," "The Cosby Show," "Full House" and "Golden Girls."

In a review of the viewing patterns of this class, the top four shows were "Fresh Prince of Bel Air," "The Simpsons," "Growing Pains" and "Who's the Boss?" Notice that not one of the programs we referred to earlier is on this list. Perhaps some of these children watch "The Road to Avonlea" but do not associate it with prime time, which they relate to the programs they watch on a regular basis during the week rather than on weekends. In one particular class, a teacher survey included a question on why they watched certain programs. One boy said of "The Simpsons": "I love it because of the comedy of badness." Another kid watched "Married . . . With Children" "because it is very funny and they are so negative it makes me feel lucky to have caring parents."

These are not the answers we would expect. If you ask your children why they watch certain programs you too may get answers that surprise you. What does this child mean by "the comedy of badness"? He obviously means it as a compliment to the program though it could be interpreted negatively. But clearly this young boy loves the show. Is this a problem?

"The Simpsons" is black comedy. In one program, for example, Homer Simpson's brother is distressingly cruel towards him. His brother is president of a car manufacturing company that is not doing well. Because of a few remarks by Homer, his brother

latches onto him as the saviour of the company, gives
him everything he wants — money, a new house, as
well as the most prominent position in the company.
When Homer finally unwraps his automobile creation
in front of all the shareholders, and it's an abysmal
failure, his brother rejects him, takes away everything
he gave him and treats him terribly. This is not the
kind of behavioural model we think children need, and
yet millions of dollars have been spent in the production of the high-quality animation in the show. You
will have to make up your own mind about this. As we
have said, no one program is going to ruin your child.
As an adult, you probably have your own favourite
escape programs to just relax and enjoy. So do children. They have as much right to this as you do.

One of the hardest aspects of dealing with television
is that when your children reach the age of twelve or
thirteen, you don't really have much control over what
they watch, or often even the amount they watch,
unless good viewing patterns have been established
from a very early age. Perhaps the main point is that,
with regard to television, you will have to begin treat-
ing your older children in a more adult manner, discussing issues of viewing time and programs as you
would with an adult. Listen to their views. You don't
always have to agree with them. Discuss. Debate.
Good conversation between people who are willing to
listen to each other's views often results in changes on
both sides.

If your children are watching an inordinate amount
of TV and you are concerned, look for the cause of the
excessive viewing. No matter how seductive we like to
think it is, television itself is not the cause of a
teenager watching the screen for five or six hours each
night. Something else is going on, and you won't find
it by blaming the talking furniture. Let's put prime-
time television, and all television, into its proper
context.

Be creatively concerned about television, and interested in it, but try not to foist your own values on your children or over-analyse programs and take the fun out of them. Being creatively concerned simply means knowing what programs your children are watching, knowing something about the programs and finding ways of discussing programs with your children, not in the sense of suggesting they not watch particular programs, but rather talking about the quality of the story or lack thereof, and the various aspects of the production qualities, such as acting, directing, camera movement, music, special effects and so on, in a natural way rather than an artificial "media literacy" classroom manner. We all discuss movies and books. Television can be the focus of the same kind of discussions.

Perhaps a few examples are in order here. One of the most popular prime-time programs among pre-teens and teens is "Beverly Hills, 90210," which focuses on a family that has moved from the American Midwest to Beverly Hills. The stars of the series are teenaged brother and sister Dylan and Brenda Walsh and their invariably good looking, fashionably dressed friends. Watch a few programs, if you can stand it, before you dare to say anything about them. Your children will jump all over you with their expertise if you don't do your research. So watch with them. What is it that they find appealing about the program? Your TV guide should be your bible. There's a lot of valuable information here about the programs our kids are watching. In the case of "Beverly Hills," at the time of writing, *The Globe and Mail's Broadcast Week* had just published an article about the series in which the producer set out the goals of the series: "We want the show to be about how the Walsh family's mores change other people's mores and morality. I agreed to do it as long as we don't have to depict everyone in Beverly Hills as idols, rich, fat and stupid." Once you know

what is intended, you can begin to make some judg-
ments about whether these goals are being achieved.
It might even be a good idea to share the article with
your children. Then you have some great openings for
discussion. In fact, you may not even have to open the
discussion. Your teenager may do this for you.

"Beverly Hills, 90210" depicts young people in
various problematic situations. The producer speaks
of doing programs about teenage shoplifting, drugs,
drinking and driving, date rape and the sensible use
of condoms. These are serious topics and demand
good, honest treatment. You can show creative
concern about a series like this, if it is one of your children's favourites, by discussing its success or failure
in relation to its stated aims, the treatment of the
problems and the credibility or "reality" of the characters and story.

A teacher who uses and discusses television a great
deal in his classroom tells us that young people have
a definition of "television reality" that identifies it as
somewhat different from everyday reality. There is of
course a difference, since a television program is a
construct, an artifact that is "not real life." However,
the kind of "reality" kids often talk about with television concerns camera movement, laugh track and so
on. They expect the camera to remain stationary, and
become annoyed when a hand-held camera is used to
give one a sense of seeing through the eyes of the character. They want the camera to be bolted down, and
they want laugh tracks. They see this as "real."

In the context of these kinds of expectations, discussion about a program like "Beverly Hills" will
begin to force kids to question some of their accepted
beliefs about television. Are the characters true depictions of young people? Since your children are also
young people, they may have some thoughts about
being portrayed in the silly, banal way most of the
characters are in this series. The characters are so

squeaky-clean and cute that they are, to us, ugly, like caricatures of some of the youngsters on "The Mickey Mouse Club." Dylan is a ridiculous parody of James Dean. The actors are grown-ups playing at being teenagers. The script is so bad that it would not have made it past first-draft reading at CBC Children's Television. The quality of camera work, direction and music is some of the lowest we have seen. Have a look at CBC's "Northwood" for enlightening comparison.

We have great faith in the critical faculties of young people. In a discussion of "Beverly Hills, 90210," we believe that you will hear your children talk about the lack of credibility in the programs, the dreadful quality of the acting and the almost insulting depiction of young people. In fact, young people have told us that the series is the topic of much discussion on the school bus, and most of them seem to agree that much of the series is "stupid." One example that kept recurring was a program about prom night and the loss of virginity. They spoke of the banality of the lines and how dumb it all was. Without going into any kind of formal teaching situation, you can explore with your children a series like "Beverly Hills" in a fun, creative way that will give them a forum for their own thoughts and opinions. They need this because of the market-driven peer pressure that is so much a part of the success of series such as "Beverly Hills." You're not cool if you don't look upon the show as cool. But, if kids can talk about these kinds of programs informally, they can begin to develop a sense that they don't have to accept television as truth, that they can have their own opinions of programs and can, perhaps, be even more cool by developing independent opinions on a series such as this.

Perhaps as adults we take this series too seriously, while the kids enjoy it as fantasy and fun. However, its success is due more to the fact that it is a well-marketed package than that it is a high-quality television series. It's a commercial for a fantasy life for kids, a way of allowing them to forget the problems in their lives for a brief time. "Beverly Hills" is industry more than entertainment.

Now we have the follow-up to "90210," "Melrose Place," which is, as one critic has aptly put it, "yet another slice of white bread," with very little content, this time featuring the "twentysomething" set, in which all the guys are hunks and all the girls are cute, and problems are solved with platitudes. We say little about this series, because we would simply be repeating, only in stronger terms, what we have said above about "90210."

"Fresh Prince of Bel Air," one of the most popular of all prime-time shows with both children and adults, is another series about which we have reservations, even though in quality it is far superior to "Beverly Hills." "Fresh Prince" draws some of the largest audiences in Canada, although again it's a U.S. series. It falls very much into the same category as Bill Cosby's show in terms of its structure, its setting and its endless stream of one-liners. Will, the central character, is not that good in school, likes to sneak out and to play tricks on people, so of course he is always getting into trouble. It is the favourite of many teenagers and pre-teens, because it's easy fantasy. The basic premise of the story, a young black person sent to live with his well-to-do uncle and aunt so that he can have a better chance in life, is not social commentary, but rather more akin to a fantasy of what you would do if you were to win a million dollars. The lottery comparison is an apt one because Will is the one-in-a-million poor black kid who is lucky enough to have rich relatives to welcome him into a house that is almost interchangeable with the Huxtables'. In many respects, "Fresh Prince" and "The Cosby Show" are the same show, only with different basic situations.

There are two ways of approaching series like these. They can be seen as either pure escapist entertainment, and as such simply innocuous fun. But they can also be seen as representations of North American societal values that need to be questioned and talked about.

So why is "Fresh Prince" so popular? Even we have to admit to enjoying the show's humour. Ever since this series hit the entertainment scene, it's been popular because of Will's ability to make fun of his uncle and aunt in a disarming, amusing way. Each show is nothing more than an expanded version of group stand-up comedy. There is nothing wrong with this. The stories are very easy to watch, because there is no dramatic tension — the problems are too trite. And while the stories are comfortable, it's out of this comfort that many of the subtle difficulties of the series grow. The characters' problems bear no relation to the kinds of concerns that we all have each day. Will's uncle and aunt never seem to work and have all the time in the world to solve the issue of the day. Their home is replete with everything one could want in one's home, including a very clever butler. All the characters are walking display cases of their many possessions — from clothes to the latest household gadgets.

As we have already said, there is nothing wrong with the program as fun entertainment. The problems arise when your children begin to want their environment to be the same as the one Will inhabits, when they want their problems solved as easily and with as much fun as Will's, and when they expect their careers to be the same kind of idle, irresponsible, obviously high-paying career as that of Will's uncle. We think that there is a subtle, not altogether desirable message in the program — the power that Will's uncle has over his family and the viewers. He is the one who has the last word, even though Will has the last laugh. His is the style of the very friendly but powerful corporate executive, who can josh, and coerce, and cajole, and seem to be giving in while all the time remaining the controlling force, moving everything into line with the vision of the company. As we said, if discerning viewers watch "Fresh Prince" as fantasy, this is fine. However, the words of one eleven-year-old are typical of how children of that age regard the show: "I like this kind of show. Everything is happy and funny, but not too crazy or silly. *It is believable.*"

The fact that children see such shows as believable indicates their need for some assistance along the road to becoming discerning viewers. How do we give children the ability to recognize that the world these programs create is totally antiseptic and unreal, sheltered from all the strands of life that wind into everything we do and affect the way we are? We talk. Simply that. We watch with them, read to them about the issues that are treated in such shows, make these series the centre of dinnertime conversation. A couple of dinnertime conversation starters: Would you like to eat at Will's uncle's home? Why? Would you like to invite Will to your place? And if you happen to be discussing another popular series, "Married . . . With Children," you can use the same approach. Would you like Al Bundy to be your father? Or Peg to be your mother? These might open up some interesting conversation. This approach is an easy way to begin to lead your children towards being more discerning when watching television.

Another problem that arises from all sitcoms is the potential confusion between real time and fantasy time. Television problems get solved in a half hour because that's the length of the program. This can become a problem when children start to expect immediate solutions to real-life problems, with minimum effort. "The Cosby Show," a series now available only in reruns, provides an instructive example. One episode, which was about studying *Julius Caesar* in school, was shown to a grade eleven class that was studying the play. The class project was to follow the example of the "Cosby" episode and turn sections of the play into rap — not an easy task. Huxtable son and friend are not happy with having to study the play, until Christopher Plummer and Roscoe Lee Brown, two well-known and accomplished actors, just happen on the scene and make *Julius Caesar* a lot of fun. Wouldn't you just love to have these two appear when your children are studying Shakespeare? The boys go upstairs to work on the play, refusing dessert in favour of their studies. Five minutes' TV time later, down they come with a beautifully rehearsed rap version of Antony's speech, "Friends, Romans, countrymen, lend me your ears . . ."

All of this is very funny, and the rap number on the show is a superb bit of entertainment. However, it took the class almost two weeks of real-time writing and revisions to arrive at workable rap numbers. And their response to the "Cosby" solution was bitter disappointment. It took some talking for the teacher to convince them that highly paid scriptwriters probably took a week to write the scene, and the kids in the show probably rehearsed the piece for several days. And then, because of the nature of television production, they probably did several takes in order to get the piece just the way they wanted it, and to time. This is the prime-time problem — subtle, funny, but the values and standards are both questionable and very seductive.

But again, what's wrong with a little fantasy? Most of us need some kind of escape. The problem is that when your fantasy becomes the driving force of your life, as it does with many people who spend large amounts of money they cannot afford on lottery tickets, then something is terribly wrong. There is nothing wrong with the fun of shows like "Fresh Prince of Bel Air," and what a wonderful medium it is that brings us such fun. It's when kids start to believe that this is real life, to talk and act like Will, that it's time for some discussion about what's real and what isn't, and perhaps about what makes kids want to live the fantasy because it's so much more inviting than real life. Once again, the phrase "creative concern" is an important one here, because "Fresh Prince" is not a show we would condemn or wish to deny to young people.

A bit more about creative concern. The following excerpt from an article by Tom Englehardt in *Mother Jones* (May/June 1991) is very applicable to "Fresh Prince," "Cosby" and many other sitcoms, even though it discusses a television show for a much younger audience than the one we're discussing here. Englehardt describes his five-and-one-half-year-old-son "chirping in wonder" as he watched "Mr. Roger's Neighbourhood," when Fred Rogers spoke directly into the screen, saying hello and asking if his child audience remembered him.

Englehardt goes on to say:

Fred Rogers' show is rare not just in having a living being on screen, but in adhering resolutely to real-time boundaries. If popcorn is popped, you wait for it to happen. No one watching a young child watching Mr. Rogers could deny the active possibilities he makes the screen offer up.

The application of this to shows like "Beverly Hills" and "Fresh Prince" is not to demand that they be produced in real time or depict real time. The nature of television constructs makes this impossible. However, it's important to find a way of making sure that your children understand that what they are watching is not in real time, that the laughter on the laugh track is not real, that the time in which problems are solved is not what it takes to solve problems in real life and that, for the most part, the problems in the programs are not the mundane, sometimes trite, sometimes tragic problems with which we must deal in everyday real life. This means knowing what your children, whether very young or older teenagers, are watching, having a sense of their responses to what they are watching, knowing something of your own response and being willing to talk about these programs. We're suggesting that you do more than just watch with your kids, more than just impose arbitrary rules about time and what your kids can watch. We recommend that you learn something about these television programs yourself and help your children to become discerning viewers. Maturity means the ability to discern, and this applies to television as it does to life.

Honest, distinctive, revolutionary. These are apt words to describe the series and programs with which we began this chapter. Series such as "Northwood," "StreetNOISE," "Degrassi Talks" and "The Road to Avonlea," and movies such as *The Challengers, The Last Winter, Where the Spirit Lives* and *Glory Enough for All* demonstrate the potential of television and its beauty as a medium of communication. These are productions that struggle to present high-quality documentaries and rich stories for young people. When we speak of prime-time television for young people, these are some of the best examples, and we can be proud that they're Canadian. However, the reality is that when we put this list alongside the rest of the prime-time schedule, and look at what there is for young people, the list looks surprisingly small.

Try sometime, as we did, setting out the prime-time schedule, 7:00 p.m. to 11:00 p.m., on a large sheet of paper. This will give you a much more graphic presentation of the overall television picture than simply looking at the pages of your TV guide. After you have the entire schedule on paper, have your children circle the programs that they watch. Then, perhaps in another colour, go through it and circle the programs that you believe are suitable programs for your children. The selection will differ with each child, but it will give you a good idea of what parts of the prime-time schedule most interest your children, as opposed to those you think are worth viewing. It will also give you an idea of how concerned you should be about your children's viewing habits, or whether you need to be concerned at all.

Chapter 4

IN THE DAYTIME

"Sesame Street" is the most important TV show in history . . . and the most influential show ever produced. . . .

Clive VanderBurgh,
Producer, "Today's Special"

Much has been written and said about "Sesame Street" in the more than twenty years since it first came on the air. Academics have fretted over its hype and fast pace, and suggested that the show contributes to children's short attention span. Reading experts cry that learning the letters of the alphabet has little or nothing to do with learning to read. Others bemoan that fact that you can't necessarily transfer learning from television to learning from a book.

But we agree with Clive VanderBurgh, who is known to parents and children for prize-winning productions such as "Today's Special" and "Cucumber," and worked on more than 100 episodes of "Sesame Street." The fact that "Sesame Street" launched the career of Jim Henson, creator of "The Muppets," is reason enough to give it a place of honour in television history.

VanderBurgh points out that "Sesame Street" was the first children's television project to be sufficiently

funded to enable the Children's Television Workshop,
which developed the program, to hire the brightest
minds in television and first-class writers and performers. And it happened in the United States, where,
except for "Mr. Rogers' Neighborhood" and "Captain
Kangaroo," children's television was a ghetto.
"Sesame Street" took everyone by storm, and when it
eventually got international distribution, it set the
standard around the world for technical excellence in
the production of television for children. Again,
because of the funding, the producers were able to
develop production techniques that had not been used
before in children's TV. They were able to afford high-
quality animation and develop significant new techniques for cueing music and dialogue with puppets
and animated characters. It was a difficult series to
produce because of the combination of education and
comedy, both of which are difficult to carry off on television, doubly difficult when they have to be combined, and for children.

"Sesame Street" made children's television
respectable. It was now acceptable for broadcasters to
work — and to say they worked — in children's TV. As
the audience grew, it was economically attractive to
broadcasters, management saw it was good competi-
tive business — and they were no longer just being
altruistic. Most important of all, according to Vander-
Burgh, it was a quality program that had a great
impact on children all over the world.

Dr. Edward L. Palmer, one of the first members of
the Children's Television Workshop, points out that
the series was originally made as part of the Head
Start program for underprivileged pre-schoolers in
the United States. In evaluating the accomplishments
of the series, Palmer comments, "As a member of the
original team, I believe its chief contribution has been
to facilitate the transition from home to school for
many generations of children aged three to five years,

which is, of course, precisely what it sets out to do."

The Bert and Ernie sketches follow traditional two-man comedy routines — the fat man and the thin man, the Laurel and Hardy, the Sir Toby and Sir Andrew, the Abbott and Costello — that have been around as long as there has been dramatic comedy. One routine combines a lesson on the parts of the body with the letter N. Ernie appears on screen with a sock over his nose and asks Bert to guess what part of the body he is thinking of. Bert, of course, says he won't go along with the game because it's too silly, it's obviously going to be his nose. Ernie encourages him to play, to guess anyway, saying he knows it will be hard because Bert can't see this part of the body. Bert refuses to go along. Finally, impatiently, he shouts, "Of course it's your nose." Ernie: "No it's not, Bert." He pulls down the collar of his turtle-neck, and says, "It's my neck. It's all covered up too." Disgusted, Bert leaves. Ernie looks at the kids, pulls the cover off his nose and says, "Gee, I wonder why he said nose?" Then, as Ernie disappears, both the words Neck and Nose appear on the screen.

Two sequences later, two animated characters appear on the screen, one large and one small. The large one, very talkative, says "Hi, neighbour," and Neighbour appears on the screen. He points out that Neighbour begins with N and then runs through a list of half a dozen other words, also beginning with N. All this time the small character is completely silent. Finally the tall figure says, "I bet you know a whole bunch of words that begin with N, too." To which the small character answers No. The figures disappear. The word No stays on the screen. The timing is beautiful. It's first-rate TV, produced by professionals, with comic timing that's as good as any we've seen.

These are typical examples of the successful combination of education and comedy that has become the hallmark of "Sesame Street." With all else that

"Sesame Street" does — such as segments about the family and its treatment of handicapped people and the elderly — it is, as both VanderBurgh and Palmer point out, one of the greats in the world of children's television. "Sesame Street" is such a strong illustration of what can be done when there is not only the budget to achieve the best-quality production, but also a genuine concern for children and the conviction that television can be an important influence in their lives. For this reason, we begin this chapter with "Sesame Street" as the touchstone by which we will judge the rest of daytime television for children.

We should point out that the Canadian version of "Sesame Street" contains twenty-two minutes of Canadian content in each sixty-minute program. The Canadian content is produced by CBC field producers across Canada, with an executive producer in Toronto. A three-day workshop is held each year to review the past year's production, and to critically assess the segments that have been produced for the coming season. At this workshop are representatives of the Children's Television Workshop from New York, Canadian consultants in various aspects of television and research of children's television and all the field producers from across the country. Over these three days a very careful examination of the structure, content and production quality of the segments for the next season is carried out. While this is expensive, it is a model of what should be done, especially with television produced for children. What a dream! To be able to spend this kind of time analysing the material being produced for children, making certain that it meets the goals and objectives of the series. This is precisely what is done on the Canadian version of "Sesame Street."

Unfortunately, as usual, this excellent program is the exception rather than the rule. Recently we flipped around the dial at 4:00 p.m. on a weekday afternoon, just to see what we might find if we were looking for a program for children, from pre-school through high school, because many kids arrive home from school at this time. As we looked at this daytime programming, what emerged was the lack of both quality and quantity of programming for young people. This is what we found:

TVOntario	Issues in Education
Global	"Batman, the Animated Series"
CKVR Barrie (Ind.)	"Gilligan's Island"
CBC	"Dan Gallagher's Video Hits"
CityTV	"Oprah Winfrey"
CTV	"Darkwing Duck"
CHCH Hamilton	"Matlock"
WKBW Buffalo	"Oprah Winfrey"
WNED PBS Buffalo	"Sesame Street" (continued)
WUTV Fox Buffalo	"Merrie Melodies"
Vision TV	"Highway"
YTV	"You Can't Do That on Television"
TSN	Badminton
MuchMusic	"Life on Venus Avenue"
Family Channel	"DuckTales"
WIBV Buffalo	"Cosby"

In all of this, if you were looking for a program for a child under nine or ten, you'd find "DuckTales," the last half of "Sesame Street," "Merrie Melodies" and "Batman," which is somewhat sombre for kids. If 4:00 p.m. is the beginning of prime time for children, what are the networks really doing for children at this time? Indeed, what are they doing for children after school to 7:00 p.m., since this is a time when many kids plunk themselves down in front of the TV set? What are they telling us about their concerns for

children? Most of the material aimed at children is
adult programming made ten to twenty-five years ago.
Talk shows like "Oprah," "Donahue" and "Geraldo"
(5:00 p.m.) are definitely not for children. The few that
are aimed specifically at children are mainly the
regular set of schlock cartoons ("Ninja Turtles,"
"James Bond Jr.") and "Kids Incorporated," a badly
produced American variety show. There are a few
bright lights in this wasteland of the darkening hours
from 4:00 to 7:00, such as "Reading Rainbow,"
"Sesame Street," "Polka Dot Door" and one of the best
science fiction fairy tales, "Star Trek: The Next Generation." But if you don't happen to subscribe to the
Family Channel, or if you don't receive YTV, your
choice is limited.

If children's viewing at this time is not regulated,
which is the case in many homes, take a guess at what
they'd be watching. Here are some entries from a
hypothetical viewing schedule for a home-alone kid,
watching television after school between 4:00 p.m.
and 6:30: "Gilligan's Island," "Growing Pains,"
"Geraldo," "Golden Girls," "Full House," "Who's the
Boss?" If your child is watching this line-up night after
night, until you get home from work and dinner is
ready, what perspective on the world is he or she
developing? Either the idealized past of "Gilligan's
Island," the sleeze of "Geraldo" or the strange family
alignments of "Who's the Boss?" and "Golden Girls."
As one critic so aptly put it, "Kids have to sift through
the idealized images of past eras in an effort to
unearth a true representation of the society in which
they live. They suffer not from information overload,
but rather misinformation overload."

Why is this what the networks think is suitable for
children? Now, do the same exercise for the morning period, from 6:00 a.m. to 8:30, during the week. Have a
look a the line-up of programs for children. The majority are run-of-the-mill cartoons, with the exception of

"Sharon, Lois & Bram" at 8:00 and "Polka Dot Door."
So what can you, as parents, do about it? In the last
chapter of this book we will give you some suggestions
about what to do if you have something to say to the networks about what your children are watching.

We're not interested in getting into criticism of the
other programs that are on, because we're concerned
about good programming for kids at all times. The
point is that you could do this at many times of the day
and come up with similar results. When we think of
daytime programming for children, we tend to think
of the morning. On a Tuesday at 10:00 a.m., we find
for children:

PBS	"Captain Kangaroo"
YTV	"The Friendly Giant"
CBC	"Fred Penner's Place"
TVO	"Riddle of Wizard's Oak"
FA	"Best of Walt Disney's True Life Adventures"

This time, five good ones: "Captain Kangaroo," "The
Friendly Giant" and "Fred Penner's Place" are all
exceptionally fine programs for young children.
However, as most parents of this generation know, the
first two are series that you yourselves watched and
enjoyed as children. Now, your own children are being
captivated by these same programs, and "Mr. Rogers'
Neighborhood" as well. These three, along with
"Sesame Street," contain many of the qualities that
make for excellent children's programming. It is significant that "Rogers," "Kangaroo" and "Giant" are no
longer in production, though they are still on the air.
Is this because there is no interest in making high-
quality programs for children? Where are the
resources? Where are the new programs that will
eventually replace these series? While the children's
audience is evergreen, as is said in the business, this

is not an excuse for these series to be forever the main-
stay of children's programming. Obviously, since they
are still being shown (in the case of "The Friendly
Giant," revived after a long absence from the screen),
there is a large market for them. There was a time
when this kind of programming was considered
important. Is it no longer important? As parents, we
need to demand more for our children than they are
presently getting on television.

Nonetheless, while we pose these questions, there
are still good things being done in children's television. For example, Fred Penner, the engaging adult
host of "Fred Penner's Place," accompanies himself on
guitar as he sings and talks directly to his young audience. His "place" is outdoors, the kind of wonderful
hideaway kids love. The show has an easygoing,
relaxed and spontaneous atmosphere. Usually there's
a theme (a smile, a rainbow, sunshine, time) but no
"message." Fred's sidekick is a puppet named Giorgio,
and every day Wordbird delivers a new word. Two
days a week the show runs for half an hour (fifteen
minutes on the other days), allowing for the appearance of guests such as Charlotte Diamond who help
Fred tell stories and sing songs. The whole show is a
delightful, friendly session — a kind of upbeat Mr.
Rogers in an outdoor hideaway.

There are several other series during the morning
worth mentioning for pre-schoolers. A superb half
hour on PBS is provided by "Reading Rainbow," hosted
by Levar Burton. The series takes viewers on various
voyages of discovery aimed at promoting a love of
learning and of good books. Each episode concludes
with three or four illustrated book reviews by likeable,
articulate children. A wide variety of topics (bees and
beekeeping, baseball, the making of an episode of
"Star Trek") and locations, and the positive and imaginative approach through reading, make this an excellent series for children from five to thirteen. Money

has been spent here — you'll see it in the quality of the program when you watch it.

Other series for children in the morning often are as follows:

10:30 a.m.	CBC	"Mr. Dressup"
	YTV	"Mr. Rogers' Neighborhood"/"Snelgrove Snail"
11:00	CBC	"Sesame Street"
	TVO	"Sharon, Lois & Bram"
	YTV	"Marie Soleil"
11:30	YTV	"Take Part"
	TVO	"Take a Look"

"Mr. Dressup," of course, belongs in that class of children's television that we mentioned above, which includes "The Friendly Giant" and "Mr. Rogers." For over a quarter of a century (he celebrated his twenty-fifth anniversary in the 1991/92 season), Mr. Dressup has entertained and encouraged children to take part in a host of activities and stretch their imaginative and creative abilities, all with minimal sets and props.

Let's look now at the Canadian network designed to cater to young people, YTV, to see what more they have to offer for children of various ages in the daytime.

6:00 a.m.	"Kid's Corner"	Pre-school
6:30	"Wild Guess"	8-12
7:00	"Romper Room"	Pre-school
7:30	"Maya the Bee"	5-8
8:00	"The Elephant Show"	5-8
8:30	"Camp Cariboo"	5-8
9:00	"Shining Time Station"	Pre-school
9:30	"Lamb Chops Play-Along"	Pre-school
10:00	"The Friendly Giant"	Pre-school
10:30	"Mr. Rogers" (M, W, F)	Pre-school
	"Snelgrove Snail" (T, Th)	Pre-school

11:00	"Marie Soleil"	Pre-school
11:30	"Take Part"	Pre-school
12:00	"You Can't Do That on Television"	Youth
12:30	"Casper"	5-8
1:00	"Shining Time Station"	Pre-school
1:30	"Size Small"/ "Time To Read"	Pre-school
2:00	"Friendly Giant"	Pre-school
	"Poddington Peas"	Pre-school
2:30	"Lamb Chops Play-Along"	Pre-school
3:00	"Camp Cariboo"	5-8
3:30	"Count Duckula"	5-8
4:00	"You Can't Do That on Television"	Youth
4:30	"Ninja Turtles"	5-8
5:00	"Rocky and Bullwinkle"	Youth
5:30	"Nick Arcade"	Youth
6:00	"Rock 'n Talk"	Teens
6:30	"Hit List with Tarzan Dan"	Teens

As we noted earlier, YTV is a young network, trying to do what is almost impossible in Canada: program entirely for the young, from pre-school to young adults. On the whole, they do a fairly acceptable job. While they are to be congratulated for some outstanding efforts in the production and acquisition areas for both daytime and prime time, there are still too many tired old fillers like "You Can't Do That on Television." But they have picked up some outstanding pre-school material, such as "The Friendly Giant," "Mr. Rogers" and "The Elephant Show"; even the locally produced "Time to Read," a fifteen-minute show about good stories for children, is worth a look for pre-schoolers. While we know these series are old, some on their fifth and sixth repeats at least, they are still high-quality children's shows with excellent content. These are the kinds of programs that should be repeated at times suitable for young children, and that parents will want their children to see.

YTV provides three other series we think are worth children's viewing time. Produced in Saskatoon by Sask Media, "Size Small" is a gentle, pleasant show for pre-schoolers, with an attractive host, Miss Helen, assisted by articulate children and delightful puppets. There's a music room for songs, a Busy Beehive for making things and lots of encouragement to join in and continue doing things after the show is over. This series fits into the same grouping as "Mr. Rogers" and "Polka Dot Door," because it too is in real time; its mood is gentle and appealing to pre-schoolers especially, and it is full of a genuine love of and concern for children.

"Waterville Gang," for pre-schoolers, features an underwater world of puppet sea creatures. The stories centre on a fantasy sea family helping each other to solve everyday problems (for example, feeling you're being left out, fear of certain noises or finding out everyone else but you has a talent). This series was originally produced for CTV and features Canadian artists and puppets. Our reservation is that it was produced in 1973 and is showing its age.

"Wild Guess" is a quiz show for eight- to twelve-year-olds, with questions based on knowledge of the animal kingdom. It has pleasant hosts and interesting content, and uses a quiz show format in which the competition between the two teams is keen but not aggressive. The live audience of children are permitted to join in with some of the answers, but they aren't the usual yelling and screaming audience one often sees in quiz and game shows for young children. "Wild Guess" is proof that there can be intelligent quiz shows for young people. The kids have to know their stuff and reason things out. There are challenges for the live audience and for the home audience too. And when the right answer is given, there are excellent slides and film clips of the creatures being discussed.

YTV is working to have young people talking to young people in many ways through the day. Their PJs (Program Jockeys), pleasant young hosts (although sometimes they are too fast, trying to be too cool), chat with the audience, read letters from children, introduce new shows, interview other young people and so on. The show demonstrates the network's encouragement and integration of young people in their productions. The PJs attract an audience their own age and younger. In this and other programs discussed elsewhere, such as "Borderline High" and "Canada's Best," YTV is offering something more for children than merely showing bland entertainment chopped up with commercials. And they are planning more of this kind of programming in the near future, such as movie reviews and book talks by and for young people.

The Family Channel, as we mentioned in the chapter on Saturday morning TV, is, by and large, the Disney Channel of Canada. Available through subscription on cable, it describes itself as "a national premium television service that features first quality entertainment for today's family." Up to sixty percent of all programming is provided by the Disney Channel, while the remaining forty percent consists of twenty-five percent Canadian and fifteen percent of the best the world has to offer. The weekday schedule is very much like the weekend's — a Disney package and a variety of adventures, films and a teen game show, "Teen Win Lose or Draw," later in the day. It's not in the same league with YTV's "Wild Guess," since it's really a game for an older audience, rather than a quiz show. It's no worse than the adult shows of the same kind, though about as vacuous. We need to ask more of kids' game and quiz shows.

In Chapter 2, we regretted the fact that there was so little Canadian content on the Family Channel's Saturday morning schedule. However, in the weekday schedule there is some promising Canadian material. Family Channel says of a series called "Take Off": "Shot on location in Vancouver and Victoria, B.C., this exuberant half-hour series combines drama, art work, music, humour, science, storytelling and more, through the magic of the ultimate-chromavision process. Targeted to children ages six to eleven . . . the purpose of 'Take Off' is to demonstrate and encourage the divergent or lateral thinking process to help children value and retain their natural creativity. By taking a theme and expressing it in many different visual, verbal, artistic and factual possibilities, each episode is experienced as a form of brainstorming." The first program, "Ideas," was a good idea. It is digressive, as it's supposed to be. As a result, however, it becomes uneven. There are several good sequences, including one about different conceptions of the horse by two artists, but we often found it too slow moving. Another program, about time, is more fun. There are some nice images, such as a time trip around the globe, lots of information, for example, about clocks, and good word plays on timely expressions. There is also an excellent, imaginative sequence about the writing of a murder detective story concerning the killing of time. We even see time fly. In a later program called "Dreams" we are given a highly imaginative treatment of a subject of great importance and mystery to children.

"The Adventures of Tintin," produced by Nelvana, one of Canada's most creative production houses, a half-hour animated series based on the adventures of the European comic book hero, received its world television premiere on the Family Channel in October 1991. It is shown at 7:00 p.m., family viewing time, and young children should watch with adults. Tintin is a young adventurer who, accompanied by his dog Snowie, embarks on many "dangerous and mysterious quests" that take him all over the world, and even into

space. Some parents may think it's a bit violent for
younger viewers. As one seven-year-old said, "He
seems to get hit on the head a lot." However, this is
fairytale, comic book violence. The animation is excellent, and the rendering of the stories is faithful to the
comic books on which they are based.

Another Family Channel series, "Eric's World," is a
wholesome but weak and disappointing little sitcom
with music, which appears once a week in the
morning. Eric, played by Eric Nagler, familiar to many
children for his guest appearances on other shows,
plays a single father who lives with his pre-teen
daughter in a friendly trailer park. They have several
friends, including a life-size puppet and a stereotypical librarian who is always saying "Sshhh." The plots
deal with relationships and growing up, and there are
a few good songs, some comedy and happy endings.
Eric does well as a guest on other shows, but on his
own, he has trouble holding his young audience. The
show is slow and boring. The only time it holds up is
when a strong guest like Veronica Tennant takes over.
The series also appears on TVOntario and other
provincial networks across the country.

"Madeline" is a beautifully animated series, an
adaptation of the Madeline books by Ludwig Bemelmans, lovingly produced by Cinar of Montreal.
The books, written in rhyming couplets, which are
retained in the animated series, transport children
into the whimsical, sometimes troubled world of the
eminently practical and courageous Madeline, her
friends in the orphanage and their teacher, Miss
Clavel. The adaptations are faithful to the content and
spirit of the written stories. Christopher Plummer,
who narrates the stories, is perfect for his role. This is
one of the best examples we have seen of how an adaptation of a book or books can be achieved with such
creativity that it takes on a life of its own, and stands
on its own alongside the original books. This is the

direction in which we hope the Family Channel, and other networks, will be headed in the development of programs for children.

In sharp contrast to these, however, is a dreadful variety series called "Kids Incorporated," which purports to deliver a fast-paced, song-and-dance-with-a-message show to pre-teens and teens. What it succeeds in doing is encompassing almost everything one can do wrong in a show for young people. The principals overact and are overdressed, and the main character strives too hard to be something she's not — a thirteen-year-old torch singer. The lip-syncing of the songs is amateurish, the dance numbers are too long and any attempt at a serious story line, for instance about a career aptitude test, is totally banal and unrealistic. The acting is terrible in the "dramatic" segments about the aptitude test, and the treatment of a situation that would in any case hardly be important to a ten- or eleven-year-old is ridiculous. The main character is depressed because her score on the test indicates that she is an underachiever. When she asks how the others did, they say they did wonderfully. (How do kids do wonderfully on a career aptitude test?) Is this the kind of message we want to impart to young people? This is rock-bottom, commercialized American fare that has no place on a Canadian channel, especially when there was a series with a similar structure, "The Rockets," on CTV on Saturday mornings, made for much less money by a Canadian producer, a series that was far more impressive in its content and in its treatment of its young audience.

Although a provincial channel, TVOntario is included here because many of its children's programs are shown on other networks. From the end of September until May, the morning schedule of TVO consists of mainly school programming designed to be used by elementary teachers and students either off air or on tape. At noon, for an hour, and some days more, there's a series of dull interview shows, ostensibly aimed at teachers, called "Daytime." Most of the rest of the afternoon is taken up with Home Studies, for adults, the main offerings for children at home beginning with the Canadian version of "Sesame Street" at 5:00 p.m., followed by "Polka Dot Door" and then a variety of programs for kids and families until 7:30. Most of the late afternoon shows, including "Today's Special," are discussed elsewhere. There are several others we'd like to review here.

First, "Join In." As the title suggests, this fifteen-minute show for pre-schoolers to eight-year-olds is full of music, movement and simply playtime activities in which the children watching are encouraged to take part. There's one young female and two male hosts who are personable and articulate. The thread of a story, often a simple problem like getting costumes ready for a play, utilizes colourful sets and keeps the interest high. Any pre-schoolers we watched with had no trouble joining in.

And speaking of joining in, the long-running "Elephant Show," also known as "Sharon, Lois & Bram," may be the ideal join-in children's show on TV. And while the main focus is on children, there's lots in the songs and dance and merrymaking of the three principals for adults to enjoy. There's often a guest or two to help along the plot (which is different in each episode), and of course Elephant herself always has a prominent role. It's not by chance that this thirty minutes of fun is scheduled in the early evening hours, because it is fine family entertainment.

Many of the "in-school" programs shown in the morning on TVOntario and other provincial educational networks are of course also suitable for home viewing, and parents would do well to seek them out. For example, TVOntario's "Music Box," written, produced and hosted by Heather Conkie (Aunt Agnes of "Dear Aunt Agnes," the series about problems faced by the pre-teen set, and writer of many episodes of "The Road to Avonlea"), is a gem of a series that awakens young children's love of music beautifully. It acquaints children with a variety of musical styles and introduces them to different aspects of music such as rhythm, tone, tempo, metre and melody. Each fifteen-minute program involves children in many musical activities, including singing, playing, listening, dancing and movement. Heather's sidekick is a magical music box in the shape of an old-fashioned gramophone. The series, aimed at primary school children, is enjoyed by adults as well as young people.

"Mainly Music," designed for older children, and also written by Heather Conkie, is a drama about young people and their music teacher that also encourages children in the musical arts. Other notable morning programs produced by TVOntario are "Read All About It," a reading show for eight- to ten-year-olds; "Readalong," the award-winning reading show for beginning readers hosted by a talking boot; "Artscape," a series that takes eight- to ten-year-olds on imaginative jouneys into the many worlds of art; and "Mathmakers," the musical math series about flips, slides and turns for seven- and eight-year-olds.

Still, there is relatively little good television for children during the daytime. The good programs, such as "Sesame Street," "Mr. Rogers," "Fred Penner," "The Elephant Show" and "Today's Special," which carry the most riches to young people, are the shows with budgets sufficient to do what they do well. Children's television needs to be well-supported. At present, it does not seem to have the funding required to produce what is needed for children. If we believe that children are our greatest resource, then they must be first, not last, in the television networks' priority list when it comes to the funding of programs.

Chapter 5

AT THE VIDEO STORE
AND LIBRARY

*Throughout the last decade there have been
tremendous advances in video technology.
These advances have provided industry,
schools and the general public with easy and
affordable access to a staggering amount of
visual material. The sheer volume of this
material has made it difficult, to say the
least, for responsible parents and educators
to effectively select suitable materials for
children of widely differing age groups.*
Fiona Zippan, video store owner

Video material now plays a large part in the lives of
children many of whom learn to operate a VCR
remote before they can even read. They can find their
favourite programs, put them in the machine, stop
and start when they want and rewind for an instant
replay, all with great facility.

When we first enter a video store as parents looking
for children's programs, we see it's not at all like a
library or a children's bookstore. At first glance, there
is very little to suggest there is *anything* available for
kids, unless it's a big promo for Nintendo amongst the
posters full of hype about recent movie attractions of
romance and mayhem for adults. In most video stores
there is a children's or at least a family section. But
we usually have to look pretty hard to find them, and

often we find they are mostly collections of stock cartoons for kids, purchased in a package from a distributor, with little of quality, and little evidence of thought about what is in the collection.

There should be a large market for children's videos. Apparently, however, this is not the case. We're not sure whether video store owners are afraid to take a chance on the children's market, or whether indeed it is true that the market is very small. One video store owner we spoke to was considering getting rid of all of the children's videos in his store, because these racks were not bringing in the revenue he needed. We believe that a lot of people who run video stores do not connect with children because children do not, for the most part, come into the stores to rent their own videos. It's the parents who do this, so the owners of many video stores see only adults, and rarely regard children as worth the bother.

In our travels through video stores, as well as public libraries, we've discovered that there *are* a few places where there is great respect for children. These outlets, which we will take you through, serve as proof that it is possible to run video stores and libraries for kids, to have large and carefully selected collections of video materials for them and to be successful. Still, there is a long way to go.

For example, let's go into a large store, one of the Rogers chain. It is a bright, airy store, with a stock of more than 8,000 titles, fewer than 500 of which are for children. The majority of these 500 programs are for children five to eight years old. Children's material, however, is at the front of the store, just to the right as we enter. Unfortunately, the first sign says "Nintendo." The physical arrangement of the children's section is circular, with a children's playground slide in the middle. Playing on a large screen at the back of the store, not visible to children at the front, is a first-run adult feature movie.

When we ask how the kids' material is chosen, we learn that all such decisions are made in the head office in Richmond, B.C., and they choose the titles according to the rental and sales record of each store. The staff we talk to have a good attitude towards children but nothing to do with the choice of materials in the store. They say that parents very seldom ask for guidance, because much of the material is fairly standard fare. They do ask for information about new releases. Most of the time, as far as the staff can tell, parents make the choices for their children.

Blockbuster Video, another chain, is also prominent in the video store market. Despite calling itself "Canada's family video store," Blockbuster is in fact an American chain, based in Florida. Nonetheless, we have some good things to say about Blockbuster. The stores are well-organized, with clearly labelled sections. The children's section in all Blockbuster stores, complete with a viewing area full of beanbag chairs, is just inside the door. One side of this section is bounded by a rack of videos labelled "Kids' Recommended Viewing," containing such titles as *Snowman*, *The Muppet Movie, Raffi in Concert, Mary Poppins* and *Ramona* — all films we recommend. Showing on the big screen at the centre of the store is always a first-run Hollywood feature or a rock concert. The average ratio in all Blockbuster stores is 3,000 adult titles to 300 children's. Most of these stores do good children's business, and staff members we talked to were, on the whole, knowledgeable and helpful. They like to "work the floor," and talk to the customers. The chief buyer for the Canadian head office confirmed that choices of both adult and children's video materials were different for each store, based on sales and rental records. She also said it was impossible to preview all the materials before they went on the shelves. This is where we have a problem with some of the big chains and many other video stores.

Children's videos should be previewed so that parents
know what they are getting for their children. We'll
have more to say about reasons for the importance of
previewing children's material.

Let's take a look now at an independent neighbourhood video store. It has 5,000 titles, 250 of which are
children's. The store, located on the second floor of a
medium-sized shopping centre, is rather crowded.
Upon entering, you are assailed with a grand visual
display of posters of the latest Hollywood offerings,
and as you go further into the store you see a large
Nintendo sign surrounded by a lot of adult action
videos. You pass the counter to reach a wall of new
releases and finally, at the very back of the store, a
small section for children, containing mostly cartoons
and Disney features. On the positive side, the first
half dozen titles in each row of the new releases are
the kind of movies that are quite suitable for family
viewing. Because it is a local store with a lot of repeat
business, parents know the staff and vice versa, and
the parents aren't afraid to ask about the family and
children's material in the store. The co-owner we
interviewed has two children of her own, and is very
selective about what they view at home. She and the
rest of her staff are very knowledgeable about all the
materials they have in the store, so parents trust their
judgment. The videos are chosen by the management
from monthly catalogues sent out by distributors.
There is a good, friendly, helpful attitude here.

We visited many video stores in larger shopping
plazas, all of which did a good business with those
aged fifteen and up, but carried a token, almost for-
mulaic selection of material for younger children,
almost all of it the stock animation video collection.
These stores usually carry around 3,000 titles overall,
about 200 of which are children's with 100 more
labelled for the family. (Wrestling, much to our
dismay, is included in the family category.) The

windows in these stores are commonly a montage of violent action posters — guns, cars, cops — and on their screens a first-run movie is always playing. In some, there is a special section for children, with perhaps a carousel display and three-dimensional posters advertising films like *The Jungle Book*. However, this special section features the stock children's package. One gets the feeling that the stores all shop at the same outlet and buy into one of two or three packages. The children's material seems like a token gesture to parents, allowing them to grab a video that has the generic label "children's." There is very little genuine concern about providing interesting, perhaps live action material for children, such as *Milo and Otis*, the popular and quite beautiful film about the journeys of a dog and a cat. These stores appear to be interested only in business, rather than serving their clients. We do not recommend that you go to this kind of store for good videos for children.

Another source of video material is the public library. By and large, Canadian libraries have good children's departments, with a varied selection of books for all ages, storytelling centres and comfortable surroundings for children's reading experiences. Now many of them have a selection of videotapes too, ranging from fairy tales and other stories based on books, through the scientific probings of "OWL TV" and classic children's broadcasts such as Sharon, Lois & Bram's "The Elephant Show," to other classic tales and short cartoon features. (See our review section for descriptions of many of these programs.) Usually, titles are chosen by a central supervisor, sometimes assisted by other librarians, from catalogues and reviews. Not all tapes are previewed, so series and features that might need careful consideration can slip by — for instance, a terrible set of fairy tales called the Davenport series (see review section), or the feature *The Peanut Butter Solution*, which is not a bad movie but has some scary scenes that require warning.

Librarians often say that they feel they don't need to review these programs because they are buying "classics," but even the classics need review. They may be badly produced, as with the Davenport series, or they may be played for adult laughs, as is the case with *The Emperor's New Clothes* (from Fairie Tale Theatre, which is usually good). This show, like several in the series, relies too much on wisecracks and corny schtick (including a lot of belching). So each episode of a series should be reviewed by someone in the library. "Classic" does not mean good.

Parents, of course, should take the time to preview tapes themselves, especially if they can be borrowed at no cost from the library, or previewed on the premises. You do not have to see a complete tape to get the gist and tone of it. We take for granted that parents know their children well. Your choices of videos should suit the ages and the tastes of your children. Sometimes what your eight-year-old might like is not what your four-year-old would want to or should watch. When there are several children in a family, often the age spread is wide enough for tastes and suitability to differ vastly. A thirteen-year-old and a five-year-old will most definitely require different programs. Don't assume that what your thirteen-year-old is watching is also suitable for the younger one.

Larger communities usually have interlibrary loan systems, and often one centre for audiovisual and film materials with several staff members. Find out what is available in your community, and make use of the facilities and the well-qualified professionals whom we have found to be very helpful in choosing suitable and interesting materials for children and families. They will also be interested in your comments about existing films and videotapes, and your suggestions.

An exception to the common practice among

libraries of not evaluating videotapes is the central library in Vancouver, which has 400 titles, all of them previewed by professional children's librarians. In this library, too, the public has access to catalogues and can preview material. However, this library is very much the exception, and outside the lower mainland of British Columbia, many libraries have no videos at all.

The children's video section of the average library holds anywhere from 50 to 100 tapes, but few libraries contain informative catalogues to guide parents in their choices. One very well-set up library did have a descriptive catalogue of 700 titles that parents could book. This was also the audiovisual centre of a Metropolitan Toronto library, with 1,100 titles for parents to browse through. Such centres are also found in other libraries in the system. However, once again there was no advisory information, other than the jacket blurbs, for parents who want to learn more about the various titles. We understand that videos are a relatively recent addition to libraries, but library administrators should be doing more to make it intelligibly accessible for parents and their children.

We have outlined above the common experience in the video market for children. Is this satisfactory in terms of serving the needs of a society of visually literate children? It does not seem so to us. The following story, which is probably not unfamiliar, in some form, to many parents, brought about the only alternative we have seen in video stores for children.

Children are most often surrounded by adult video material, and adults all too often are not able to distinguish between videos suitable for adults and those suitable for children. The fact that the typical video store carries 5,000 titles for adults and only 300 for children speaks volumes about the priority given to children here. They are at the bottom of the heap, as they are in the world of television. One woman has tried to change this situation — Fiona Zippan, the founder of the original Kids' Video Store in Toronto.

One October day, during a teachers' strike, Fiona Zippan picked up her daughter as usual after school. The child, normally a bright, bubbly, energetic ten-year-old, was uncharacteristically silent and withdrawn, and when asked what the matter was, she replied with that gloomy old standby: "Oh . . . nothing." Fiona decided to take her daughter to the local hamburger place to cheer her up. While they were sitting there her daughter stared off into space, alternately shifting her gaze and smiling faintly.

"What are you doing?" Fiona asked.

"I'm trying to think of nice things," her daughter replied, "So I don't see those awful pictures in my head."

"Awful pictures of what?" Fiona asked. Then it all came out. The teacher had treated them to a movie that afternoon, *The Changeling*.

In case you don't know the movie, it features the brutally graphic murder of a crippled child and the horrific haunting that follows. It would frighten many adults; it's almost certain that the majority of the children who saw it were profoundly and adversely affected. According to Fiona's daughter, just about all the children were badly frightened by the film, and one of her friends actually vomited afterwards.

Fiona went to the school the next day and demanded to see the principal, who was too busy to see her. She was directed to the vice principal, who in response to her concerns replied, "Oh no, that shouldn't have happened. What a terrible mistake! But don't worry, children are resilient. She'll get over it." When Fiona asked where the supervising adult might have obtained a film like that (under the naïve assumption that the school had some sort of systematic method of selecting materials presented to its pupils), the vice principal responded: "The teachers usually just go to the video stores, like everyone else."

For Fiona, a young mother of two, this was the last straw. "It just seemed like another area where children are exposed to material that isn't aimed at them, like the local corner store with its magazines, the innocent-looking gift shops with adult cards and, of course, video stores." She had thought for some time that it would be wonderful if somebody in the city established a video centre geared exclusively to children, where kids could go, whether accompanied by an adult or not, to pick out a movie without being exposed to an array of violent, pornographic images, and without risk of inadvertently selecting a nasty surprise. Seeing her daughter's reaction on that particular afternoon finally galvanized her into acton. As she put it: "I was so sickened. I felt like my child had been violated in some way. I was outraged. It was my outrage that finally motivated me, pushed me into doing something, not just for my own daughter, but for all the other children who were in that class that afternoon, forced to sit through that film because the adult in question abused the privilege of supervising them.

"I don't want anyone to get the wrong idea," she says. "I'm not a religious fundamentalist book-burner type. I'm not intent on eradicating everything I feel doesn't meet my particular code of ethics. We don't censor here, nor do we sit in judgment on anything or anyone. All we do is watch the films before we put them on the shelf. It's a pretty simple premise, but it works, I think. We watch the films, we review them, and then we list them in a catalogue for the parents, with a short summary of the plot and a basic description of any event that might be considered too violent, frightening or mature for a child of a certain age. We also place films in a general age category, which we feel will enable the parent, or whoever else is selecting on the child's behalf, to quickly and confidently make a reasonable choice, without having to worry about coming into the TV room halfway through making dinner to find their six-year-old watching a guy in a goalie mask chainsawing co-eds."

This approach is the basis of a neat little store on Bayview Avenue in Toronto, the only one of its kind that we know of in Canada. When we enter Fiona Zippan's store with two eight-year-olds, they of course first discover the popcorn machine just inside the front door, at kid level. Being just turned eight, and knowing we are anxious to see how they feel about the store, when asked if they notice anything different about this store, they appear blasé at first, and give a nonchalant "No," as they are down on their hands and knees exploring the shelves, munching from their bags of popcorn. Left on their own, they soon set about exploring the premises.

There's lots to explore. The shelves are no more than five feet high so that most children can read or at least see all the titles and pictures on the video boxes. The signs above each shelf and section clearly indicate age and interest groups. There is a wide range of titles, from popular cartoons to *A Child's Christmas in Wales*, to *The Nutcracker* and *Swan Lake*, to sections entitled Just Great Movies (*National Velvet, A Hole in the Head*), Lots to Sing and Dance About (*Oliver, Oklahoma, Fiddler on the Roof*) and Extra Great Hits From Extra-Terrestrials (*Spaceballs, Star Trek, Star Trek TV Episodes*). And much more that takes this place far beyond the average video emporium.

As we move further into the store there is a viewing area, a tiny theatre draped in black, complete with a marquee and carpeted steps to sit on (there is usually a first-class children's show playing on the screen), where, on request, you can preview part of a tape if you are unsure about content or level. The staff of the store are knowledgeable, helpful and, most important, truly interested in children and in what interests them.

For parents and other adults, an adjacent room, really another store, offers a wide variety of titles for general viewing, but even here the young people are not forgotten. There is an adult side of fine movies, organized and situated so that teenagers who have moved out of the children's side can begin to look here for good video material. It is extremely well organized, with the most adult material at the top and out of the reach and sight line of younger children. In one section, for example, the comedy videos have been selected with younger teenagers in mind, while on the opposite wall, the comic material is aimed at a more mature level.

Again, the shelves and sections are clearly labelled and it's obvious which areas contain good family viewing material. In every section there is no sex or violence on the lower shelves for children to stare at. In conversation with Fiona, we learned that she developed her video placement techniques by observing young children with their parents in video stores. She recounted situations in which very young children would be staring straight into blood and guts on video covers, right at eye level for these youngsters, while their parents were searching for a movie. No one had taken the time to think of the children who come in with their parents, and what a child three feet tall will be confronted by. Parents who frequent Fiona Zippan's store, and there are many, are confident that they can allow their children to explore on their own and make their own choices.

Fiona and her partner Douglas Atkinson preview every tape that goes on the shelves. This is done in very few video stores. The reason given in most cases is that there are simply too many titles to preview and they don't have the time. As we will see below with Academy Movie Rentals in Toronto, which is a combination adult/children video store, one of the best, this statement does not hold up.

Even in the children's section of Kids' Video, some tapes are marked for the attention of parents and children, with an indication on the box that there are scary or violent passages that may be frightening to some children. The eight-year-olds we were with carefully read all the notes on the boxes with great interest, and suggested some of their own from their own viewing experiences. As our eight-year-olds discovered, this is a fun place for kids. May there be more of them in the future.

During our survey, we wandered through several other video establishments, if one could call them that. Not much to see in these places, which we will not name. The one that stands out is one into which we hope no child ever has the misfortune to set foot. As we walked in, a line of dialogue from the movie playing on the screens sounded out loud and clear: "But I've only got a fucking G-string on . . ." To match this was the sight of a neon-lit room straight ahead called "X-rated Adult." When asked where the children's material was, the clerk pointed straight ahead to a column with perhaps sixty titles of the regular nondescript video-store package type. When asked why there was so little children's material, the answer was that there was very little demand, that there were not many children in the neighbourhood. In Toronto?

After similar experiences, we discovered Academy Movie Rentals, run by partners Jerry Phinney and Danny O'Hara, with great relief. This outlet is well known as one of the best video stores in Toronto, and fits into the same category of excellence as Kids' Video in terms of its concern for children. A feeling of excitement greeted us as we walked in the door. We filled our bags with popcorn, pausing at the rack of new releases, turned and looked at the wall of classics, which is like a painting with all the jackets of the same pattern, and then were struck by the children's section in the next room. It's not ostentatious,

with three circular racks, each containing about 145
boxes, and a wall of another 150. Looking through the
boxes, we were taken by the following titles: *Bye, Bye
Red Riding Hood, Mr. Magoo's String Band, War Boy,
The Bellstone Fox, The Orphan Train, The Dog Who
Stopped the War, The Point,* and *Dr. Seuss's 5,000
Fingers of Doctor T,* among many others. Now, this is
not your regular children's fare. It was obviously
selected with care by someone who is knowledgeable
about many unusual sources of video material for
children.

Next we talked to Jerry Phinney, the person responsible for a lot of the choices. How many titles were
there in the store? Five thousand. How many children's? Five hundred — but very carefully chosen.
Jerry looks at everything before it goes on the rack.
He spoke to us about a title called *Plague Dogs,* which
is an animated film about animals being used in scientific research, an adaptation of the Richard Adams
novel of the same name. The movie opens with a horrendous scene in which a dog is almost drowned
during an experiment by two scientists, who comment
clinically on the proceedings. In another scene, a dog
has its head blown off as it tries to attack a man. Jerry
mentioned this one as an example of a video that could
easily go out as a children's program because of the
cover, if parents did not know what it was really about.
It's a fine movie for older teenagers and adults, but not
for young children. This points to the importance of
having knowledgeable staff in video stores and
libraries, when it comes to children's material. Jerry
spends much of his time recommending movies to
parents. When we asked what sells best, we got the
usual *Mary Poppins,* the animated *Robin Hood* and
standard Disney titles. But something more was
added here — musicals. *The Sound of Music* and *Oklahoma,* for example, which are recommended to
parents and taken out regularly.

How refreshing it is to find a place in which such care is taken about children's video materials. Why is this true here, and why is so little care taken in most other video stores? We think it's just downright lack of concern for children. People talk about marketing, about the fact that things don't sell, but they obviously do sell. The Kids' Video Store and Academy Movie Rentals stand out as models of what is possible when people who run video stores focus on children as well as adults, and see children as having their own intrinsic value and needs. The wide-ranging lists of titles in both these locations demonstrate this positive attitude towards children. This does not mean that these stores exclude the fun stuff or the animation. Kids need to relax and lunch out just as adults do. But it's possible to provide a lot of good titles and exclude the schlock packages that seem to monopolize many video-store kids' sections.

Jerry talked about parent-child input playing a large role in what is stocked in the children's section. This says a lot to parents. Look for places where people care about children. Look for places where care is taken with choices for children's video material. Look for people who talk to you about your choices, who make recommendations if you ask. Look for places that care about kids.

Start looking at your local video stores in a different way, not only for the number of titles of children's programming, but also for what kinds of programs are offered. Are they mostly cartoons, or programs that can be watched on network television, such as "Ninja Turtles"? How much floor space is devoted to children's programming compared to the total area of the store? Are there more space and more titles in the horror section, or in the adult section? If it's a large chain, talk to some of the staff and find out how interested and how knowledgeable they are about children's video. Are they concerned, or is it just another sales item? Ask, as we did, how the children's material is ordered and decided upon and how much of it is previewed. Ask the same questions at your local library. Are they as careful cataloguing and categorizing the children's videos as they are the other children's materials? If not, why not?

Remember, your dollars support local video stores and libraries. Your questions and concerns should be welcomed and acted on. Too often parents feel that they have no say in the content or policies of such places. Not true. It's your money. So put your mouth where your money is when it comes to your child and video outlets. You can make a difference to the quality of materials and service available to your children.

Chapter 6

INTO THE CLASSROOM
AND BEYOND

I think educators and producers who work in educational television are going to be the ones who are going to spearhead education via television. It's going to be in the hands of computer technologists in conjunction with universities, who are going to be constructing programs for the classroom.
Carolann Reynolds, executive producer

Do you know how much television/video your child is watching in school, and how it is being used? How large a part of the current curriculum should it be? According to a recent TVOntario survey, 61 percent of all elementary and secondary level teachers in Ontario used educational TV or videocassettes in their teaching of subjects as diverse as music, mathematics, family studies and space education. We hope that this chapter will give you a sense of the place of television in the classroom today, so you can measure the role that TV has in your child's education, and can judge, by the end of the chapter, what effect new technologies will have in education, both formal and informal.

In the 1990s, nearly all teachers in Canada have access to television programs via videocassette. As far as we can determine from the few surveys available, and from our own contacts across the nation, still fewer than half of all teachers in all subjects make use of the fine materials available. Those who do use TV are usually teachers of science, social studies, English and language programs. In the elementary grades, ready-to-read and reading programs are most popular.

Surveys have found that teachers who tend to use television in their classes are those who have been trained in the effective use of the medium. (A sad footnote here is that TVOntario, once the leader in training classroom teachers, has cut back this service so drastically that their training programs are virtually non-existent. In June 1992, TVO eliminated almost all of its educational services personnel, trained teachers who were expert in the use of television in the classroom.)

Still, the chances are that many of your children have been, or will be, exposed to television in their classrooms. Just how the television is used is a very important matter. Are television programs used merely as fillers, as a comparatively unimportant supplement to the more important print material? Or are teachers using television in creative ways, as an integral part of their curriculum in many subject areas?

In Canada one out of every three students drops out of high school before the end of grade twelve. This is an alarming statistic for parents. Will your child be the one in three? Perhaps you should ask yourself what the reason is for this high drop-out rate.

We believe that many students do not find the educational system relevant in either form or content. What is relevant to today's students who walk in to the classroom with baseball caps on backwards, connected up to their Walkmans? Somehow we must plug into the students' world and their experience of daily living, which includes television, radio and computers. Television is but one part of this array of technology, but a most important part, since it is so ubiquitous. To the kids, it's a fact of their existence. They were born into a world in which television was not a new thing, but an everyday presence. Yet somehow the medium always seems too esoteric for the adults teaching these kids.

The radio age passed teachers by without their making much creative use of it. Now the television age is passing them by, and teachers had better get a move on before they let this opportunity go as well. Television, both the formal educational programming and much of the regular fare, is an important educational force, both for good and for ill, in the lives of all of us. The education system must take heed of this and learn to use the medium well.

Almost every kid in a classroom has at least one television set at home — many have a VCR too — and all of these kids are TV literate. Television is their medium. They've grown up with it. Teachers in the classroom can do one of two things about this. They can say that kids are watching much too much television as it is, and it's rotting their brains, and it should never, never be allowed into the classroom, because the classroom is for serious learning. Or they can look at the situation, recognize the power and importance of this medium in the lives of children and integrate it into the classroom. The second option is the wiser decision, since this is the medium with which children are most familiar, and teachers who ignore it are nothing short of technological ostriches.

Educational television is different from our usual perception of television, the "furniture that talks" that we watch to be entertained. When we speak of educational television, at school or in the home, we mean most definitely the kind of television from which children learn. Now this needs to be qualified, because there is educational television and instructional television. The first can be a play or a drama, like "The Road to Avonlea" or "Northwood." It is the context that makes this kind of television educational. The second is explicit how-to television instruction, based squarely on curriculum, designed to teach certain concepts and skills, and structured to be a part of the classroom learning process. Both have their place in the learning spectrum.

Consider the things that television can do that no other medium can achieve as easily and with as much flexibility. The most obvious is that it can deliver the world to you and your children in the comfort of your own living room. Many of us will have learned something of the war in the Persian Gulf, with the attendant media assault and abuse of our senses and our intelligence. This was a powerful example of the world becoming a part of our homes, whether we want it to be there or not. It is also an especially good example of television as an educational tool, because of the way it was used by the powers running the Gulf War in 1991, who were dictating the terms of the media coverage, in order to educate the television viewing world, not about the war, but about the version of the war that the ruling power, in this case the United States, wanted us to see, hear and accept.

We call this educational television for a number of reasons. First, if all we got was an unbiased stream of pictures from the war in the Middle East, this would have been an education in itself. We would have been taken directly into the war to see all that was happening, and could have made up our own minds about what was, indeed, taking place. This happened during the Vietnam War, when for the first time we began to get pictures, right under our noses, of the horrors of war — and this was when the United States started to lose support for what it was doing.

During the Gulf War, the sensation was more akin to being inside a video game, in which the rules had been made up in advance. We saw very little of the real war. What we did see was a lot of graphics and military personnel giving video workshops in hotel rooms, making sure that we understood clearly why this war was necessary, how carefully the assault was being carried out to avoid harming innocent people and how precise was the weaponry being used. We got to see bombs falling out of planes, follow them to their delivery point, watch them as they exploded, then listen to the commentary explaining how they had hit their target precisely to destroy only the military assets of the enemy. The educational value of all this depended on whether you and your children talked about these events. Children could not avoid a barrage of this reportage if they turned on the television set during the Gulf catastrophe, but what would they make of it on their own? As one prominent Canadian political commentator so aptly summarized: "It was almost like one long commercial for the arms manufacturers, to show the world what weapons they had for sale."

After the war, a group of educators and journalists put together a media unit — a case study — for teaching and helping students understand the Gulf War as shown on television. The Association for Media Literacy in Ontario published the unit, which is available to parents and teachers. To give you some idea of the scope of the study, we quote a few lines from the preface:

Aware that our classrooms contain diverse nationalities and conflicting points of view, many school boards issued guidelines cautioning teachers to discuss the war with extreme sensitivity. Certainly, our students were generally fascinated by the events in this censored living room war, a phenomenon in which the more we saw on our TV screen, the more confused we became. And the less we seemed to know.

Some school boards prepared study kits which touched on historical, political, and geographical background, as well as the ethical issues generated by the conflict. What was generally missing, however, was an understanding of the media's crucial role in framing the discourse for discussing the Gulf War.

The project provides educators with a superb case study for media and global issues. By examining the media, especially television coverage, of the war, and beginning with student response, the unit takes a cross-curriculum approach to the whole phenomenon. There are ideas and materials for language study, multiculturalism, history, geography, popular culture and satire. While this unit is about the Gulf War, the material in it and the suggestions given can be applied to many other events and issues of importance to young people.

Not enough schools are doing this kind of media work in their classrooms. For too many teachers, television is still a frill, something to introduce a lesson or review some material (if used at all), but not something about which, and with which, they can teach. Too few teachers see television as a flexible teaching tool that they can use in their lessons.

There are several educational television networks and broadcasters across Canada, and their roles in providing programs, materials and ideas for use in the curriculum vary.

TVOntario is a network set up to serve schools and to create and acquire the best in educational television. We expect TVOntario to be a leader in the field. It is the oldest of the educational television networks in Canada and has developed an international reputation for its work in this area. In 1990 TVO celebrated its twentieth anniversary, having won awards and kudos in North America and around the world. Its instructional programs for elementary and secondary schools were some of the best in the world. Unfortunately TVO has moved its resources away from children's programming to meet adult home studies and prime-time needs. There is nothing wrong with the latter concerns, but their development has come at the expense of children's broadcasting, especially educational broadcasting.

What TVOntario offers now, as an excuse for educational broadcasting, is a phenomenon known as "Daytime." "Daytime," as its name implies, is a daily feature, at noon, ostensibly aimed at teachers and any others interested in education and educational trends. It presents interviews with prominent educators, and panels dealing with contemporary educational issues. Most days it runs for one hour, while on Fridays it extends till 3:00 p.m. Originally, when the technology to introduce this program was being considered, it was intended to broadcast to students over the lunch hour in school libraries. This was not practical: students are not in libraries over lunch.

The technology required to produce and broadcast "Daytime" cost approximately $1.3 million to acquire and install. It now costs $59,000 per week to run, $30,000 above the projected $29,000. At $59,000 per week, this nine hours of cheap, simple and totally ineffectual programming is costing taxpayers $3,068,000 per year to broadcast keynote speakers, dull talking-head discussions about educational issues and clips of programs to teachers who are not watching because they're either eating lunch, monitoring halls or teaching when the series is broadcast. And not a thing for the student in the classroom. What a waste!

TVO's overall budget is $80 million. Of that, only about $3.5 million goes into children's programming. Along with this, TVO's children's programming budget has been flatlined for the last seven years. This means that it has taken drastic cuts without anyone ever saying so. Its youth programming for grades seven to the end of secondary school has been cut drastically as well.

In the past, TVO programs were produced or acquired to address Ministry of Education guidelines. An Educational Services Department, whose personnel comprised highly skilled teachers, developed methods of teaching teachers how to use television creatively in the classroom. A provincial network of television resource teachers, one in each school, was developed and became a model on which many American departments of education based their implementation of television in the classroom. Programs could be taped off air, or ordered directly, at very low cost, from TVOntario. It was an institution in which educators and television experts worked side by side in the creation and delivery of excellent programming. It was a model educational television broadcasting organization, filled with excitement about education at all levels. Now, however, it has become a model of top-heavy bureaucracy, with little evident concern about high-quality television, and even less concern about its delivery to schools.

The new programming for schools coming from TVO for 1992–93 is revealing. In the TVO *School Broadcast Magazine* that is sent out to schools, in a section called "What's New" we learn that a total of sixty-eight hours of programming is produced for schools. This includes a little over twelve hours of new programming for primary and junior levels, and a total of seven hours of original production for intermediate and senior levels. Not much for an educational broadcaster, an important part of whose mandate has always been, and still is, to serve schools. One of the dangers of the cutbacks is that five years from now TVOntario may run out of materials for teachers, who will become tired of using the same old programs and print materials. And what teachers don't like, students won't see.

In contrast to TVOntario, Access Alberta has an annual budget of approximately $17 million, with which they do a great deal for schools. Sadly, Access too has recently suffered severe budget cuts, and has had to downsize drastically. However, as then acting general manager Jean Campbell told us in 1992, they are still producing, they are still on the air and they are still providing their very important service to the schools. The concern of this administrator is that parents see only what is on air, and do not see the volume of programming that is produced and acquired for schools that goes directly to schools without ever being broadcast. Several million dollars annually are spent on production that doesn't get to air. Broadcast quality and quality of content are uppermost in the selection and production of materials, since, as Jean Campbell put it so well, "Television is the single most important technology in the lives of children today." It helps them at all developmental stages, she said, and also helps pre-schoolers make the transition from home to school.

Access produces approximately 125 hours of new material each year. An example is "Homework Hotline," a series for junior high students that helps them with their homework by giving them the opportunity to call in to qualified teachers on air. Produced in collaboration with the Alberta Teachers' Association, it has been on the air for six years now, and has been very successful with its target audience. Tapes are distributed to teachers from the Media Resource Centre. Access used to have eight field officers, who worked in eight regions of the province, dealing directly with teachers. However, due to budget cuts, this most valuable face-to-face contact has been lost. Material is now distributed through the Department of Education.

The mandate of Knowledge Network, the educational broadcasting organization in British Columbia, is to provide open learning opportunities for all learners in the province. Through Schools TV, Knowledge Network, provides a service to the Ministry of Educa-

tion by assisting with the identification, evaluation
and broadcast of educational programming in support
of the Year 2000 initiatives. In return for this service,
the Ministry of Education provides an annual grant.

The Schools TV area is funded to deliver materials
to the schools, not to produce them. They broadcast
650 hours a year, five days a week, fifty-two weeks of
the year. This is all curriculum-based programming
acquired in collaboration with the Learning Resource
Branch. The goals of this branch of Knowledge
Network are:

1. to enhance the curriculum,
2. to reduce inequalities (of educational opportunity) and
3. to provide remedial learning opportunities (30
   minutes per day at home).

The schools unit also provides ancillary print
resources to assist teachers with the use of television
in their classrooms.

One of the major problems the Schools TV sector of
Knowledge Network faces is that it receives no direct
funding from the Ministry of Education. It has a
$300,000 budget for staffing, acquisitions and travel,
but schools also expect French as a Second Language
materials.

Despite this small budget, the Schools TV sector of
Knowledge Network is doing a massive amount for
schools. In addition to acquiring many series, it is producing an excellent magazine show for young people,
"Kidzone," which we described in an earlier chapter.
However, it receives no money from the Ministry of
Education for this, because the ministry does not fund
the development of programs. To continue this series,
funds have to be found from other sources. This situation can only aggravate an existing problem in the
province: teachers turn to the American education
broadcaster PBS for school materials. Some schools

even buy PBS "utilization services," which provide
teachers with workshops on the use of television in
their specific curriculum area, and print materials to
help facilitate the creative use of television in the
classroom. KTCS, the educational broadcaster in
Seattle, gets $1.2 million from British Columbia
through membership and subscribers. It has purchased TVO materials but not the rights to broadcast
in B.C., but it broadcasts into Canada anyway, deliv-
ering educational television to B.C. schools. Since the
Ministry of Education does not provide the funds for
Knowledge Network to work with teachers in schools,
an American educational television broadcaster is
providing these services to Canadian schools. What is
missing is a real commitment by the Ministry of Education to an educational broadcast policy. The situation in Ontario, Alberta and B.C. is typical across
Canada. There is a chronic problem with underfund-
ing everywhere.

When one looks at television as a beautiful, powerful
medium that affects our lives profoundly, then one
begins to read it as one does a book or a newspaper.
Often teachers will bring in a column from a newspaper, some stimulating piece to use as a model for
writing. The excitement comes in the understanding
of what it says and *how* it says what it says. The same
can be true of television. Recently, teachers have
shown students episodes from series such as "Northwood" and "Degrassi High," not just to explore the
subjects they cover, but also to study how they are
made. By using a VCR, stopping the video, rewinding
and reviewing, teachers can explore the techniques
used by filmmakers — plotting, pacing, scoring,
development of characters, point of view, camera
angle and so on. The result is a new kind of literacy in
students, an understanding of the most important
medium in their lives.

In 1989, the Ontario Ministry of Education made the study of media, or media literacy, mandatory for grades seven through twelve. While this is innovative for Canada, we were not the first country to see the importance of this field of study. Such countries as the United Kingdom, Denmark, Holland and Australia have led the way for years.

As a result of the Ministry of Education mandate, many schools now have credit courses in such areas as TV production, journalism and screen education. In one school, typical of many, the grade eleven students write weekly reviews of TV shows and movies, learn the use of small-format video equipment through hands-on instruction, develop on- and off-camera interviewing techniques and spend time critically viewing and appraising video and print materials. In grade twelve there is further video production (even some editing when equipment is available) and much in-depth study of weekly news magazines, newspapers and other periodicals that are available in the community. By the end of these courses, students will have examined all types of media, and through their involvement in production will have discovered various techniques we use to communicate with each other through sound, picture and print.

Ask your children if their teachers are using television in the above ways. Ask them how often television is used in their classes. If the answer is "not much" or "it's boring when the teacher shows a program," you might want to have a closer look, and ask some questions of the teachers and administrators.

Some people ask why students are "fooling around with cameras, tape-recorders and other gadgets" when they should be spending their time with the "basics" of reading and writing. What are the basics for young people who are going to live most of their lives in the twenty-first century? Surely the basics must now include the ability to understand the world of technology, including the computer, the video camera and desktop publishing, as well as pen and paper. Communication — clear, concise and creative — is always basic to learning. It is just the tools that change, and we must know how to use them.

Another complaint, not heard as often now as it was when we first became involved in media education over twenty years ago, is that by teaching students to make TV programs we're only creating a lot of frustrated and unemployed producers. This narrow-minded type of argument has often been directed in the past to teachers of such subjects as music and drama. But children don't take the music option in school and learn to play the clarinet just to become professional musicians, nor do they study dramatic arts just to become professional actors and directors. The more we know about a subject or skill, the more we develop a talent, the richer our lives will become, and we will be able to love and appreciate the arts throughout life. The same applies to learning media skills. The more we learn about how a thing is made or done, the more we will appreciate it and the better equipped we will be to be constructively critical of those who do it professionally. Students who learn about, and develop skills in, media will become adults who are not easily duped by the image makers and the hucksters of the great consumer society that surrounds them.

Video materials available to teachers cover everything from arts and visual arts, language arts and literature, health education and mathematics to science, values education and Canadian studies, and there are also programs and series for most other curriculum areas. Television programming spans all grade levels, from primary through to the end of secondary school. If you are interested in learning more about what programs are available in your area, look up the address and phone number of the educational broadcasting organization for your province. Catalogues and broadcast schedules are readily available. There is a plethora of curriculum material — not television that can be used incidentally, but programming that can and should be used by teachers as an integral part of their course work in many subject areas. The cost is by no means prohibitive, so if you find there is not a lot of television being used in your children's school, you now know it's not because there is no material available, but rather for reasons that lie within the individual board system, or with individual teachers. Find out, and make some noise!

Since the technology of information distribution is changing daily, what might happen in the classrooms of the future? As this book was being written, we gained two glimpses into the future.

The first case concerns the "immediate future," as it is already happening in one school in Canada, River Oaks Public School in Oakville, Ontario. We interviewed Gerry Smith, the principal of the school, and discovered that River Oaks is not your traditional K-8 school. It was three years in the planning stage, with the recurring question, "If we had a chance to build a brand-new school, what changes would we look at in preparing children for the future, especially a future in the work place?" The main emphasis in the preparation was on restructuring the curriculum. Principal, teachers and board consultants interviewed many people in the community, especially those in business. It was decided that the students of the future should be trained to become people who:

1. are collaborative,
2. can think logically,
3. can solve problems,

4. are highly literate (in both print and electronic media) and
5. can communicate well.

Therefore the curriculum was divided into four main areas:

1. Literacy
2. Life Skills
3. Arts
4. Creative Application (the application of the first three to all the five skills listed above).

The idea was that the students could apply all their learning to real-life problems, through many different forms of communication — written, oral and other, such as the electronic media, drama, music, physical movement and visual arts.

Computer technology became the main integrated learning tool. Elements of the technology include text, graphics, sound and video capability. One good example of the creative application of the curriculum and tools available in this school was provided in a unit on endangered species, at grade seven level. Two girls decided to do a project on the African elephant. As any student would, they first went to the library and examined an encyclopedia. The next step was a visit to the video library. Here they pulled various video clips about the elephant, which they inserted into a multi-media-based computer. They then added music and their own voice-over narration, and put together a complete presentation for their peers. The important thing is that they shared their information with others using all the tools available.

Of course, as the principal points out, today's students must still know the basics of mathematics, writing and reading. But in this age of the information explosion, these are now not the only "basics."

Students must develop the specialized skills of accessing and processing information that are meaningful to them and serve their needs. In the above example, the video material was central to the students' presentation. The selection and integration of this material, and the manipulation of it, was also crucial.

Television/video begins to take on an entirely different role in the lives of young people when it is used in this way. It becomes another medium of communication. Television literacy is an understanding and appreciation of the medium of television, and an ability to manipulate it as one would print.

CDI (Compact Disk Interactive) technology uses what looks like a compact disk, but is actually much more sophisticated: with CDI, voice, data, music, sound effects, video and audio compression and graphics can all be integrated on the same screen, If, for example, you are going to work with an encyclopedia on a disk, and you want to know about elephants, you call up the menu called elephants or mammals. The program goes through the menu and takes you where you want to go. Eventually you see a picture of elephants, with some sort of reference, such as comparing it to the size of a man. You have a tremendous power behind you to search out that kind of material. If you want to see this elephant move, the screen shows it in full motion. A level of artificial intelligence can then be overlaid onto this image. As you select your options, the computer analyses your requirements. A program has been created that instructs the computer to watch for the clues. At some point it stops you and asks, as a teacher would, "Have you ever considered this?" or "What about that?" It will point out relationships between subjects and suggest other directions for your investigation. Then it can direct you as to how to manipulate the material that's in front of you. Using this new form of interaction between the medium of video and all

sorts of other media, you and your children will be able
to create your own programs, made up of material that
other people have created combined with your original ideas. The power of all this is incredible.

CDI also has implications for television. We need no
longer be purely passive as viewers; we can work with
the medium and it can work with us. This changes the
way we might use television. In terms of training or
education, whether casual or formal, at home or in
school, the whole business of being able to make direct
inquiries, of being able to go in and manipulate a
program, is soon going to become a reality. If the
industry giants get into this and push the technology
to the home market, the implications will be as far-
reaching as the arrival of the home VCR.

Another potentially enormous development is "compression" of video signals so that at home or in school
people will be able to choose from as many as 200 "channels," though perhaps a new word will have to be
coined. Compression technology is being used now by
the private sector to deliver home entertainment programming — news, sports, weather, movies — none of
which is really interactive. Compression replaces
broadcast terminals with fibre-optic lines that deliver
signals from a transponder to your television set. If you
want to watch "Cheers" over and over again, you can
just keep calling it up on your screen by using an
interactive device connected to your television.

SkyPix Inc., the international movies-via-satellite
service that hopes to introduce the technology here, is
facing all kinds of problems with the CRTC. Broadcasters and cablecasters are against it because SkyPix
represents what has been referred to as sky cable. The
dish that they will have you buy is twenty-four inches
across, and you'll put it in your attic. A little box will
sit on top of your television, and you'll plug it in. The
SkyPix system is going to be challenged by the courts.
Think about this. Broadcast legislation in this country

requires that Canadian content rules apply, but the SkyPix process isn't broadcast. The only way you can get it is by buying it; it's the equivalent of a telephone call. SkyPix lawyers and other supporters are saying it is private communication, and if the CRTC is going to regulate them, then they must regulate phone calls, because you choose and you pay in just the same way. It's not offered for general broadcasting consumption; it's simply a signal in the sky, and if you want it, you buy it.

Broadcast television to schools went out a long time ago. Video allowed for control of material by teachers. They could stop and start, use a freeze frame, and use video information as quickly or as slowly as their students required. Now, with the interactive technology, there are companies in the United States offering full credit courses at a distance. And there are all sorts of teacher education programs, and programs for gifted and disadvantaged kids.

There will be problems in bringing this material into Canada, since these are U.S. programs with U.S. teachers. The problems include accreditation and dealing with teacher unions and ministries of education. Magic Lantern, a distributor of educational videos that wants to hook up with SkyPix, contacted the Ontario Ministry's Independent Learning Centre and asked them to look at some material. They had called the "Tie-in Network" in Texas, which was transmitting a German lesson the morning of their meeting with the Ministry. At 10:00 a.m., the Ministry people dropped in on the German class via satellite, that class being broadcast live, with students in twenty-three states calling in with questions. They could hear the questions coming in, and they could see the responses. When the teacher announced the hook-up with Canada, the American students decided that they would welcome the Canadians to their class. The Canadians sat and watched as kids communicated via

computer, by fax, by teleresponders and by telephone.
The teacher was trained to handle the whole situation. She had a system in front of her that indicated
the source of each student signal. At the end of the
class they had arranged to go via teleconference to the
teacher, the administrator, the engineer — eight of
them in a boardroom in Texas — to ask questions
about the process, about evaluation, costs, effective-
ness and the results of their research.

If this kind of distance education were going to be
done in Canada, what steps would have to be taken?
These courses can't just be delivered into Canada as is.
The teachers involved are not qualified to teach in this
country. This is not to say that we don't have excellent
teachers here. Rather, it illustrates the possibilities of
this technology with appropriately trained staff. If
there happens to be student in Opiongo or Eganville
who wants specific courses for which there is not sufficient demand to justify a teacher in each school, such a
student should be allowed to take courses that will get
him or her into engineering, science, medicine or whatever is his or her chosen area of interest.

Secondary schools across the country are starting to
look at satellite receiving time — in Western Canada
almost every secondary school has a satellite receiving dish on its roof, and in other areas more than
eighty percent of schools have a dish and bring in programming from various sources. One teacher we know
receives information from weather satellites. The students built the dish, using a shortwave radio, a box
and software for the classroom PC. This brings the
signal down from the satellite through the shortwave
radio and translates the digital signal into a video
signal and onto the television screen. The students are
bringing the satellite images down, using them for
mapping the weather. They watch environmental con-
ditions, and they are able to focus on a fire and see
what it looks like as it happens.

Broadcast, as we think of it, may not be a reality much longer. It's satellite today, compression tomorrow, digital video or CDI after that. There's a lot of work being done on how CDI can be delivered by satellite or by fibre optics. There may be a host hub or unit with a library of programming on it that could be called up either by satellite or by fibre optics on a keypad and paid for as it is used, like "pay per view" television today.

Dedicated teachers don't stand still. They want to be knowledgeable, and their professional spirit and ambition will drive them to find out about all of this.

We all know that in our world it is no longer enough simply to learn to read and write. We leave you with this statement from *Television and America's Children*:

> In a world where students are deluged with messages from every side, we must help them become sophisticated as message senders and receivers.
>
> The challenge is not to view technology as the enemy... [but] to build a partnership between traditional and non-traditional education, letting each do what it can do best.

Conclusion

The reason I work in children's television —
and I'd like this to be kept a secret — is that
children's television is the most rewarding
part of television.
    Clive VanderBurgh, producer / director

The technology of television has brought us full-circle, back to the image that was so important to our preliterate ancestors, and it has made the world of our children very much a world of images. Some people may decry this, and bemoan what they consider to be the passing of the age of print. We don't believe this: it's just that we have developed new methods of communication in addition to those we already had. It takes strong parenting and creative teaching to bring all of these together. And this is just what is needed.

We have written about the future directions of television, with CD-ROM and satellite transmission. However, we don't want to get too far away from the basics of television, the image on the screen. It matters very little whether you receive your programs via cable service, or satellite, on video or by coathanger. The basic principles of parenting, or knowing what's on the screen, what programs your children are watching, which videos they are seeing with their friends, and what is suitable for them are still the same. The number and variety of programs available may increase, but this only increases the importance of your parenting where television is concerned.

We hope that this book will serve as a guide for evaluating new material for many television seasons to come. Even though the programs will be new, the guidelines that we have given here should serve as a starting point from which parents can judge this ever-changing, very exciting medium.

Remember: by being actively involved in your children's viewing, you can help shape what they take from it. Watch with them, talk to them — and to other parents and teachers. If you object to programs, write to the networks; if you rent an unsuitable video, let the store know. It is only through constant participation and dialogue that we will be able to improve television and video, and our children's experience of them.

In this collection of some 400 reviews, we have tried, for your convenience, to place titles in age categories. This way, if you're in a hurry, you can quickly leaf through and select a video that will be suitable for your children. However, the age categories are somewhat arbitrary. "The Simpsons," for instance, can be suitable and entertaining for one nine-year-old and not for another. Who decides? And how?

The decision is yours. You know your children best. If you are not sure of a program and have some doubts as to its suitability for your children, either because of level of difficulty of content, or perhaps because of elements that might be frightening to your children, we suggest you preview the program, or at least a part of it, or err on the side of caution.

We have included some negative reviews where we think they may be useful, and we have tried to indicate where certain programs might frighten younger children. We have not specifically included a "Family" category, because we take for granted that ideally most viewing will be family viewing, but in many reviews we have indicated programs most suitable for family viewing.

Where a director or cast is well known, we have included their names. The letter T indicates a program or series that can be seen on television; V indicates a film, program or series available on video.

We hope that these reviews will prove useful as another tool to help you select video material for your children. The following video is also a valuable source of information.

Choosing the Best in Children's Video
The American Library Association (1990), 36 min. Hosted by Christopher Reeve

This program is a must for all parents concerned about their children's viewing choices, and should be viewed with a pencil and paper handy before the next trip to the library or video store. The tape gives an excellent overview of first-class videos for children — fiction and non-fiction. Tips are provided on where to get videos, how to choose and reasons for each choice. Between excerpts of programs there are useful comments from librarians, educators, critics and psychologists about children's television and reading.

Ages 1–5

Shari Lewis's 101 Things to Do
Random House (1987), 60 min.
Director: Jack Regas
Starring Shari Lewis and Lamb Chop   **V**

Not too cute, not at all condescending. Just a load of clever fun. The title is a bit misleading as the "Things to Do" include simple little tricks such as, "How do you write the number 1000 without taking your pencil from the paper?" They are all easy to learn and well explained, and use household items. Shari encourages the viewer to "stop the tape, rewind and try it yourself." It's not necessary to do everything the tape suggests straight away; after all, 101 things is quite a lot for any rainy day. Humour, professionalism and charm are only three reasons why Shari Lewis is still one of the best children's entertainers around.

The Adventures of Rufus and Andy — The Drug Decision
Educational Services of Credit Valley Hospital (1989), 20 min.
Animation / Live action   **V**

An appealing story with animated puppets and live action, aimed at young children but good for parents to watch too. "Drugs and booze are not cool, dude" is the message. A fun lesson saying it's okay to say no. Complete with a rap song, "It's Your Body."

Babysongs, Vol. 1
Hi-Tops Home Video (1987), 30 min.

Director: Dorian Walker
Animation, claymation and live action **V**

The first in a series of videos, which includes "More
Baby Songs," "Even More Baby Songs," "Turn On The
Music," "John Lithgow's Kid-Size Concert" and
"Babysongs Christmas." Aimed at children under four
years old, these videos are a collection of original
songs by Hap and Martha Palmer (songbook is
included). The songs are introduced by claymation or
animated sequences and move quickly from one song
to the next. Each contain children and babies singing,
dancing and moving to the soundtrack. A high-quality
production, effective for capturing the attention of
very young children.

Beethoven
Universal Pictures (1991), 108 min.
Director: Charles Gradin Bonniettut
Starring Dean Jones and Oliver Platt **V**

An amusing tale about dogs, kids and parents.
Beethoven, a Saint Bernard, grows from a lovable little puppy into a huge, slobbering monster of a dog, in a
household where the father does not like dogs. But the
story is mainly about a crooked vet who is stealing dogs
for experimentation — to test exploding bullets. In the
end, Father saves Beethoven, Beethoven saves all the
dogs, Father and dogs become friends.

Beethoven Lives Upstairs
The Children's Group (1992), 52 min.
Director: David Devine
Starring Neil Munro, Illya Walowshyn,
Fiona Ried, Paul Soles, Sheila McCarthy
and Albert Schultz **V/T**

A disappointing adaptation of the very fine audiotape

series, which includes Mozart and Haydn. Apart from
snippets of some beautiful music, and one interesting
scene between a boy and Beethoven, we learn only
that Beethoven was bad tempered and eccentric.
Badly directed and badly written, this is a waste of a
talented cast.

Best ABC Video Ever! (Richard Scarry)
Random Home Video (1989), 30 min.
Director: Tony Eastman
Animation   **V**

A terrific animated adaptation of Richard Scarry's
books. All your favourite characters are there —
Bananas Gorilla, Grocer Cat, Sergeant Murphy,
Smokey the Fire-chief, Huckle Cat and Lowly Worm.
Miss Honey teaches the alphabet using the "Alphabet
Song." A vignette describes a word for each letter.
Children's voices are used, not adults trying to be chil-
dren, and the accompanying music is charming. This
is also a good reading tape. Simple, amusing and pos-
itive. See also Richard Scarry's "Best Counting Video
Ever!"

A Bunch of Munsch
Cinar Productions (1991/92), 24 min.
Director: Bill Speers
Still animation   **V/T**

Thomas's Snowsuit, 50 Below Zero, David's Father
and *Pigs* are a pleasure to watch, with pastel drawings in the style of Michael Marchenko, the illustra-
tor of most of Munsch's stories. The first two are a bit
on the loud side. The visualizations are great, and the
stories work well, even though some of them are
stretched a bit far. They extend Munsch's stories into
the visual world of television in a most pleasing way.
For the most part, they are different from the books

and work in the way that this kind of adaptation should work. They create something new with the stories. Look for more in this series from a fine Canadian company, Cinar Productions of Montreal.

Canadian Wilderness Journal: The Wood Duck
Keg Productions (1992), 24 min.   **V**

A charming presentation of the conservation message confirming that preservation of habitat is important for the long-term future of the wood duck. A child viewer said about this program: "This is the most interesting nature program I've ever watched, because most of them aren't made for kids and use a lot of big words." This one doesn't, and works well.

Mr. Rogers Talks About Dinosaurs and Monsters
Mr. Rogers' Home Video (1986), 64 min.
Starring Fred Rogers   **V**

Mr. Rogers, America's trusted family friend, helps young children understand what scary monsters are — and aren't — about. Childhood fears are real fears, even though many things that give rise to them are only fantasy. Dinosaurs, for instance, were real, so Mr. Rogers visits a museum where dinosaur skeletons are exhibited. In the "neighbourhood of Make-Believe," the puppet Prince Tuesday has been having scary dreams about dinosaurs, and Lady Aberlinn and Handyman Negri help younger neighbours understand what is real and what is not. "Mr. Rogers Talks about Dinosaurs and Monsters" is a video special that can help your family talk about feelings too.

Fairy Tales: Sharon, Lois & Bram's Elephant Show, Volume 2
MCA (1989), 60 min.

Director: Wayne Moss
Starring Sharon, Lois & Bram   **V**

The three veteran children's entertainer-musicians
have put a number of episodes from their hit TV show
on video. In this one the lively trio include Mother
Goose, which features various musical numbers in a
"fairy glade" and King Bram's four and twenty black-
birds. Snow White Elephant presents the traditional
fairy tale with more than a bit of a twist, and features
a rap song (with Eric Nagler), "Walk Right In, Sit
Right Down," kid dwarfs, and "Polly Wolly Doodle."
Other titles in the series are Vol. 1: "Mysteries"; Vol.
3: "Sports Days"; Vol. 4: "Magic"; Vol. 5: "Trunk Troubles"; and "The Sharon, Lois & Bram Elephant Show
Concert."

✓ **Five Lionni Classics**
Italtoons–Random House (1986), 30 min.
Animation and Direction: Giulio Gianini   **V**

These five stories for young viewers (two- to six-year-
olds), based on the wonderful picture books created by
Leo Lionni, are fables for the very young, with animal
characters, dealing with such themes as sharing,
living together in harmony, enjoying one's own world
and celebrating the power of the imagination. For
example, Frederick the Fieldmouse shows his friends
how to use the warmth of the sun and the bright
colours of flowers as well as the food they've gathered
to survive the winter. Each five- to six-minute episode
is beautifully animated, with gentle, quiet narration.

Fred Penner in Concert
A & M Video (1990), 45 min.
Director: Tony Dean   **V**

The lively Mr. Penner, a star in the Canadian

children's entertainment scene, appears in his first
live concert video. Unpretentious as usual, he likes
and respects his audience and this comes through in
the fresh, enthusiastic presentation of such songs as
"You Are My Sunshine" and "I Am the Wind." A
terrific addition to the library of children's concert
videos.

Free To Be . . . You and Me
Children's Video Library (1974), 44 min.
Director: Bill Davis
Starring Marlo Thomas, Michael Jackson,
Rosy Greer and Dustin Hoffman   **V**

A very dated educational video that tries to help children feel that it's all right to just "be themselves."
Uses a combination of live sketches, songs, puppets
and poetry recitations. Don't miss Michael Jackson in
very fashionable seventies gear singing "When We
Grow Up" with Roberta Flack. Still a very good
message video for children up to eight years old.

Frère Jacques
Cinar / France (1991), 24 min.
Director: Chris Randall
Animation   **V**

There are thirteen shows in this series (entitled "The
Real Story") of fun twists on tales familiar to children. Kids like them because they can get the joke of
each story. In this episode, Frère Jacques is a monk
whose job it is to ring the morning bells. He constantly falls asleep and forgets, much to the chagrin
of the head monk. The King of Insomnia, on the other
hand, can't sleep. Eventually their stories come
together and Jacques helps the king get some sleep.
Wizards and animals, and fine animation, make this
a fun story for kids.

Frog

Orion (1987), 55 min.
Director: David Grossman
Starring Shelley Duvall, Elliott Gould,
Scott Grimes and Paul Williams   **V/T**

Arlo has an awesome reptile collection, is rather short, wears glasses and gets great marks in school. When he finds an unusual frog who can talk and claims to be an Italian prince, Arlo's world becomes even stranger. The frog tells Arlo that the spell will be broken if Arlo can find a girl who will kiss the frog. Of course, what girl in her right mind would kiss a frog? When one of the most popular girls in class thinks she can get a better science mark by being Arlo's science partner, he sees an opportunity. A great ending makes this a delightful story for all ages.

Halloween Package Number 1

Walt Disney Education Media Company (1980),
18 min.
Animation   **V**

Two short adventures entitled "Trick or Treat" and "Haunted Halloween." The first is strictly cartoon fun with Donald Duck and all his pals. The second has more laughs and imagination, and gives us a good history of Hallowe'en and the superstitions that surround it. There are also some good common-sense tips for today's kids about safety on Hallowe'en.

The Island of the Skog

Weston Woods (1975), 13 min.
Still animation   **V**

A charming story, told with voice-over narration, of a group of mice who on "national rodents' day" escape the terrors of their city and its cats and dogs, board a toy ship and sail to an island, which has a population of one — a Skog. Monster or friend? This is a nonviolent tale about relationships and co-operation, good for two- to six-year-olds.

It's the Great Pumpkin, Charlie Brown
Hi-Tops Home Video (1966), 25 min.
Director: Bill Melendez   **V**

Charles Schultz's Peanuts gang gets together in a celebration of Hallowe'en centred around Linus's near-religious devotion to a seasonal deity of his own invention: the Great Pumpkin, a gift-giving spirit who rises from the "most sincere" pumpkin patch on the big night and bestows his largess on the faithful. Linus and Sally spend the evening awaiting this event, while the rest of the gang engage in the usual Hallowe'en high jinks.

Join In
TVOntario (1988), 15 min.
Director: Jed McKay   **V/T**

Music, movement and simple playtime activities. One young female and two male hosts who are personable and articulate. Simple, colourful sets with good props. This show works well for pre-school children to age eight.

Keats' Stories About Peter
Weston Woods, 30 min.
Animation   **V**

  "Goggles": directed by Isa Wichenhagen, 1974 (a bit grainy)
  "A Letter to Amy": directed by Cynthia Freitag, 1979
  "Peter's Chair": directed by Cynthia Freitag, 1980

These three stories together make a good family
package. They are sympathetic and realistic stories
about inner-city black children, based on books by
favourite children's author Ezra Jack Keats. The animations are based on drawings from the books, with
good voice-over readings. Very suitable for young children, two to five years old.

King Cole's Party
Wee Sing Productions (1987), 60 min.
Director: Susan Shadburn   **V**

This is a lively, upbeat song and dance production,
with live action and puppets, featuring familiar
nursery rhymes for children to sing along to. A loose
story line is built around each song and its characters. A colourful show, appealing to ages two to
eight.

The Land of Faraway
Norstar Home Video (1988), 104 min.
Director: Vladimir Grammatikov
Starring Nicholas Pickard, Christian Bale,
Timothy Bottoms and Christopher Lee   **V**

This tale by Astrid Lingren concerns a young boy who
runs away, encounters an imposing spirit in the park
and is whisked off to the Land of Faraway. There he
discovers that his father is king, and that he is actually Prince Mio. According to destiny, Mio is forced to
seek out and do battle with the evil knight Cato, who
is invincible by virtue of his heart of stone. Cato
imprisons his victims in the tower of Eternal Hunger
and turns the unfortunate children he has captured
into birds doomed to circle his dark castle forever. The
story is stylish and subtle but may be too intricate and
scary for the very young.

Madeline
Hi-Tops Home Video (1989), 30 min.
Director: Stephan Martiniere
Animation; featuring the voice of
Christopher Plummer   **V**

Based on the first of the famous children's stories by
Ludwig Bemelmans, "Madeline" is exquisitely animated; in fact, it is just as if the original books had
been brought to life. Madeline, the irrepressible
twelfth of the "twelve little girls in two straight lines,"
contracts appendicitis during a trip to the zoo, and
then effects a recovery. Featuring musical interludes.

Milo and Otis
RCA/Columbia (1989), 76 min.
Director: Masanori Hata
Featuring the voice of Dudley Moore   **V**

A charming film (with no dialogue, only narration)
follows the shenanigans of Milo, a ginger kitten, and
his close buddy, Otis, a pug puppy. Together they get
into and out of scrapes and share humorous moments.
A thoroughly entertaining animal film suitable for
young children.

Mother Goose's Video Treasure
Junior Home Video (1987), 28 min.
Directors: Frank Brandt and Caroline Hay   **V**

Each of the four videos in this collection has eight or
nine Mother Goose stories performed in lively song
and dance, in very colourful settings and costumes.
The setting is Gooseberry Glen, and Mother, flying on
her goose, launches each story. The singing and
dancing in these stories is clear and well done for
young ones. This is one good for mom and dad to watch
with very young children, one to five years old.

Norman the Doorman
Weston Woods (1985), 15 min.
Director: Cynthia Freitag
Still animation   **V**

Based on the book by Don Freeman. One in a series of
Weston Woods stories based on children's books. A
charming tale in still picture animation of a mouse
who acts as a doorman to other mice in the basement
of a great art gallery, practises his art as a sculptor
and manages to enter and win a great contest.

101 Dalmations
Walt Disney Home Video (1989), 79 min.
Directors: Wolfgang Reitherman, Hamilton Luske
and Clyde Geronimi
Animation   **V**

This is a remake and an update of the original production of thirty years ago. It's an excellent example
of a Disney animated feature film with endearing,
cute dog heroes outsmarting the "evil" human dog-
napper villains, headed by Cruella DeVille. With love
stories thrown in for a bonus, this one is for all ages.
Much good humour, and a very funny chase scene.

Polka Dot Door: Dinosaurs
Golden Home Video (1983), 30 min.
Director: David Moore
Starring Cindy Cook and Dennis Simpson   **V**

The popular children's television show tackles the most
popular children's subject: dinosaurs. Dennis and
Cindy sing songs about different dinosaurs and their
attributes, the toys build a dinosaur landscape in the
sandbox, geologist Hedy Hoberlin pays a visit to show
fossils and bones, Dennis reads "If the Dinosaurs Came
Back" by Bernard Most, and Polkaroo shows a film of

his trip to a dinosaur theme park. Informative fun for little ones.

The Racoons
Nelvana (1984), 24 min. each
Animation   **V/T**

A series of twenty-four-minute animated cartoon adventures suitable for young children. At times they are almost cartoon music videos with standard cartoon heroes and cartoon villains and catchy tunes. The stories are pleasant enough, with little violence and usually some attempt at a moral or meaning. On the whole, rather dull, though.

Reading Rainbow
PBS (1990), 28 min. each
Hosted by Levar Burton   **V/T**

In this series, Burton appeals to both children and adults, leading viewers through various voyages of discovery aimed at promoting a love of reading and good books. Episodes conclude with three or four book reviews by likeable, articulate children. The wide variety of topics and locations and the positive and imaginative approach to reading make this an excellent series for children.

The Red Balloon
Embassy Home Video (1956), 34 min.
Director: Albert Lamorisse
Starring Pascal Lamorisse and Georges Sellier   **V**

In this magnificent and endearing film, a boy is adopted by a big red balloon. It follows little Pascal everywhere, even to school, where it hovers outside the window until school's out. When the street bullies of Paris throw stones at the balloon, Pascal gets the surprise and the ride of his life! This film, made in France, has no dialogue. The story unfolds with clarity and charm. Winner of an Oscar for Best Original Screenplay and a Golden Palm at the Cannes Film Festival.

The Reluctant Dragon
Magic Lantern, Walt Disney Educational Media Company (1985), 20 min.
Director: Hamilton Luske   **V**

A good old-fashioned animated comedy from a factory full of Disney artists. It's a wonderful satire on the old knight versus dragon theme. Fun for all ages.

Rupert
Playhouse Home Video (1988), 57 min.
Director: Mike Trumble
Still animation   **V**

Long a favourite of British children, Rupert Bear is now becoming more familiar to North American audiences. The magical stories are presented in traditional storybook fashion: the narrative is supported by tasteful music, and the camera moves constantly over rapidly shifting still drawings, giving a very strong impression of animation where there is none. This video contains twelve episodes: "The Magic Ball," "The Secret Boat," "The Pepper Rose," "The Icicle Flowers," "The Lost Fiddle," "Morwenna," "The Ozzie Kangaroo," "The Hazelnut," "The Sea Sprites," "The Winter Woolly," "The Dragon Sweets" and "The Black Imp."

Rupert and the Runaway Dragon
Playhouse Home Video (1990), 35 min.
Director: Mike Trumble
Still animation   **V**

Another, shorter offering involving the gentle bear in a wide range of adventures. This video contains seven episodes: "The Runaway Dragon," "The Shy Robins," "The Pirates," "The Crystal Ball," "The Flying Buttons," "The Fire Bird" and "The Tree Goblin."

Rupert Bear
Nelvana Productions (1991), 30 min. each
Director: Dale Schott
Still animation   **T**

The beautiful opening of each story sets the tone for the stories and for the entire series. Some excellent classical music creates the feel of an overture to a ballet. The stories are good ones, gentle yet exciting and interesting enough to hold eight-year-olds. There is a warm Rupert/Mom relationship and some good characters, like Constable Growler, who, gently but with authority, takes command of situations. Great Saturday morning viewing.

Sharon, Lois & Bram Sing A to Z
Elephant Records Production (1992), 50 min.
Director: Don Allan   **V**

If you've never had the opportunity to take your kids to a Sharon, Lois & Bram concert, here it is. The popular trio plus Elephant sing and dance their way through the alphabet. Fifteen of the letter songs are contained in clips from several live concerts, while the other eleven are illustrated by clever, colourful animated sequences combined with the three live actors. While this video has not been seen on TV, the concert sequences will be familiar to many viewers. With the usual wonderful songs, movement and audience participation, this video can be a join-in treat for all ages.

The Small One
Magic Lantern / Walt Disney Productions (1980), 30 min.
Director: Don Bluth
Animation   **V**

This is a beautifully animated Disney musical tale of a young boy and a small donkey. Forced to sell the donkey because it is old and can no longer work hard enough for its keep, the boy goes to the city and the marketplace, where he endures ridicule, and many dangers, before finding a very suitable buyer, who needs such a beast to carry his pregnant wife, as they travel towards Bethlehem.

The Smoggies
Cinar Productions (1989), 24 min.
Director: Douglas Petterton
Still animation   **T**

There is a gentle quality to the pace, the music, the drawing and the stories that makes this environmentally focused series more appealing than most Saturday morning cartoons. The stories are always centred on some aspect of environmental problems, always caused by the Smoggies, headed by Miss Emma, the not-so-evil villain, and her sidekick Polluto, who dumps garbage from their ship, the "Stinkypoo." Princess Leila runs the nature school that all the kids attend. She is helped by Uncle Boom, a scientist who solves environmental problems. This series works well for kids both artistically, and for the focus on environment.

The Snowman
Sony (1982), 26 min.
Director: Dianne Jackson
Animation   **V**

This superbly animated film based on the Raymond Briggs book is one of a kind. Visually beautiful, without any dialogue (as in the books) and accompanied only by the award-winning score, the story is about a boy who spends a magical evening when his snowman comes to life. A must for every family's video collection.

The Tale of Mr. Jeremy Fisher
Sony (1988), 30 min.
Director: Mark Sottnick
Still animation; narrated by Meryl Streep   **V**

Two well-known children's tales are brought to life by David Jorgenson's wonderful illustrations, Ms Streep's engaging storytelling, and a knockout score by jazz-fusion star Lyle Mays. In the first, Mr. Jeremy goes on a minnow-fishing trip, and turns into the hunted when a giant trout shows up. In the second, the famous Peter Rabbit ignores his mother's warning about Mr. McGregor's garden, and soon regrets it.

The Tales of Beatrix Potter
HBO (1971), 90 min.
Director: Reginald Mills
Starring the artists of the Royal Ballet   **V**

A rare treat for ballet lovers. This beautiful film features costumes that bring Beatrix Potter's endearing characters to life. Jeremy Fisher, Mrs. Tiggywinkle and the most adorable mice dance in little pink point shoes.

The Tales of Beatrix Potter
Children's Video Library (1986), 43 min.
Director: Brian McNamara
Still animation; narrated by Sidney S. Walker   **V**

This "Show Me a Story" video is not animated; rather, it is similar to watching the pages of a book while the story is being read. The illustrations are faithful to Potter's books, and the stories include: "The Tale of Tom Kitten," "The Tale of Peter Rabbit," "The Tale of Two Bad Mice," "The Story of Miss Moppet," "The Tale of Benjamin Bunny" and "The Tale of Jeremy Fisher." At the end of the video is a read-along of Cecily Parsley's nursery rhymes "Three Blind Mice," "Tom Tinker's Dog," "Little Garden," "Goosey, Goosey Gander," "Three Little Pigs," "Ninny, Ninny Netticoat" and "Pussycat, Pussycat."

Tooth Fairy, Where Are You?
Lacewood Productions (1991), 24 min.
Director: Paul Schibli
Animation   **T**

A heartwarming story of a little girl named Lori who discovers and befriends an apprentice tooth fairy called Dottie. How the two meet accidentally, become fast friends and learn from and help each other is charmingly told in this lovely animated special. Well produced, with good characterization, an interesting story and great voices.

The Rockets: The Tooth Fairy
CKY-TV (1991), 26 min.
Director: John Cuccaro   **T**

There are no scripts for any of the "Rockets" programs. The subjects and methods of presentation are worked out by the cast during a round-table brainstorming session and in subsequent improvisational performance. This one is lots of fun, the tooth fairy myth treated in a way that leaves the myth intact for young ones.

Three Favorite Stories
Marvel Productions–Little People Video (Fisher-Price)
(1985), 30 min.
Animation   **V**

The three short stories on this video might be subtitled
"The Adventures of the Tiny Perfect Little People Family." There's mom and dad and three squeaky clean
kids, including a Babykins, and of course a dog. All are
happy, all get along, all work together, all are comfort-
ably off and all are white. Cute is the operative word to
describe these straightforward and simplistic stories.
They are very much like an afternoon jelly donut —
harmless enough, gooey and soon forgotten. Mildly entertaining for the very young children aged two to six.

The Three Fishkateers
f.h.e. (1987), 22 min.
Directors: Jerry Reynolds and Russ Harris
Animation; featuring the voices of Adam
Dykstra, Russ Harris and Jerry Reynolds   **V**

Three adventurous guppies meet a girl fish and avoid
a predatory pike on a trek across the ocean floor to
relocate a particularly important pearl. This short
little three-man effort (Dykstra, Harris and Reynolds
did everything, even the music) is witty and fun, and
especially popular with pre-schoolers.

The Tin Soldier
Hi-Tops Home Video (1986), 30 min.
Director: Chris Schouten
Animation; narrated by Christopher Plummer   **V**

This Canadian-produced animation is based on Hans
Christian Andersen's story of the steadfast tin soldier
(the last one left from a box of twenty-five) with only
one leg, who falls in love with a wind-up ballerina

figurine. Accidentally knocked out of the window, the toy soldier is cast adrift in a paper boat by a little boy, and eventually melts in the fireplace. Competent animation and voices highlight this story.

Today's Special: Shoes
TVOntario (1984), 28 min.
Director: Clive VanderBurgh
Starring Jeff Hyslop and Nerene Virgin,
Bob Dermer and Nina Keogh   **V/T**

This episode, like so many others in this superb series by one of TVOntario's most prized producer/directors, introduces young viewers to outstanding Canadian talent, in this case Karen Kain. The music, written by Clive VanderBurgh, is excellent, and the dancing most exciting for children.

Today's Special: Storms
Golden Home Video (1984), 30 min.
Director: Clive VanderBurgh
Starring Jeff Hyslop, Nerene Virgin,
Bob Dermer and Nina Keogh   **V**

Loaded with songs, puppets and sight gags, this particular episode from the hit show concerns familiarizing young children with the concept of storms, and overcoming their fears, in particular, of thunder and lightning.

There are seventy-five programs in this series, all of them of the quality of the program reviewed above, and all dealing, in many entertaining ways, with subjects that are important to the lives of children aged three to eight.

Tom Thumb
MGM/UA (1958), 92 min.
Animation/live action; starring Russ Tamblyn   **V**

Although made thirty-four years ago, this video holds
up well. It's an ingenious piece for kids, with a wonderful energy, great creative spark, animation that
works very well and sets that create the illusion of
gigantic and tiny very successfully. There are some
great dance numbers, such as the scene at the fair
where we see "Talented Shoes," Tom's dance in the
magic shoes, which shows Russ Tamblyn to be a
superb dancer and acrobat.

Too Smart for Strangers with Winnie-the-Pooh
Walt Disney Home Video (1985), 40 min.
Directors: Philip F. Messina and Ron Underwood **V**

Winnie-the-Pooh, Tigger, Piglet, Rabbit, Eeyore, Owl
and Roo help children understand the dangers of
talking to strangers and playing in deserted areas.
This video is not animated. It is live-action with
people in effective costumes superimposed on painted
backgrounds. Songs illustrate principles like "Say No,
Run Away and Tell," and live-action sequences with
children help to demonstrate possible dangerous situations. A difficult subject well handled. Professionals
were consulted in the preparation of this material. For
children aged three and up.

Troupers
Golden Home Video (1983), 30 min.
Director: Jim Bach
Starring Robert Munsch, Merrytime Clown
and Puppet Show, Abraham Adzinyah and Nexus **V**

This episode from the up-tempo television show is a
mixed bag of entertainment. Robert Munsch tells "The
Mud Puddle" and the story of Mortimer who wouldn't
go to sleep; four kids play a clapping game; Abraham
Adzinyah and Nexus perform a rhythmic African

song. A fun show for little ones featuring top-quality Canadian entertainers.

√ **The Ugly Duckling**
Magic Lantern / Disney Productions (1955), 8 min.
Animation   **V**

This short animated version of the familiar fairy tale is a little gem. There is no dialogue, only the sounds of the quacks of ducks and swans, and music. The animation is superb, and the effect of the story is quite powerful because of the brevity of the treatment.

√ **The Velveteen Rabbit**
Thomas Howe Associates (1985), 24 min.
Director: Pino Van Lamsweerde
Animation; narrated by Christopher Plummer   **V**

This production is based on the story by Margery Williams. It's a great story, well told and animated, with fine voices and music, and some gentle comic touches. The rabbit is told by the other toys that he's not real, but he becomes real through the love of a little boy. A nice surprise ending. Excellent for the very young.

√ **Winnie-the-Pooh and the Honey Tree**
Disney Home Video (1965), 25 min.
Director: Wolfgang Reitherman
Animation; featuring the voices of
Sterling Holloway and Sebastian Cabot   **V**

The first in a series of Winnie-the-Pooh videos based on the stories by A.A. Milne. When Pooh's attempt to steal honey from some very angry bees by disguising himself as a "little black raincloud" fails miserably, he then loots Rabbit's pantry and becomes so fat that he

gets stuck in Rabbit's doorway while trying to leave.
His friends Christopher Robin, Owl and Rabbit decide
he should just stay there until he gets thinner. Songs
make this nicely animated series good for little ones.

Zoo Babies
TDF Pictures (1989), 30 min.
Director: Denice Evans
Narrated by Toby Styles   **V**

An appealing documentary about animal young born
in the Metro Toronto Zoo, their needs and habits, and
the measures taken to keep them safe and healthy. We
see the new-born of familiar North American species,
wood bison, Canada geese and beavers, and of such
exotic creatures as snow leopards, green water
dragons and African crown cranes. Younger children
will be enthralled by the footage of these baby
animals. Older children and their parents will enjoy
the narration describing the care of the young animals
and the environmental concerns that lead to the
carefully organized breeding of endangered species
in zoos.

Ages 5–8

The Absent-Minded Professor
Walt Disney Home Video (1961), 96 min.
Director: Robert Stevenson
Starring Fred MacMurray, Keenan Wynn
and Tommy Kirk   V

The wonders of modern technology meet the wonders of Disney in this computerized colour version of a classic black and white film. Fred MacMurray plays the quintessential "absent-minded professor," Prof. Ned Brainard, who accidentally invents "flubber." This amazing anti-gravity "flying rubber" is, of course, incredibly useful for making the professor's Model-T Ford fly and helping the college basketball team win the tournament. But when the Pentagon and some small-time con artists get wind of the discovery, the high jinks begin. Still great, silly fun. Also available in black and white.

An American Tail
MCA (1986), 81 min.
Directors: Don Bluth and Steven Spielberg
Animation; featuring the voices of Dom DeLuise,
Madeline Kahn and Christopher Plummer   V

Feivel, the little mouse, and his family emigrate to nineteenth-century America from Russia because "there are no cats in America." But he is separated from his family and spends the rest of the film searching for them, encountering a variety of characters, some trying to help him and others bent on using him. A kind of rodent Oliver Twist story. The animation is

superb. There are a number of frightening episodes for
the very little ones. There is also a loud and noisy
soundtrack, typical of Spielberg action films.

A Dog of Flanders
Paramount Home Video (1960), 96 min.
Director: James B. Clark
Starring David Ladd, Donald Crisp and
Theodore Bikel   **V**

A wonderful dog story featuring charming children
and a beautiful stray retriever. Nello is a young boy
with a great talent for art, who hopes one day to be as
good as his idol Rubens. He expects to win an art
contest and to give the prize money to his ailing grandfather, with whom he lives. When he doesn't win the
prize and his grandfather dies, the boy is left to pay
the rent on the farm by taking over his grandfather's
milk rounds, having his devoted dog pull the cart. But
an art patron proves to be more of a guardian angel
than Nello could imagine.

Babar the Movie
f.h.e. (1989), 79 min.
Director: Alan Bunce
Animation; featuring the voices of Sarah Polly,
Gordon Pinsent and Gavin McGrath   **V**

The characters Babar the elephant, his lady-love,
Celeste, and Zephyr the monkey are all from Jean and
Laurent de Brunhoff's books of the same name, but
that is where the comparison ends. This full-length
cartoon has none of the subtleties of the original or the
soft, simple pastel colours of the illustrations. It's pure
Saturday morning cartoon adventure, complete with
the evil and menacing rhino warlord Rataxes who
wreaks havoc on Celesteville and commits various
atrocities; violent and noisy.

Babes in Toyland
Walt Disney Home Video (1961), 105 min.
Director: Jack Donohue
Starring Annette Funicello, Tommy Kirk,
Ray Bolger, Ed Wynn and Tommy Sands   **V**

This was Disney's first musical film using the then
popular talents of Annette and Tommy Sands. In
Toyland, Mary Contrary and Tom Piper prepare for
their wedding, much to the consternation of the villainous Barnaby. Wanting Mary for himself, he
kidnaps Tom and the adventure begins. Full of fantasy
and effects, great songs like "I Can't Do the Sum" and
a wonderful toy soldier battle are the highlights of this
family-oriented film. Entertaining for even very little
ones.

Babes in Toyland
The Finnegan Company (1990), 96 min.
Director: Clive Donner
Starring Drew Barrymore, Richard Mulligan,
Eileen Brennan, Keanu Reeves, Jill Schoelen,
Googy Gross and Pat Morita as the Toymaster   **V**

This updated version wraps the original story in an
adventure, beginning with a snowstorm, during
which Lisa slides out of the back of a four-wheel-
drive jeep, slides down a hill and bumps into a tree,
and from there we are taken into her adventures in
Toyland. What children like about this version is
that it has an adventure, based on one situation. In
this version, Barnaby, who lives in a bowling ball, is
more threatening and more fun, and Lisa always
speaks up for herself. Children prefer the songs in
this version to those in the earlier version. This
update definitely gets more votes from young
viewers.

The Ballad of Paul Bunyan
Broadway Video (1980), 25 min.
Directors: Arthur Rankin and Jules Bass
Animation   **V**

The animated story relating the legend of Paul
Bunyan and his battle with Panhandle Pete and the
creation of Niagara Falls. The tale is pleasantly told,
with fine animation and music and good voices,
though it's somewhat dated in its information about
cutting and planting trees and other environmental
issues that kids know about.

Batman (The animated series)
Fox Productions (1992), 24 min.   **T**

A rather sinister series that seems to be centred on
fear and cynicism. This seems to be a reflection of the
somewhat difficult times in which we live. "It's a sad
fact," says Batman, "you have to accept violence on
Crime Alley." Another character says, "This used to be
a beautiful street. Good people used to live here."
These words are spoken as we watch a sad picture of
a mother and her child who seems to have died on the
street. The sinister voices, Batman's hard-edged chis-
elled face, make for a tough series. We question its
need in the world of children.

The Bear
RCA/Columbia (1990), 92 min.
Director: Jean-Jacques Annaud
Starring Jack Wallace, Tcheky Karyo and
André La Combe   **V**

Based on the novel *The Grizzly Bear* by James Oliver
Curwood, this is the story of Youk, an orphaned cub
who attaches himself to a wounded grizzly. Together
they must escape their enemy — man. This film treats

these animals as if they have human emotions, even
showing the little cub having nightmares. It contains
some amazing footage but generates concern in some
children for the animals' safety. (Of course, none of
them is hurt.)

Bearskin
Davenport Films (1985), 20 min.   **V**

Based on the Grimms' fairy tale, "The Man Who
Didn't Wash for Seven Years." Shades of the Faust
legend with Cinderella's ugly sisters thrown in for
good measure. A young soldier makes a contract with
the Devil that he will not wash for seven years.
Another in this series, "Bristlelip," a twenty-minute
adaptation of a fairy tale, indicates that this series
features very decorative costumes and sets, but
overly simplistic plots and dialogue and uninspired,
at times downright poor acting. Not very exciting or
entertaining.

Beauty and the Beast
Cannon (1987), 93 min.
Director: Eugene Marner
Starring Rebecca de Mornay and John Savage   **V**

A visually stunning production about a devoted
daughter who trades places with her father in order
to save his life. She must live in a castle with a very
strange and hideous beast. However, Beauty finds
that when one looks a little deeper, everything is not
as it seems.

One in a series of beautifully produced fairy-tale
films, all feature length, starring well-known actors
and actresses and filled with terrific songs. The viewer
never gets the impression that these films are musicals, however. The songs seem to arise spontaneously
and the singing is natural and unaffected. Other titles

include *The Emperor's New Clothes, Hansel and Gretel, Little Red Riding Hood, The Frog Prince, Snow White* and *Sleeping Beauty.*

Beauty and the Beast
Walt Disney Pictures (1991), 108 min.
Directors: Gary Trousdel and Kirk Wiser
Animation   **V**

A work of art, probably the best ever to come from the Disney Studios, this is one to purchase now that the video is available. Superb animation that brings together the Disney tradition of animation with the latest in computer animation technologies makes this a wonder to watch. Belle is a beautifully rounded character, a self-reliant young woman who can best the beast with her intelligence and feistiness. The music and song carry this piece into the realm of musical theatre. Clever characterization, great humour and an extremely intelligent script that appeals to children and adults alike make this a classic and a touchstone of what should be the quality of film and television for children.

Ben and Me
Walt Disney Productions (1953), 25 min.
Director: Hamilton Luske
Animation   **V**

This animated tale is a combination of the original theatrical and television versions. Sterling Holloway narrates Bill Peet's story of Benjamin Franklin and his inventions, told from the viewpoint of Amos Mouse — Ben's best friend and the real genius behind his contributions to technology. This little film gives children some insight into the workings of a printing press, bifocals and electricity. The animation is standard Disney Studio — competent but not brilliant.

Big Bird in China
Random Home Video (1982), 60 min.
Director: Jon Stone   **V**

Filmed in China, Big Bird and Barkley the dog introduce children to Chinese culture through stories, language and songs. As they embark on a "treasure
hunt" to find the magical Phoenix, we see the Great
Wall of China, little girls doing the "duck dance," tai
chi in the park and children playing games in the
schoolyard. A naïve and simplistic look at Chinese
life. Watch out for the line "We have to find someone
who speaks American." This tape also features,
although perfunctorily, Oscar the Grouch, Bert and
Ernie, Cookie Monster, Grover and a Monkey King
who sometimes (inadvertently) frightens little children. Not nearly as good as "Sesame Street," as it's
much too commercial.

Big Red
Walt Disney Home Video (1962), 89 min.
Director: Norman Tokar
Starring Walter Pidgeon and Gilles Payant   **V**

From the novel by Jim Kjelgaard about a wealthy
sportsman (nicknamed "Le Boss") who hires a young
backwoods Quebecois orphan to exercise his champion
Irish setter, Big Red. A bond develops between Big
Red and René. This causes a problem, as the dog's
attachment to the boy is disturbing the dog's training
to be a champion. En route to a stud farm, Red and his
mate Polly escape. They raise a family in the bush and
when René finds them, boy and dogs together save "Le
Boss" from a mountain lion. Subsequently, René gets
a new home. Disney "boy and dog" story at its best.
The film is not too sentimental or dated, and provides
interesting exposure to some French-Canadian
idioms.

The Blue Bird
Playhouse Home Video (1940), 83 min.
Director: Walter Lang
Starring Shirley Temple, Spring Byington
and Nigel Bruce   **V**

Based on the play by Maurice Maeterlinck, this film
was 20th Century Fox's answer to *The Wizard of Oz*,
and it, too, starts in black and white, then turns to
colour as Mytyl (Temple), a spoiled, selfish girl who
doesn't appreciate anything, falls asleep. She and her
brother Tyltyl and their dog and cat (who have been
magically humanized) must find the "Bluebird of Happiness." Their quest takes them to the future, where
children are waiting to be born; to the past; and to the
Land of Luxury. Excellent special effects considering
that this film was made in 1940.

Bobby's World
A Levey Production (1992), 24 min.
Starring Howie Mandel   **V**

This interesting combination of live characters and
animation is fun and witty, and deals with issues that
are important to its young audience, such as swimming, lying and selfishness. The episode on swimming
worked well, with Bobby heading off the diving board
and finding himself at the deep end of the pool. He
ends up on the bottom of the pool, terrified, and is
rescued by his brother Derek. His parents enroll him
in swimming classes, much to Bobby's delight. He
passes the first level, and quickly moves on to the
highest level, illustrating what can be accomplished
in the right circumstances. We wish, however, that
there was more live footage.

Captain Planet
Fox (1990), 24 min. each
Animation   **T**

A fine example of a well-produced animation series that will grab kids quickly because of its environmental focus. The central characters are Gaia, Captain Planet and four multi-ethnic characters who are constantly on the lookout for dangers to the environment. Each episode is built around one or several evil characters involved in some nefarious business that is polluting or threatening to destroy parts of the environment. However, when you have watched enough episodes, the pattern of racism, sexism and stereotypical plot handling becomes quite blatant. The question, in this case, is whether the program has enough to offer kids in the way of content that is relevant to environmental issues and the lives of the viewing audience. We think it has a great deal to offer, despite its problems. It has dealt with the drug issue in a very strong way, but in a way that kids are able to handle. It has introduced young children to many important issues. Too bad there aren't more cartoons like this series.

Charlotte's Web
Paramount (1972), 85 min.
Directors: Charles A. Nichols and Iwao Takamoto
Animation; featuring the voices of Debbie
Reynolds, Paul Lynde and Henry Gibson   **V**

This animated musical version of E.B. White's beloved children's book has been aired on television regularly. Wilbur the runt pig is scheduled for dinner, but he is saved from certain death by the farmer's daughter Fran, who promises to take care of him. However, it takes Charlotte (no ordinary spider) to ensure Wilbur's continued survival by spinning masterpieces that say things like "Some Pig" in her webs above Wilbur's pen. As it turns out, Charlotte is also very wise. She imbues Wilbur with confidence and teaches him how to deal with everything from the ups and downs of daily living to the eternal cycle of life and death.

Cheetah
Disney Home Video (1988), 83 min.
Director: Jeff Blyth
Starring Keith Coogan, Lucy Deakins
and Collin Mothup   V

Based on the book *The Cheetahs* by Alan Caillou. A summer vacation in Africa turns into an adventure involving Ted and his sister Susan, their Masai friend Morogo, an orphaned cheetah cub named Duma and some corrupt gamblers. All children find that there is much to be gained from sharing and respecting each other's culture.

Chitty Chitty Bang Bang
MGM / UA (1968), 147 min.
Director: Ken Hughes
Starring Dick Van Dyke, Sally Ann Howes,
Benny Hill and Lionel Jefferies   V

Based on the novel by Ian Fleming with an Oscar award-winning title song, this is the story of a very special car with a very silly name. A magical flying car takes inventor Caractacus Potts, his two children and their lady friend Truly Scrumptious on an adventure to Vulgaria where the Evil Baron Bomburst and his wife kidnap the children and steal the car. Of course, Potts invents a scheme to save them all.

A Christmas Story
MGM / UA (1983), 95 min.
Director: Bob Clark
Starring Peter Billingsley, Darren McGavin
and Melinda Dillon   V

Christmas 1947 comes to Holman, Indiana, and nine-
year-old Ralphie Parker plans to ask Santa for a
"Genuine Red Ryder Carbine Action Two Hundred
Shot Lightning Loader Range Model Air Rifle." But
to accomplish this he must neutralize his mother's
greatest fear: "You'll shoot your eye out." A fantasti-
cally appealing "film for the whole family." Jean
Shepherd deftly narrates this hilarious film adaptation of his own novel *In God We Trust, All Others Pay
Cash*.

Cinderella
Playhouse Home Video (1964), 84 min.
Director: Charles S. Dukin
Starring Lesley Ann Warren, Stuart Damon,
Ginger Rogers and Walter Pidgeon   **V**

First seen on television, this version of the classic
fairy tale plays the story traditionally. Lesley Ann
Warren is a wide-eyed Cinderella with an average
singing voice but pleasant personality. Rodgers and
Hammerstein's songs include "In My Own Little
Corner," "Do I Love You Because You're Beautiful?"
and "Impossible." Cheap studio sets and saccharine
acting are glaring.

Cirque du Soleil
VCA (1989), 55 min.
Director: Jacques Payette   **V**

If you can't go to the circus, bring the circus home!
This very special circus is unlike any other. Since
there are no animal acts, Cirque du Soleil uses unique
and inventive acts involving contortionists, clowns,
acrobats and trapeze artists in a combination of
music, dance and theatre. This video is the winner of
a number of awards.

Clarence the Cross-Eyed Lion
MGM / UA (1965), 93 min.
Director: Andrew Marton
Starring Marshall Thompson, Betsy Drake
and Cheryl Miller   **V**

Clarence, Doris the chimp and Paula, the teenage
daughter of Marsh Tracy the animal doctor, must save
the giant gorillas from poachers. Authentic film
footage of gorillas in natural habitat highlight this
film.

Classic Tales Retold
Astral / Hi-Tops Video (1977 / 78), 90 min.
Director: Fred Laderman
Animation   **V**

One of the few fairy-tale videos that stay with the traditional stories without "updating" them. The animation is of Saturday morning cartoon grade and the
music is unrelated and irritating. Of the stories presented on this tape, the last two — "Goldilocks and the
Three Bears" and "Aladdin and His Lamp" — have the
best animation. Other stories include: "Jack and the
Beanstalk," "Thumbelina," "Hansel and Gretel,"
"Wild Swans," "Little Match Girl," "Wolf and Seven
Kids" and "The Ears of King Midas." Not one we
highly recommend.

Conan the Adventurer
Chase / Rucker Productions (1992), 24 min.
Animation   **T**

This is the stuff that drivel is made of: Conan with the
wrestler's raspy voice, the muscles, the somewhat
weaker woman companion, the silly stories, kung fu,
the black man with the phoney African accent. This is
about the worst we've seen in the genre of animation.

A Cricket in Times Square
f.h.e. (1973), 30 min.
Director: Chuck Jones
Animation; featuring the voice of Mel Blanc **V**

Based on the book by George Selden, this is the story of a little country cricket named Chester, transported in a picnic basket to a newsstand in Times Square in the big city of New York. He makes friends with Tucker the mouse and Harry the cat. Chester has an unusual gift: when he rubs his wings together he makes beautiful violin music. When his friends at the newsstand have financial problems, Chester helps them by drawing a buying crowd with his wonderful music. Winner of a Parents' Choice Award.

The Dancing Frog
f.h.e. (1989), 30 min.
Director: Michael Sporn
Animation; featuring the voices of
Heidi Stallings and Edna Harris **V**

Based on the story by Quentin Blake and narrated by Amanda Plummer. This beautifully animated tale concerns Gertrude and her talented frog George, whose dancing brings him fame and fortune around the world. There are songs and lots of music by James Laev. A rare treat.

The Dancing Princesses
Faerie Tale Theatre / Playhouse Video (1984), 50 min.
Director: Peter Medak
Starring Lesley Ann Warren, Peter Weller
and Roy Dotrice **V**

One of the better shows in this uneven series. The story is well told by Dotrice, as the father, and engagingly performed by a large and attractive cast.

Darkwing Duck
Walt Disney TV (1990), 24 min. each
Animation   **T**

An upscale, modernized Donald Duck who has become a sort of Indiana Jones of the little set. Guns and zapping machines abound, as do raspy-voiced villains. To all of these, Darkwing Duck addresses himself: "I am the chill that runs up your spine. I am Darkwing Duck." The animation is slick, but the sounds of guns and machines puts this into the class of the fifty or sixty other series of zap 'em kids' cartoons.

Diamonds and Dragons
CBC Vancouver (1990), 30 min.
Director: Tony Wade
Starring Charlotte Diamond and
the Hug Bug Band, and Jackson Davies   **V/T**

An entertaining, fast-paced video full of inventive arrangements of songs. Grannie's trunk in the attic is the springboard for talented singer Charlotte Diamond to perform ten great songs: "Slimy the Slug," "Hug Bug," "Animals Have Personalities," "La Bastrange," "La Bamba," "The Unicorn," "Dickie, Dickie Dinosaur," "Competition," "The Laundry Monster" and "A Happy Street" are sung in different styles and languages. A great program that children love to watch over and over.

Digby: The Biggest Dog in the World
Prism (1974), 88 min.
Director: Joseph McGrath
Starring Jim Dale   **V**

Digby the dog gets more trouble than he bargained for when he accidentally eats the experiment that his owner Jeff has been preparing for the army.

Unfortunately, it is a growth serum and Digby grows
by leaps and bounds until he is as big as a mountain,
causing no end of chaos. Some good special effects
highlight this silly film in the shaggy dog vein.

Dinosaur, An Amazing Look At . . .
Vestron / MCA (1985), 60 min.
Director: Robert Guenette   V

Host Christopher Reeve (*Superman: The Movie*) takes
the viewer on a journey through time to see what we
know about the creature that arouses so much curiosity today. There are a variety of techniques used to
examine the dinosaurs: stop-motion animation, interviews with scientists, artists' re-creations and lots of
monster-movie footage. This video is endorsed by the
National Education Association.

Doctor DeSoto, The Dentist Mouse
Weston Woods (1984), 10 min.
Animation   V

This story by William Steig, published in 1983, is
about a dentist mouse and his wife who run a dental
clinic for animals large and small. The only restriction
is that no cats or other "dangerous species" are
allowed. A fox with an abscessed tooth tries to outwit
the dentist after the dentist has kindly extracted his
tooth, but the fox is foiled. Engaging animation, good
humour and suspense. Five years old and up.

Doctor Doolittle
20th Century Fox (1967), 152 min.
Director: Richard Fleischer
Starring Rex Harrison, Samantha Eggar
and Anthony Newley   V

The classic story of an unusual man who prefers the

company of animals to humans. It works out quite well since he understands everything they say. A child's dream come true. Unfortunately, this film is far too long to hold a child's attention. A couple of good songs like "If I Could Talk to the Animals" are the highlights of this otherwise slow-moving film. Nominated for an Oscar for best picture.

Dr. Seuss: The Cat Comes Back, There's a Wocket in My Pocket, The Fox in Socks
Praxis Media Inc./Random House Video (1974), 30 min.
Still animation   **V**

Sally and her brother soon learn that C-A-T spells trouble. Charmingly narrated by child and adult voices, this tale is full of good drama for children, and is an excellent reading and visual presentation of the story, being very faithful to the original drawings and story. The other two stories on this tape are equally good, with fine voices and good visual effects that will delight children. Don't use this instead of the stories in print. Use them alongside each other, for the one will enhance the other.

Dog City
Nelvana/Jim Henson Productions (1992), 24 min.
Puppets/animation   **T**

Here's a unique concept for kids that combines animation and puppets. The puppets are in the animation studio, drawing the story. The story is about Ace Hart, detective, who, in the episode we reviewed, was solving the mystery of stolen rubber toys. The combination of animation and puppetry, and the focus on animation techniques, makes this one of the more interesting of the new Saturday morning series.

Don't Eat the Pictures: Sesame Street at the Metropolitan Museum of Art
Random House Video (1987), 60 min.
Director: Jon Stone   V

Big Bird is accidentally locked in the Met overnight, learns about art and helps a 6,000-year-old Egyptian prince defend his soul in a trial by Osiris. An educational and entertaining video for those a little older than the regular "Sesame Street" watchers.

The Donuts
Weston Woods (1963), 27 min.
Director: Beth Sanford   V

A mediocre live-action comedy, this is a tale of a boy who is looking after his uncle's coffee shop and donut machine. With the help of a couple of customers, he gets the donut machine going, but then he can't get it stopped. The corny plot is complicated by the loss of a diamond bracelet and the various stereotypical characters who come into the shop. Based on a book written in the early forties, the film is very dated.

The Dragon That Wasn't . . . Or Was He?
MCA (1983), 83 min.
Directors: Bjorn Frank Jensen, Bob Maxfield
and Ben Van Voorn
Animation   V

Baby dragon Dexter has a problem: he seems to think that Ollie the bear is his father. This is fine for a while but Dexter has another slight problem: whenever anything upsets him, he grows to gigantic proportions. Ollie knows that what is best is to take Dexter to the Dragon Realm beyond the Misty Mountains where he can be with others of his kind. After harrowing experiences with a couple of thieves and an unjust internment in jail, Ollie finally returns Dexter to the Dragon Realm. Features songs and good animation, but has an overly complex plot.

Draw and Color Your Very Own Cartoons
CBS / Fox (1985), 60 min.
Director: Fred Lasswell **V**

Finally a drawing tape from which children can actually copy and produce a recognizable picture. "Uncle Fred" (alias Fred Lasswell of "Barney Google" and "Snuffy Smith" fame) shows kids how to draw five wild animals. All you need is a pencil or crayon and twenty sheets of paper. "It's great if you want to learn how to draw because it's really easy!" says eight-year-old Ariana. For kids four to eight.

DuckTales the Movie: Treasure of the Lost Lamp
Disney Home Video (1990), 74 min.
Director: Bob Hathcock
Animation **V**

When Scrooge McDuck, his nephews Huey, Dewey and Louie, and Webbigail Vanderquack make off with the loot from Collie Baba's ancient pyramid, they don't realize that a magic lamp they have contains a wish-granting genie. The excitement begins when the evil sorcerer Merlock heads after them to steal the lamp. An animated parody of the Indiana Jones film *Raiders of the Lost Ark*. Disney studios continue to produce above-average animations. However, this one has the same Saturday morning cartoon feel as the television show from which it was derived.

Dumbo
Walt Disney Home Video (1940), 64 min.
Director: Ben Sharpstein **V**

The story of a little elephant born into the circus who has the largest set of ears ever seen. His mother, after attempts to fend off the insulting jibes of the other elephants, is wrongly diagnosed as "mad," taken away from her little son and bound in chains. Dumbo, left on his own, is befriended by a compassionate mouse named Timothy, who attempts unsuccessfully to establish Dumbo as a circus star. After ruining an act and accidentally consuming a bucket of beer, Dumbo has a terrible nightmare (the surreal "Elephants on Parade" scene that sometimes frightens young children) and awakens with Timothy in a treetop. Timothy then realizes that Dumbo must be able to fly. Dumbo and Timothy return to the circus, become a sensation, and set things to rights. This is one of Disney's best heart-tugging stories.

The Elephant's Child
Random House Video (1985), 30 min.
Director: Mark Sottnick
Still animation; narrated by Jack Nicholson   **V**

The video version of the audio cassette based on the story by Rudyard Kipling. This "Just-So Story" of how the elephant got his trunk is told with beautifully drawn illustrations. Not a fully animated video, it is like watching a book being read with someone turning the pages. The camera moves over the pictures so there is some movement. Jack Nicholson's reading is perfect for Kipling's dry humour and wordplay. Some younger children have trouble with the slow pace and lack of movement.

The Elves and the Shoemaker
Hanna-Barbera (1990), 30 min.
Director: Carl Urbano
Animation; featuring the voices of
Jobeth Williams and Ed Begley, Jr.   **V**

One of a series called "Timeless Tales" introduced by
Olivia Newton-John, and based on the story by the
Brothers Grimm, this is the story of Bertram and
Bettina, shoemakers experiencing financial troubles.
They are helped out by three tiny elves who do
tremendous work while the shoemakers sleep. Not
having any children of their own, Bertram and
Bettina thank the elves by making them tiny clothes.
There is music throughout, and a nice song segment
in the middle. At the end of the tape, Olivia gives a
little "environmental" lecture.

The Emperor and the Nightingale
Rabbit Ears Productions (1987), 40 min.
Director: Mark Sottnick
Still animation; narrated by Glenn Close   **V**

Glenn Close narrates this famous tale about the
emperor who learns, almost too late, the difference
between real beauty and the artificial. The story is
beautifully told through superb story-book stills animation of paintings by Robert Van Nutt and music by
Mark Isham. A visual and aural delight.

The Emperor's New Clothes
Cannon Home Video (1988), 85 min.
Director: David Irving
Starring Sid Caesar, Clive Revill
and Robert Morse   **V**

Great songs, classic comic performances and beautiful
costumes and sets highlight this feature-length film. A
king who worries more about his appearance than about
his subjects or affairs of state hires two wily tailors to
make him a suit of clothes like no other. Being the con
men they are, they pocket the money and make the king
a garment that can only be seen by men "who are suited
to their office." Wait for the scene where Sid Caesar as

the king does his "foreign language gibberish" routine as
he deals with tailors from different countries. A classic.

The Emperor's New Clothes
Faerie Tale Theatre / Playhouse Video (1984), 55 min.
Starring Dick Shawn, Art Carney
and Alan Arkin   V

One of the series hosted and produced by Shelley
Duvall. This one is very disappointing. The series, on
the whole, is very good, but there are a few shows like
this one that rely too much on wisecracks and corny
(almost vulgar at times) banter aimed at adult
viewers. Thus the tone is lowered, and the overall
appeal to children is weakened.

Fern Gully: The Last Rain Forest
Fox Video (1992), 72 min.
Director: Bill Koyer   V

This is an imaginative, beautifully animated tale
with some delightful songs based on "The Fern Gully
Stories" by Diana Young. The story is a good one, concerning the saving of the fairyland rain forest from the
"monsters," the human machinery of earth and tree
destruction, great bulldozers, and tree cutters.
Although the environmental message is at times a
little heavy, the characters and their adventures, combined with engaging touches of humour, keep the
interest high. We had our usual young critics along for
this review, and the notices ran from good to rave. Lots
of fun for the whole family.

Flipper
MGM / UA (1963), 91 min.
Director: James B. Clark
Starring Chuck Connors, Luke Halpin
and Flipper   V

Sandy Hicks, the son of fisherman Porter Hicks, rescues a wounded dolphin and nurses it back to health, and in the process the boy and animal become fast friends; however, the friendship interferes with Sandy's family duties, so his father sends Flipper back to the open sea. Porter won't acknowledge Flipper's usefulness to the family, even when the dolphin saves his fishing business by guiding the boat to stocked waters. Only when Flipper rescues Sandy from a marauding shark does Porter finally realize the dolphin's true worth. The original environmentalist film.

Follow That Bird
Warner Home Video (1985), 92 min.
Director: Ken Kwapis
Starring Carroll Spinney, Joe Flaherty and Dave Thomas

V

Trouble starts for Big Bird when Miss Finch of the Feathered Friends Society decides that Big Bird should be with a family of his "own kind," and places him with the Dodo family of Oceanview, Illinois. But family life is not what Big Bird had imagined, and when the Dodos won't let him be friends with Snuffelupagus he decides to walk back to Sesame Street. Big Bird is pursued by Miss Finch, by the Sleaze brothers, who want to paint him blue and make big bucks by exhibiting him as the Blue Bird of Happiness, and by his friends from Sesame Street, who want to prevent him from falling into the clutches of evil. After various adventures and comic situations, Big Bird is restored to his rightful place. A typically excellent and hilarious entry from the Children's Television Workshop, featuring great songs and cameo performances from a number of star comedians (including Chevy Chase, John Candy and Sandra Bernhard).

The Fool and the Flying Ship
Rabbit Ears Productions (1991), 30 min.
Director: C.W. Rogers
Still animation; featuring the voice of
Robin Williams   **V**

Robin Williams demonstrates the versatility of his considerable talent with his Yiddish narration. Tim Raglin's drawings and the Klezmer Conservatory's rambunctious polkas power this excellent rendition of the Russian folk tale in which a country fool (who never thinks very far, because fools never think very far), with the help of his superhuman companions, must perform a variety of impossible tasks in order to win the hand of the Czar's daughter. Viewers who have seen or read versions of "The Fabulous Adventures of Baron Munchausen" will notice distinct similarities between the helpers in both tales.

Freaky Friday
Disney Home Video (1977), 95 min.
Director: Gary Nelson
Starring Jodie Foster, Barbara Harris,
John Astin, Ruth Buzzi and Kaye Ballard   **V**

Adapted from the book by Mary Rogers, this film shows again that Disney did all the great themes long before everyone else. A junior high school girl and her mother wish simultaneously that they were in the other's shoes and, lo and behold, the wish comes true. The mom gets to do school with all its traumas over again, and the daughter sees that it isn't as easy as she thought to be a housewife. The acting is competent, the situations a little dated. The end degenerates into pure slapstick, but the film is loads of fun for children under ten.

The Frog Prince
Cannon Video (1988), 86 min.
Director: Jackson Hunsicker
Starring Aileen Quinn and Helen Hunt   **V**

What qualities would a girl need to be a true princess?
Long hair, grace and a beautiful face to be sure. That
puts Princess Zora out of the picture, because she is a
tomboy with short hair who likes to play ball down
near the well. When she drops the ball into the well a
magic frog retrieves it and makes her promise to be
his friend. So starts a very unusual commitment.
Lessons are learned about the true qualities of friendship, gratitude and dignity in this beautiful, feature-
length film of a classic fairy tale. Actress Eileen Quinn
of "Annie" fame performs a number of songs, though
it doesn't seem like a musical as the song or dance
sequences arrive naturally and subtly. This is not for
fairy-tale purists, though, as the story contains
several subplots to fill out the running time.

General Spanky
MGM / UA Home Video (1936, black and white), 73 min.
Directors: Fred Newmeyer and Gordon Douglas
Starring the "Our Gang" comedy group   **V**

It's civil war in the south and the Our Gang army, "The
Royal Protection of Women and Children Regiment
Club of the World and the Mississippi River," engages
in comic battles with Union forces. Lots of pratfalls
and laughs. Nostalgia for grandparents, and grand-
kids love it too.

A Good Tree
Magic Lantern / Atlantis Films / NFB (1984), 26 min.
Director: Giles Walker   **V**

A charming Christmas story about three youngsters

who trespass onto a crotchety old neighbour's farm to
cut down a tree for Christmas. On Christmas
morning, they feel so guilty about stealing the tree
they decide to visit the neighbour and take him some
of their presents. He turns out not to be the miserable
old man they feared, but just a lonely old sailor, who
enthralls them with his tales of the sea, and gives
them some presents in return. Well played and
directed, this is good family Yuletide viewing.

The Goose Girl
Davenport Films (1984), 18 min.   V

One of the Davenport series, with modern American
actors trying to use the language of another century,
but they are inconsistent. This story, which has been
recommended for five-year-olds and up, is simple, but
very violent. We watch a beautiful white horse being
decapitated; we watch the maid try to strangle the
women of whom she is jealous; we hear about a horri-
ble punishment — of being dragged along on a bed of
nails until dead. The acting is uneven, hammy at
times. Avoid this one.

Gregory the Terrible Eater
*Reading Rainbow/Canadian Learning Co. (1989),
28 min.*
Hosted by Levar Burton   V

Levar Burton visits the goat paddock of the San Diego
Zoo to check out the eating habits of the goats. Here
he introduces the animated story by Mitchell
Charmat about Gregory the goat who was a terrible
eater. This five-minute animated tale is narrated by
Marilyn Michails. It's a cute little story about a goat
who wants to eat greens and vegetables. His parents
allow him to have his greens only after he has eaten
the can. They bring him around to better eating

habits. The rest of the program is devoted to the eating habits of many animals, plus a cooking session for kids given by a New York chef. The tape concludes, as usual in this series, with a review of three good books for youngsters, delivered by three articulate and attractive kids. It's good to have some of the programs from this excellent PBS series available now on video.

Hallowe'en Is Grinch Night
Playhouse Home Video (1977), 25 min.
Director: Gerald Baldwin
Animation; featuring the voice of Hans Conreid   **V**

It's back to the familiar locale of Whoville, as the "sour-sweet" wind returns to cause havoc, setting in motion a chain of noisy events that irritate the Grinch, who begins "a-prowling," and, with his faithful if reluctant sidekick Max, descends on Whoville with his dreaded "paraphernalia wagon." Only one little Who, Eukariah, stands in his way. With a combination of wit and courage, Eukariah succeeds in delaying the Grinch until the weather vane changes. A scary tale for Hallowe'en night not about Hallowe'en.

Hans Christian Andersen
Embassy (1952), 120 min.
Director: Charles Vidor
Starring Danny Kaye, Farley Granger,
Roland Petit and Jeanmaire   **V**

Highly romanticized view of the famous storyteller. The best thing about this movie is Danny Kaye's delightful version of the song "Thumbelina." A wonderful film.

Hansel and Gretel
Playhouse Home Video / Faerie Tale Theatre (1984), 51 min.
Director: James Frawley

Starring Ricky Schroder, Bridgette Anderson,
Joan Collins and Paul Dooley   **V**

Probably the best piece of acting Joan Collins has ever
done. This is the Grimms' tale of a young brother and
sister who are abandoned in the woods by their selfish
stepmother and weak father. But even after they are
captured by a wicked witch, Hansel's intelligence and
Gretel's courage save them.

The Happy Prince
Random House Video (1986), 30 min.
Director: Michael Mills
Animation; featuring the voices of
Christopher Plummer and Glynis Johns   **V**

Oscar Wilde's classic story is beautifully adapted in
this fine animated effort. After the untimely death of
a happy young prince, his spirit inhabits a beautiful,
gold-plated statue, where he is forced to oversee the
misery of his poverty-stricken city. Aided by a courageous young swallow, the Happy Prince distributes
pieces of his gold covering to alleviate the suffering of
the masses.

Heidi
Vestron Home Video (1968), 110 min.
Director: Delbert Mann
Starring Maximilian Schell, Jean Simmons
and Michael Redgrave   **V**

Based on the well-known Johanna Spyri novel about
a young orphan girl in the Swiss Alps sent to live with
her suspicious, reclusive grandfather. Heidi is sweet
and endearing and reminds her grandfather of his
lost daughter. She finally breaks down his resistance
and they become inseparable. However, others have
plans for Heidi that don't include her staying on the

mountain with her grandfather, including a rich
industrialist with a crippled daughter who comes to
depend on Heidi for emotional support and the will to
overcome her disability. But her grandfather's fierce
love overcomes all obstacles, and all ends well. A solid
version of the classic tale.

Horton Hears a Who
MGM / UA (1970), 26 min.
Director: Chuck Jones
Animation; featuring the voice of Hans Conreid   **V**

An enjoyable adaptation of a favourite Dr. Seuss story
about the elephant Horton who, with his giant ears,
can hear the voices of the inhabitants of Whoville who
live on a speck of dust. Horton must convince the other
creatures of the jungle that there is indeed a city full
of Whos on that speck of dust before he is carted away
as being quite mad and the Whos are destroyed. Can
he do it? Yep!

Ida Fanfanny and the Three Magical Tales
LCA (1981), 49 min.
Director: Paul Fierlinger
Animation   **V**

Four witty and ironic animated stories that entertain
and educate. Subjects include the value of good education, the pleasures and pitfalls of the changing
seasons, the causes of thunder and lightning and the
geological structure of the earth. Don't let the word
educational deter you. These stories take any pain out
of potentially dull topics and are delightful for young
ones and adults alike.

The Incredible Mr. Limpet
Warner Home Video (1963), 99 min.
Director: Arthur Lubin

Starring Don Knotts, Andrew Duggan,
Jack Weston and Carole Cook
Animation / live action   **V**

A combination live-action and animated story of a
man whose love for fish makes him long to be one.
When he is rejected from the U.S. navy, bookkeeper
Henry Limpet's fall off a Coney Island pier magically
makes his dream a reality. Using his underwater
powers as a fish to detect Nazi U-boats in Atlantic
waters, he becomes the navy's secret weapon in World
War II. After being honoured with a medal, he finds
his true love and lives the life he always wanted,
happily under the sea. A thoroughly silly and delightful fantasy film.

Ira Sleeps Over
Phoenix Films (1978), 17 min.
Director: Andrew Sugerman   **V**

Eight-year-old Ira is going to sleep over at a friend's
house for the very first time. He worries all day about
the fact he has never slept without his teddy bear. If
he takes his bear along, will his friend laugh at him?
His sister chides him, but his parents encourage him
to take it along. Of course, all turns out happily. His
friend sleeps with a teddy too. Like other films produced and directed by Andrew Sugerman, this one
deals with the problems of upper-middle-class, afflu-
ent people living in a charming neighbourhood. The
relationships and problems dealt with are real, but
the setting and characters are just a little too wholesome and sweet. Young children may enjoy this.

Jack and the Beanstalk
Interglobal Home Video (1967), 51 min.
Director: Gene Kelly
Animation / live; starring Gene Kelly   **V**

In this song and dance version of the well-known tale, Kelly plays the salesman who dupes the naïve Jack into swapping his mother's cow for a handful of beans, and in a significant twist, Kelly accompanies Jack up the stalk to eventual fame and fortune. A decent effort, remarkable in that it foreshadows *Pete's Dragon* (1977) and *Roger Rabbit* (1988), with its emphasis on combining live action and animation. Suitable for just about any age.

Johann's Gift to Christmas
O'B & D Productions (1991), 24 min.
Director: René Bonnière
Animation, claymation and live action; starring Heath Lamberts, Sarah Polly and Gary Quigley   **T**

This adaptation of the story by Jack Richards about the origin of the Christmas carol "Silent Night" is one of the finest examples of beautiful television for children, using the best of modern technologies, without the zap and the high voltage that many people think must be in successful children's television. The clay animation is superb in the creation of the two main characters, Johann and his old tutor, Viktor, who are enchanting in every detail. The combination of animation and live action is brilliant. The movement back and forth between the two, and the simultaneous use of both in many scenes, is a delight. The cat and mice scenes, the sequences of the mice playing the organ by hopping from key to key, as well as the humourous interaction between Lamberts and Quigley, who play Father Mohr and Herr Gruber, the organist, all add up to fine television viewing for both children and adults. This is an example of what television for children can and should be.

The Last Unicorn
ITC Films (1982), 95 min.

Animation; featuring the voices of Alan Arkin,
Jeff Bridges, Tammy Grimes and Angela Lansbury **V**

A beautiful white unicorn, who has never shared the
love and comfort of her own kind, learns the secret of
all the other lost unicorns being held in Ramsgate,
guarded by the infamous Red Bull. The Lady
Almathea is not to be won by great deeds. The prince
wishes to serve her, but she will not speak to him.
The old king, who keeps the unicorns imprisoned in
the sea, knows that she denies herself and pretends
to be human. Good animation, fine music, a great
story for children, with a lot of excitement.

The Lion, the Witch and the Wardrobe
Vestron (1985), 95 min.
Director: Bill Melendez
Animation; featuring the voices of Rachel
Warren, Stephen Thorne and Beth Porter **V**

This feature-length cartoon is based on the first book
of C.S. Lewis's *Chronicles of Narnia.* While staying at
their uncle's house, four children discover a strange
land inside an old wardrobe. Animals can talk and
time is completely different. They meet an evil White
Witch, who knows the threat the children pose to her
reign, and the real king, a majestic lion named Aslan,
who teaches them special lessons. The animation is
fair and the children (in an originally British story)
have American accents.

The Little Drummer Boy
International Telefilm / Broadway Video (1989),
25 min.
Directors: Arthur Rankin, Jr., and Jules Bass
Animation; featuring the voices of Greer Garson
and Jose Ferrer, with the Vienna Boys' Choir **V**

A musical animated puppet story based on the famous Christmas carol of the same name. Aaron is a poor, embittered orphan shepherd boy who wanders the desert, with his drum and three animals he saved from the terrible fire that killed his family and the rest of the livestock. Through various encounters, both comic and serious, he is led to the stable at Bethlehem at the moment of Jesus' birth. There, through the miracle of the gift of love, his life and world are changed. The animation is superb. Good family viewing for Christmas time.

The Little Mermaid
Walt Disney Pictures (1989), 83 min.   **V**

Ariel, the little mermaid who was supposed to stay under the sea, but just couldn't because she so much wants to be a part of the enchanting world on land, is the courageous and endearing heroine of this delightful movie. The animation is lovely, many of the songs superb, especially from the reggae-singing crab, Sebastian. Another Disney masterpiece, we think that this one belongs in your library of classics along with "Beauty and the Beast."

The Little Mermaid
Walt Disney TV (1992), 24 min. each
Director: Jamie Mitchell
Animation; featuring the voices of Jodi Benson
(Ariel) and Samuel E. Wright (Sebastian)   **T**

There is much that puts this series many cuts above regular cartoon fare. The stories, well scripted, are about issues that young children have to deal with. One episode, "Message in a Bottle," deals with a funny, lovely giant, Simon, who can never make friends because he always breaks other people's toys. Ariel and her friends Sebastian and Flounder dutifully help

teach Simon that he can indeed make friends. The
series is equal to the movie in technical quality, music
and characterization.

Mary Poppins
Disney Home Video (1964), 140 min.
Director: Robert Stevenson
Starring Julie Andrews, Dick Van Dyke,
Glynis Johns and Karen Dotrice   **V**

Based on the books by P.L. Travers about a magical
nanny who is blown in by the wind to the Banks home,
where she shows the children Jane and Michael that
life isn't always as it seems and that it can contain
many marvellous, magical moments. In the Disney
adaptation the heroine is more saccharine sweet than
the original literary character; however, this film
remains a favourite because of its charm, Oscar-
winning songs and combination of live action and
animation.

Misty
Paramount (1961), 91 min.
Director: James B. Clark
Starring David Ladd, Arthur O'Connell,
Anne Seymour and Pam Smith   **V**

A conventional tale of two children and their over-
whelming love for a wild pony, Phantom, and her foal,
Misty. After the yearly roundup of wild ponies, the
children buy Phantom with money they've earned and
carefully saved. They enter the pony in an important
race, but they soon learn that some creatures are best
left in the wild, and shortly before the big event they
set her free. Made by the same people who created
A Dog of Flanders, and based on the book *Misty of
Chincoteague* by Marguerite Henry.

The Mouse and His Child
RCA/Columbia (1977), 82 min.
Directors: Fred Wolf and Charles Swenson
Animation; featuring the voices of Peter
Ustinov, Cloris Leachman and Andy Devine   **V**

The story of a toy wind-up mouse and his child who find themselves in the big scary world outside. They fall into the hands of the villain Manny Rat, who makes them toil laboriously, but the burden is lightened when they meet other delightful toys. When they are broken into pieces by Manny, they are aided by a performing tin seal and a pink elephant. Of course, Manny gets his just deserts and the mouse gets to fulfil his dream of being "self-winding." Based on the book of the same name.

Muppet Moments
CBS/Fox Henson Production,
Playhouse Video (1985), 56 min.   **V**

A dusting off of Muppet classics, with the Muppets and guest artists Pearl Bailey, Lena Horn, Zero Mostel, Bernadette Peters, Liza Minnelli and Andy Williams. Kermit and friend are cleaning up the attic, and each time they move an object or a prop it reminds them of a favourite moment from a favourite show. Watch it all the way through, or watch just parts. Watch it together. Watch it many times over. It contains some of the funniest Muppet sequences we've ever seen, including the famous Swedish chef, a Miss Piggy space take-off, and a brilliant sequence of an Egyptian mummy singing "Night and Day." Delightful family entertainment, typical of the brilliant Jim Henson.

My First Video: My First Nature Video
Sony Kids' Video (1992)   **V**

The jacket of this video describes the series as "a colourful easy-to-follow guide for fun activities using everyday materials from around the house." Yes, this one is colourful, the activities much fun and very creative, and all activities do use materials readily available around the house. The opening explains to kids how to use the Pause button and the Rewind button on their VCR's, to enable them to follow instructions, make lists, gather materials, and indeed turn this video into an interactive experience. There are very careful instructions, offered in an easy-to-listen-to voice, which set up the entire video, including such items as when to ask for adult help, and how to put together your own nature diary. The twelve activities on this tape range from sprouting seeds, to making interesting bird treats, making a worm farm, to making animal tracks in plaster of paris. We are sure that children would be able to do all of these. The instructions are excellent, the video most informative, and the potential outcome superb. Others in the series include "My First Activity Video," "My First Science Video," and "My First Cooking Video" which instructs kids to watch for the oven mitt that will appear in the top corner of the screen, signalling the need to get adult help. A most interesting, creative series for both children and adults. Teachers will find this once, along with the *My First Activity* books, most useful.

Noah's Ark
STR (Stories to Remember) (1989), 27 min.
Directors: William T. Morrison and Steven Majaury
Animation; narrated by James Earl Jones **V**

Based on the book by Peter Spier, this is a rather slow-moving version of the biblical myth, but it is beautifully animated and well narrated, and there's just enough action to keep the interest up. Families and children interested in Bible stories will enjoy this one.

Pee Wee's Big Adventure
Warner Home Video (1985), 90 min.
Director: Tim Burton
Starring Paul Reubens, Elizabeth Daly
and Mark Holton   **V**

Pee Wee's prized possession is his shiny red bicycle, but
when he comes out of the Magic Store . . . it's gone! He
knows his next-door neighbour Butch has it because he
has been eyeing it, but getting it back is not easy. Full
of satire, silliness and great laughs, this is the better of
the Pee Wee Herman films. Directed in his distinctive
style by ex-cartoonist wonderman Tim Burton. Note
Pee Wee's similarity to early Jerry Lewis!

The Pied Piper of Hamelin
Faerie Tale Theatre/Playhouse Video/Glen Warren
Productions (1984), 30 min.
Starring Eric Idle   **V**

Eric Idle plays the Piper and is supported by a fine
Canadian cast in this familiar story about the Piper
who rids the town of the plague of rats, and eventually of all the children. Based on the poem by Robert
Browning, the tale is presented as a bedtime story told
to a young boy in England in 1840. There are some
good touches of humour mixed with a sad note or two.
This is fine family viewing, well performed, with well-
spoken verse.

Pinocchio
Faerie Tale Theatre/Playhouse Home Video (1983),
30 min.
Director: Peter Medak
Starring Carl Reiner, Paul Reubens,
Lainie Kazan and James Coburn   **V**

Poor carpenter Geppetto wants a son more than

anything. But he must be content with the wooden
marionette of a boy he has carved with loving care. A
magic fairy casts a spell that makes the puppet, Pinoc-
chio, come alive, and together he and Geppetto go
through many adventures that lead to a magical revelation. Well-cast version with good effects. This is one
of the best episodes of producer Shelley Duvall's
twenty-six-episode Faerie Tale Theatre series.

Pippi Longstocking
Vid America (1974), 99 min.
Director: Olle Hellbom
Starring Inger Nilsson and Par Sundberg **V**

The first in a series of four Pippi movies based on the
book by Astrid Lingren. Pippi is a strange little girl
who lives by herself because her father is at sea and
her mother is an "angel in heaven." She is not quite
alone, however, as she has a horse, a monkey and her
neighbours Tommy and Annika to keep her company.
Her strange ways precipitate many adventures
during which she always remains capable. She is self-
reliant and very strong, and has a chest of gold in her
basement. This Swedish film is badly dubbed into
English, but the story is so charming that children
don't seem to mind.

The Plucky Duck Show
Warner (1992), 24 min. each **V**

A song and dance routine opens each episode of this
series about a duck hero who wants to be a movie star.
Each story then evolves around a take-off on a particular movie or TV show, such as "The Return of Bat
Duck." Lots of biff and bam but also some fun and
satire on movies, the characters and types, and TV
shows and lore that kids will know and understand.
Better than average Saturday TV.

Pollyanna
Walt Disney Home Video (1960), 134 min.
Director: David Swift
Starring Hayley Mills, Jane Wyman,
Richard Egan and Agnes Moorhead   **V**

Pollyanna is an irrepressibly cheerful orphan sent to live with her aloof Aunt Polly Harrington. When a tragic accident befalls Pollyanna, it inspires a warmth long forgotten in Aunt Polly and a charity long submerged in the townsfolk. Mills won an Honorary Academy Award for Most Outstanding Juvenile Performance of the Year.

Prancer
Nelson Entertainment (1989), 103 min.
Director: John Hancock
Starring Sam Elliot, Cloris Leachman,
Abe Vagoda and Rebecca Harrell   **V**

A sentimental but, on the whole, charming and well-played Christmas story about a young girl who finds a wounded deer in the woods near her farm in a northern American town. Her insistence on saving the deer's life and caring for it has a profound effect on the town's many characters. The usual magical Christmas ending. A fine performance by the young Rebecca Harrell, and by the supporting cast of Hollywood regulars. Syrupy, but good family viewing for young ones at Christmas.

Ramona
Lorimar (1987), 30 min.
Director: Randy Bradshaw
Starring Sarah Polly   **V**

One of an excellent five-part series of thirty-minute videos based on the popular stories of Beverly Cleary.

These are outstanding productions with fine Canadian casts that, unlike most similar series, contain very believable family scenes and school situations. The precocious eight-year-old Ramona is played by Sarah Polly, and her adventures will entertain and delight youngsters and families alike. A wonderful antidote to so many of our dreadful thirty-minute "family" sitcoms.

Ramona: Mystery Meal
Lorimar (1987), 30 min.
Director: Randy Bradshaw
Starring Sarah Polly, Barry Flatman,
Lynda Mason Green, Lori Chodos   **V**

When Ramona Quimby, a delightful and typical eight-year-old, and her sister Beezus refuse to eat the dinner their mother has prepared, she suggests they make their own — with surprising results. Superior casting helps these television adaptations of the Beverly Cleary novels come alive.

Rapunzel
Davenport Productions (1984), 15 min.   **V**

By far the worst show in this mediocre series. The first five minutes is so badly shot and spoken that a six- or seven-year-old who did not know the story would be completely confused. An insult to children's intelligence and a waste of their time.

Rapunzel
Fairie Tale Theatre/Playhouse Video (1982), 45 min.
Starring Shelley Duvall, Jeff Bridges
and Gena Rowlands   **V**

A much better version than the Davenport. It has a clear story line and is well narrated, played and produced. The violence is toned down, and Rapunzel's banishment, even the blinding of the prince, are handled with care. Interesting and quite suitable for five-year-olds and up.

The Red Room Riddle
Marlin Motion Pictures (1982), 24 min.
Director: Robert Chenault   **V**

Based on a novel by Scott Corbett, this is a good old-fashioned haunted-house adventure for six-year-olds and up. It concerns two young boys who are curious about an old neighbourhood house that is supposed to be haunted. As their initiation, they have to report to their club that they have been inside the house and seen what it's all about. They encounter various odd characters, including a strange boy who leads them through the house and traps them in a glowing room. Needless to say, they escape. For fans of haunted-house stories, though it's not terribly scary.

The Rescuers Down Under
Disney Home Video (1991), 77 min.
Directors: Hendel Butoy and Mike Gabriel
Animation; featuring the voices of George C. Scott,
Zsa Zsa Gabor and Bob Newhart   **V**

In the Australian outback, two brave little mice named Bernard and Miss Bianca are sent by the Rescue Aid Service to save a young boy named Cody who has been kidnapped by a ruthless poacher after having interfered with the poacher's capture of a magnificent golden eagle. Superior animation, wonderful interpretation of characters suggested by Margery Sharp and a great music score by Bruce Broughton make this one of the best efforts to date from the new Disney studios.

Rock Along With Bob Schneider
Golden Home Video (1991), 30 min.
Director: Ron Meraska
Starring Bob Schneider and the Rainbow Kids   **V**

Bob Schneider leads his musical group in a number of funky up-tempo songs. This video won't disappoint Schneider's following. Includes "Rock Along," "One Big Family," "Kemo Sabe Hobby Song," "Over and Over," "The Eat Song," "Got a Hat Hat" and "Funky Expressions."

The Rockets
CTV (ongoing), 24 min. each
Director: John Cuccaro
Starring Janis Dunning and group of children   **V**

Rehearsing shows, song and dance numbers, and the development of ideas for shows is the subject of this lively musical drama series, peopled with attractive and talented young people from about eight to sixteen years old. Subjects range from the tooth fairy to clowning. In this last show, for instance, the kids in the show, and therefore the young audience, learn much about clowning from a real clown. Children like to watch other children rehearse, and this is exactly what they get in this show.

Rumpelstiltskin
Cannon Home Video (1987), 84 min.
Director: David Irving
Starring Amy Irving, Billy Barty and Clive Revill   **V**

A beautifully presented version of the old Grimms' fairy tale, with lavish costumes and songs. This is the first in a series of feature-length fairy tales by the Cannon film studios. A fine effort not to trivialize or oversentimentalize these traditional stories. Amy

Irving's singing voice is a little thin, but she is charming as the poor girl who is pressed into an odious
bargain with a demon, and Billy Barty is great as the
nefarious evil spirit; however, the ending, where
Rumpelstiltskin is banished back to the infernal
domain, may be too frightening for younger viewers.

Saint Nicholas and the Kids
O'B & D Productions (1990), 24 min.   **T**

A strange little Christmas story about two children in
a poor family with an ailing mother. In the haunted
forest, Pierre meets a weird man, who is the partner
of a witch-like woman. Estelle meets St. Nicholas.
Both Pierre and Estelle are captured by the weird pair
who love "yummy children" and stuff them into
barrels. St. Nicholas saves the day. An interesting but
not entirely successful story. Children don't quite
understand it, and adults find the story incomplete.

The Selfish Giant
Weston Wood (1971), 14 min.
Director: Walter Reiner
Animation   **V**

A well-told story in excellent black and white animation with voice-over. An allegorical fairy tale by Oscar
Wilde, in which a giant learns to love little children
and is rewarded.

Shining Time Station
Catalyst Entertainment Inc. (1990), 60 min.
Director: Stan Swan
Animation/live action; starring Ringo Starr   **T**

This Christmas show is a strong example of an excellent series. Set in a railway station, it stars Ringo
Starr as the tiny station master. The mix of live action,

which is often very funny, and the rich animation of "Thomas the Tank Engine," the fine British series much loved by many children, moves along well over the hour. This is a well-directed, prettily shot show. The cast of characters — Stacey Jones, the warm and helpful clerk, Midge Snoot, the busybody, Schemer, the shyster, and the two children, along with special guest Lloyd Bridges — tell a touching and important story about a little girl who can't get along with anyone, but just needs some gentle understanding and love. Mr. Nicholas (Bridges) helps the girl to smile, and helps the other children to understand her. Some beautiful songs by the puppet country rock band make this a beautiful, moving Christmas story for children and adults. We are left with the line, from Mr. Nicholas: "Whenever you bring light and joy into another person's life, you find Santa Claus."

Sign Me a Story
Random Home Video (1987), 30 min.
Director: Steve Zink
Starring Linda Bove, Elaine Bromka,
Tim Scanlon and Ed Waterstreet   **V**

Linda Bove ("Sesame Street") begins with some simple signs, then the entire group acts out two familiar fairy tales, "Little Red Riding Hood" and "Goldilocks and the Three Bears." An excellent little effort that combines signing and narration and is thus accessible to both the hearing and the hearing-impaired.

Silverhawks: The Origin Story
Scholastic-Lorimar (1986), 101 min.
Animation   **V**

Tells of the origin of these half-machine, half-human cyborg heroes and how they defend the peaceful people of the universe of 2839 against the evil forces of Mon Star. The jacket invokes the viewer to "Join Commander Stargazer, Quicksilver, Smiley, Mumbo-jumbo, Steel-heart and Melodia in keeping the galaxy safe for mankind" — a dreadful insult to the intelligence of children. The animation is poor, the characters' voices of wrestler quality. There is nothing more to be said about this series.

Sparky's Magic Piano
f.h.e. (1987), 51 min.
Director: Lee Mishkin
Animation; featuring the voices of Mel Blanc,
Tony Curtis, Cloris Leachman and Vincent Price   **V**

Eight-year-old Sparky hates practising the piano, but his mother insists on one hour a day. Then Sparky's piano takes on a life of its own and will play anything Sparky asks. Sparky becomes a star over overnight, and develops a titanic ego to match, until the piano itself loses patience and refuses to play properly in the middle of a major concert. Sparky emerges from the embarrassing climax of his fantasy to discover himself seated at home before his ordinary piano with his loving parents nearby. He makes a vow right then and there: henceforth he will practise hard, and learn to play himself.

Stories and Fables
Walt Disney Home Video (1981), 50 min.   **V**

These live action stories, which all take place "long ago and far away," are completely narrated. The stories are filmed on location throughout the world. In each two-story package, one usually deals with royalty of Anglo times, and the other with people on exotic islands.

In "The Widow's Lazy Daughter," the daughter of the title is taken away from her poverty by a handsome prince. But the queen's mother sets three gigantic tasks for the girl to complete before they can marry. The beautiful young bride is helped through her chores by three mysterious and magical old ladies.

In "Hinemoa," a Maori tale, a chief's beautiful daughter struggles to overcome her father's wrath about her determination to marry the man she loves.

The stories are rather tame, but well narrated, nonviolent and quite suitable for young children.

Strega Nonna
Weston Woods (1977), 14 min.
Director: Gene Deitch
Animation   **V**

One of a series based on books using the illustrations from the books as the basis for the beautiful animation. *Strega Nonna* is the story of Grandma Witch, who lived long ago in southern Italy, helping all the people in the village with her magic powers and her magic pasta pot.

Swiss Family Robinson
Walt Disney Home Video (1960), 128 min.
Director: Ken Annakin
Starring John Mills, Dorothy McGuire,
James McArthur and Tommy Kirk   **V**

A fun adventure film about a family shipwrecked on a desert island, who come up with ingenious devices to make everyday living possible and to defend their homestead from pirates. A great family film, based on the Johann Wyss book.

Teeny Tiny and the Witch Woman
Weston Woods (1980), 14 min.
Director: Gene Deitch
Animation   **V**

Based on an old Turkish tale about three boys named Big One, In The Middle and Teeny Tiny. In spite of constant warnings from their mother not to venture into the woods where a wicked witch lives, they do just that, although Teeny Tiny is reluctant. The witch has a reputation for eating young children and using their bones and skulls to decorate her house and property. Sure enough, the boys come upon an old woman whose home is surrounded by a human bone fence. After the witch convinces them that there is nothing to fear, they all bed down for the night. Teeny Tiny has his doubts and stays awake and manages to outwit the witch, and all ends happily. There are a few very scary moments that may be too much for very young children, but the tale is well told.

Tell Me Why
Video Encyclopedia (1988), 15 min.
Director: Arkady Leokum   **V**

This British information series is beautifully shot and presents straight information. We call it a "when the need arises" video. It's the kind of program that is most valuable when children have school projects to develop or when children are being schooled at home. These programs provide opportunities for parents to work with children. The episode that deals with fishes has some fine footage, and talks about such things as the first fishes and the nature of eels.

The Three Caballeros
Disney Home Video (1945), 70 min.
Director: Norma Ferguson
Animation / live action; starring Carmen Miranda
and featuring the voices of Sterling Holloway
and Clarence Nash   **V**

This family favourite uses a combination of cartoons

and live-action travelogue sequences seen on "The Wonderful World of Color." The opening animation features a little penguin who can't stand the cold. Next, a charming fantasy of the little gaucho who discovers a burro with wings and enters him in the greatest horse race in all the land. And finally, Donald Duck and his friends south of the border, José Carioca and Panchito, take us on a panoramic tour of Latin America. Watch out for the hysterically funny song "The Three Caballeros" with the line, "We're three happy chappies in snappy serapes." The Steve Martin, Martin Short, Chevy Chase film *Three Amigos* is a send-up of these characters.

Toxic Crusaders
Troma, Inc. (1990), 24 min. each
Director: Fred Wolf   **T**

Dr. Killemoff is the central villain of this dreadful series that features strange mutants and the Crusaders who fight the evil machinations of Killemoff. Also features the beautiful dumb blonde secretary Yvonne, with the bimbo voice. Action takes place at the Traumaville Mall. Lines such as "You've got to be the biggest idiot I've ever been attached to" abound. One of a series capitalizing on current environmental issues and being presented to kids in school. Dreadful.

Ty's Homemade Band
Phoenix Films (1983), 20 min.   **V**

Based on a popular children's book, this is the engaging story of a ten-year-old boy who joins with a strolling musician and some of his friends to present a concert for the community. There are lots of fun ideas for putting musical sounds together using common household objects such as a washboard, thimbles and various kitchen utensils. Ty's parents, and other adults, doubt very much that he can get a concert together in a short time, but he has faith in his friend the musician, who gathers the kids together and teaches them how to accompany themselves on various pots and pans. Before the show is over the whole community is joining in, singing and dancing.

We All Have Tales: Finn McCoul
Rabbit Ears Productions, Inc. (1991), 30 min. each
Director: C.W. Rogers **V**

As the dust jacket of this one says: "The Rabbit Ears series is a celebration of music and storytelling traditions of peoples around the world." In this story, so finely told by Catherine O'Hara, with beautiful Celtic music by The Boys Of Lough, the famous Irish hero Finn McCoul and his more than clever wife Oonagh play some shrewd and very funny tricks on the brutish giant Cucullin, to defeat him once and for all and send him scurrying off, having been reduced to the size of a mouse. The still watercolour drawings,by Peter de Seve, are elegant, and the shooting of them makes them almost animated. Rabbit Ears presents these stories, all twelve in the series, from various cultures, in a most entertaining, intelligent manner for the whole family. Television can be allowed to become the bedtime story with this series of ten stores, which include: "Anansi" told by Denzel Washington, music: UB40; "East of the Sun and West of the Moon," Max von Sydow with music by Lyle Mays; an Indian story, "The Tiger and the Brahman" told by Ben Kingsley, music by Ravi Shankar; "King Midas and the Golden Touch," told by Michael Caine, music by Ellis Marsalis; "Koi and the Kola Nuts," a classic Swahili tale, told by Whoopi Goldberg, with music by Herbie Hancock.

Willie the Operatic Whale
Disney Home Video (1940), 29 min.
Directors: Hamilton Luske and Clyde Geronimi
Animation; featuring the voice of Nelson Eddy

This quirky selection concerns Willie, a magnificent opera-singing whale, who dreams of performing all the great roles in opera houses around the world — that is, until he is shot by an unimaginative whaler. This tape also contains well-made versions of "Ferdinand the Bull" and "Lambert the Sheepish Lion."

The Wizard of Oz
MGM / UA (1939), 101 min.
Director: Victor Fleming
Starring Judy Garland, Jack Haley,
Ray Bolger and Margaret Hamilton   **V/T**

This classic of all classics still works as well today as the day it was released, and now it is hard to imagine anyone else in the characters created by L. Frank Baum. We all know the story of little Dorothy and her dog Toto, swept away by a tornado to Munchkin Land where she must follow the yellow brick road to the land of Oz to meet the great Wizard who will show her the way home. It doesn't seem too complicated either . . . it's only the part about killing the "Wicked Witch of the West" that Dorothy and her companions, the Tin Man, the Scarecrow and the Cowardly Lion, are not too pleased about. Margaret Hamilton's witch has been scaring kids for over fifty years. One of the greatest scores of all time. Winner of numerous awards.

The Woman Who Raised Her Son as a Bear
Lacewood Productions (1990), 24 min.
Animation   **T**

This story of an old Inuit woman who raises a bear cub as her own child is animation storytelling at its best. The bear can only be saved from the irrational hunter if it is given its freedom. Great music, representational animation beautifully coloured, and an excellent script make fine viewing for young and old. Warm, witty and wise, this is a well-told modern television fable.

Ages 8–12

Abel's Island
Random House Home Video (1988), 30 min.
Director: Michael Sporn
Animation; featuring the voices of
Tim Curry and Lionel Jefferies **V**

Academy award nominee Michael Sporn has brought
William Steig's lyrical story to life using stunning
full-colour animation. Young and old alike will fall in
love with Steig's wonderfully romantic Abelard
Hassam di Chirico Flint, an elegant mouse who,
while picnicking with his beloved wife, Amanda, gets
caught in a furious storm and is swept away to a
desert island, where he spends his time living by his
wits and charm, and his newly awakened creativity.
This is a sophisticated story, delicately realized and
beautifully animated.

The Addams Family
Paramount Pictures (1992), 103 min.
Director: Barry Sonnenfeld
Starring Angelica Huston, Raul Julia
and Christopher Lloyd **V**

Tish takes Fest on a tour of the family cemetery to
remind him of their roots: psychopaths, fiends, this
sort of thing. Fester has returned after twenty-five
years, and he's a bit too "normal." Tish speaks very
slowly, and the movie moves in just this way, all too
slowly. It may have some entertaining bits for kids,
and there's not much very problematic with it. It's just
a bore.

Amazing Adventures
Macmillan "Let's Explore" Series based on the
Macmillan Illustrated Almanac *(1985), 30 min.*   V

Each program in this series contains several explorations. This one deals with a journey into space and a fascinating examination of the life and times of the stars and planets in the universe, followed by a close look at volcanoes and the formation of land. Program three deals with the properties of soap bubbles, and the last segment explored the windy world of kite flying. These last two items have many do-it-yourself hints. The fun of these programs is discovery, and there are hands-on ideas and sources for further information included on the cover and on the tape. This may not be the things that youngsters themselves would choose, but they make great viewing for a day home from school or for general information gathering for the whole family. The programs are well produced and easy to follow.

The Adventures of the Black Stallion
Alliance Communications (1992), 28 min.
Director: Mark Defriest
Starring: Mickey Rooney, Richard Ian Cox,
Marianne Filali   T

This series, set in New Zealand, is aimed at the preteen market. There are good relationships established between Uncle Henry (Mickey Rooney) and the kids, and there are one or two good scenes per episode. On the whole, however, the stories and situations are cliché ridden, and the characters are stereotypical. Little violence. Fairly good family viewing.

The Adventures of Tom Sawyer
Playhouse Home Video (1938), 93 min.
Director: Norman Taurog

Starring Tommy Kelly, Jackie Moran,
Walter Brennan and May Robson   **V**

The antics of Tom Sawyer and the whitewashed fence
have become synonymous with cleverness, trickery and
fun. In this restored, original version of Selznick's film,
based on the book by Mark Twain, mischief-maker Tom
leaves home to become a pirate. He stumbles upon adventure in the form of a foreboding cave and "evil Injun
Joe." His friends Huck Finn and Becky Thatcher get
drawn into the misadventures as well. This passionate
and visually rich film will appeal to fans of the genre.

Alice in Wonderland
Walt Disney Home Video (1951), 75 min.
Directors: Clyde Geronimi, Hamilton Luske
and Wilfred Jackson
Animation   **V**

Lewis Carroll's wonderful story about little Alice,
who, falling asleep from boredom one afternoon, imag-
ines herself falling down a rabbit hole and arriving in
a fantasy land full of colourful, frightening and perplexing characters. Alice manages to maintain her
dignity in this ridiculous place. Disney, by injecting
charm into the bizarre and famous characters (the
March Hare, the Dormouse, the Cheshire Cat and of
course the Queen of Hearts), tones down some of the
more frightening elements. The film also features
some of Disney's best songs, including "A Very Merry
Unbirthday," "We're Painting the Roses Red" and "I'm
Late." Definitely a classic.

All Dogs Go To Heaven
MGM/UA (1989), 85 min.
Director: Don Bluth
Animation; featuring the voices of Burt Reynolds,
Dom DeLuise and Loni Anderson   **V**

German shepherd Charlie B. Barkin, aided by his dachshund sidekick Itchy, breaks out of the Pound and returns to his gambling joint. His evil partner Carface is none too glad to see him, and promptly has him bumped off. Charlie gets into Heaven on a technicality (all dogs go to Heaven), but he isn't ready for it (too boring, no surprises) and so, despite the fact that once he leaves he can never return, he conspires to escape back to Earth, where he sets up a betting scam, using Anne-Marie, an unwitting orphan girl who can communicate with all animals. But Charlie eventually sees the light, and sacrifices himself for his friend. Former Disney animator Don Bluth brings his usual superbly crafted animation, voice-overs and characterization to the screen; however, the convoluted plot with its themes of damnation and redemption may be too much for little ones.

Amazing Grace and Chuck
HBO Video (1987), 116 min.
Director: Mike Newell
Starring Jamie Lee Curtis and Gregory Peck   **V**

After a school visit to a Minuteman III missile silo, Chuck, an all-star little-league pitcher, decides to take a stand. He refuses to throw another pitch until the United States and Russia have totally disarmed. His actions are publicized in the local papers and eventually reach the notice of Boston Celtic basketball star Amazing Grace Smith, who is so taken by the boy's sense of purpose that he too makes the same stand. These actions cause a snowball effect throughout the athletic world, until the very foundation of the military-industrial establishment is shaken, with violent, far-reaching, and eventually significant results. A terrific film that stresses that a single determined individual can indeed affect things on a global scale.

Angel Square
Cineglobe (1991), 106 min.
Director: Anne Wheeler
Starring Jeremy Radick, Nicola Cavendish,
Brian Dooley, Leon Pownell and Ned Beatty   **V**

This Genie Award-winning film, directed by Anne
Wheeler (*Loyalties* and *Bye, Bye Blues*) is a delightful
treat for the whole family. Loosely based on the book
by Ottawa's Brian Doyle, it is full of humour and
flights of fancy, and features a mixed bag of characters
and families in a very believable urban Canada of
Christmas 1945. The main character, wonderfully
played by Jeremy Radick, is obsessed with war comics
and radio adventures. Inspired by his hero, The
Mystic, he and his pals set out to solve the mysterious
beating of the father of one of his friends. The supporting cast is superb. It's a good story well told with
an excellent setting.

Animation '91
YTV (1991), 60 min.
Animation   **T**

This compilation of animated shorts from the Children's Animation Workshop and the best of the
National Film Board makes for excellent viewing of
this genre for both children and adults. Children from
across Canada introduce and show their animation
productions. They talk about the process of making
their short films. Some lovely pieces of work here to
inspire children to explore this medium and to
become involved with enterprises like the Children's
Animation Workshop. Watch for these kinds of YTV
presentations. They are great celebrations of children's creativity.

Anne of Green Gables
Nova Home Video (1985), 195 min.
Director: Kevin Sullivan
Starring Megan Follows, Colleen Dewhurst
and Richard Farnsworth   **V**

A beautiful and touching version of the classic Lucy
Maud Montgomery book about Anne, a dreamy, intelligent orphan sent to live with Marilla Cuthbert and
her brother Matthew. The problem is, however, that
the Cuthberts had asked for an orphan boy to live with
them. Anne, terrified of being sent back, asks for a
trial period, during which everything she does seems
to go wrong. However, Marilla, unconvinced at first,
comes to recognize something of herself in the girl,
and a bond grows between them. Superbly cast, acted
and directed, this film and its sequel should be part
of everyone's video library. (The sequel is based on
Montgomery's novels *Anne of Avonlea* and *Anne of the
Island.*)

Annie
RCA / Columbia (1981), 128 min.
Director: John Huston
Starring Aileen Quinn, Albert Finney,
Ann Reinkin and Carol Burnett   **V**

A film version of the musical *Annie,* based on the
comic strip "Little Orphan Annie." Aileen Quinn is
superbly cast as Annie, the poor little orphan who
dreams of having a real mother and father, but instead
lives at the orphanage with a number of other little
girls (who all sing and dance like they've had ten years
of musical theatre training) under the supervision of
the alcoholic, sexually frustrated Miss Hannigan.
When Annie is sent to stay for a day with millionaire
Daddy Warbucks, she is determined to be adopted by
him and his secretary Miss Farrel, but things become

complicated when Miss Hannigan arranges for two co-conspirators to pose as Annie's long-lost parents to bilk Warbucks of a $50,000 reward. This box-office smash features the huge hit song "Tomorrow."

Arctic Diary
Lauron Productions (1991), 10 min. each   **V**

This series of thirteen programs traces the progress of a four-man international team led by Canadian Richard Weber and Russian Mikhail Malakhov. This first Canadian-led expedition, an official Canada 125 event, travelled from Ward Hunt Island, off the northernmost point of Canada near Greenland, to the North Pole and back. Each program opens with a list of classroom activities and materials needed to take part in that particular day's event. The program body has interviews, voice-over and excellent footage of the trek. Each show ends with a weather report and questions from various students, relayed to and answered by the explorers. It is excellent classroom fare for grades six to ten, or anyone interested in science, geography and international adventure.

Are You Afraid of the Dark? "The Tale of the Twisted Claw"
Cinar Productions (1991), 24 min.
Director: D.J. MacHale
Starring Maxwell Medeiros, Noah Plener
and Ann Page   **V**

One of an excellent series of thirteen half-hour programs, this is a well-told, just scary enough story, recounted by one of the members of the Midnight Society around their campfire. In this story of Hallowe'en, two young boys are given the claw of a vulture by an old woman they believe to be a witch. The claw will give them each three wishes, but they

are warned to be careful — they just might get what
they wish for. And they do — literally. The old be-
careful-what-you-wish theme. This is a great series
for campfire-aged young folk, nine and up. A bit scary
for younger ones.

Baby . . . Secret of the Lost Legend
Walt Disney Home Video (1985), 90 min.
Director: Bill Norton
Starring William Katt, Sean Young
and Patrick McGoohan   **V**

A surprise favourite with the younger crowd, mainly
because of special effects that create a very appealing
and lifelike baby dinosaur. Two paleontologists discover a living family of Brontosaurs in Africa. After the
adult dinosaurs are killed by crazed soldiers (in true
Bambi fashion), the orphan is left in the care of the couple. But an unscrupulous scientist (McGoohan) will
stop at nothing to obtain the infant, and the story ends
in tragedy. Parents of young viewers should be warned
that the film contains one especially brutal murder.

Bach and Broccoli
Roch Demers, Tales for All, Number 3 (1986), 95 min.
Director: Andre Melanson
Starring Mahee Paiement and Raymond Legault   **V**

A delightful tale of a nine-year-old girl suddenly
orphaned and forced to live with her musician uncle,
whose life is completely absorbed with his music,
leaving very little room for a young girl. This is a
charming story of relationships, ambition and understanding. Both main characters are convincing. This
is a fine family show for those aged seven and up.
Excellent performances, good direction, interesting
Canadian scenery and pleasing music make for a fun
family viewing experience.

Back to the Future
MCA (1985), 112 min.
Director: Robert Zemeckis
Starring Michael J. Fox, Christopher Lloyd,
Lea Thompson and Thomas F. Wilson   **V/T**

The first film in a trilogy that includes *Back to the Future II* and *III,* this film also stands alone. Because of the incredible attention to detail, it can be watched over and over and only gets better. The story revolves around Marty McFly, a typical American teenager, who is transported back in time by his old friend "Doc" via a DeLorean car converted into a time machine. Arriving in 1955, Marty must make sure that his parents meet and marry; otherwise Marty and his siblings won't exist. But Marty's interference in the past creates a very different, and better, future. This is a brilliantly conceived sci-fi fantasy full of adventure and excitement.

Ballet Shoes
BBC Young Classic Collection (1975), 120 min.
Director: Timothy Combe   **V**

Based on the novel by Noel Streatfield about three little orphans, Pauline, Posy and Petrova, who "vow to become famous and be written about in the history books." They live with their guardian Sylvia, and financial crises constantly threaten their dreams of fame and fortune. But when the local ballet school gives them a chance to take acting and dancing lessons, it seems their prayers are answered. Somehow, everything turns out to be better than they expected. A charming and gentle film.

Bambi
Disney Home Video (1942), 69 min.
Director: David D. Hand
Animation

This exquisitely animated film is based on Felix Salten's heart-wrenching story of a little faun and his friends Flower the skunk and Thumper the rabbit. The story follows Bambi growing up and the eventual emergence of Bambi as a proud buck with a family of his own. A rather adult story despite the animated presentation. Don't forget the scene of his mother's death, which can frighten younger ones.

Banjo the Woodpile Cat
Children's Video Library (1979), 30 min.
Director: Don Bluth
Animation   **V**

Banjo is a country cat who's always in hot water for one reason or another. Full of self-pity after being disciplined, he runs away to Salt Lake City, but he soon discovers that the big town isn't all it's cracked up to be, and enlists the aid of an alley cat named Crazy Legs to help him get home. This fine little film represents Don Bluth's first work after leaving Disney Studios, and one can clearly see the style that would later come to maturity in *The Secret of N.I.M.H.* and *An American Tail.*

Barnyard Commandos: Back to the Farm
Sachs-Finley Programming (1989), 30 min.
Director: Fred Wolf
Animation   **T**

Simple but interesting animation and fun voices fill this somewhat perplexing tale. Episode one of a series, this story takes us into the war zone of pigs versus sheep, in which they do battle with veggies as weapons. It matters little whether the weapons are guns or veggies, the war message is still the same: might is right. So watch out for this one. It's one of those insidious little entertaining cartoons that has weapons as its focus.

Batman Returns
Polygram Pictures (1992), 104 min.
Director: Tim Burton
Starring Michael Keaton, Danny DeVito,
Michelle Pfeiffer   **V**

Very much in the style of Burton's "Edward Scis-
sorhands," this one is hardly as endearing, and much
further away from the world of children's viewing.
Sombre, brooding, full of adult witticisms such as
Bruce Wayne to Cat Woman: "No hard feelings?" to
which she replies, "Actually, semi-hard, I'd say,"
pushing her body close to his. Violent, ugly birth,
infanticide, implied sex, grotesqueries everywhere,
heroism by violence, this is definitely an adult comic
book film. Penguin drools bile. Cat Woman, in her first
violent, life-saving encounter, says to her opponent:
"Be gentle. It's my first time," before she rips his face
into squares with her claws. Definitely one to stay
away from, at least with younger children.

Batteries Not Included
Steven Spielberg Productions (1987), 106 min.
Director: Matthew Robbins
Starring Hume Cronyn, Jessica Tandy, Frank
McRae, Elizabeth Pena and Dennis Boutsikaris   **V**

A whimsical, sometimes sugary story that is fun for
children of all ages, from eight to ninety. The aliens,
friendly little fix-it flying saucers, come to the rescue
of human beings, the tenants of an apartment building cum 1950ish fast-food restaurant run by Frank
and Faye, played beautifully by Cronyn and Tandy.
The amazing, tiny saucers swoop down and fix things,
plug themselves into wall sockets for energy, have
babies and generally make things miserable for the
crooked developers and just fine in the end for the
good folk. Frank McRae plays an ex-boxer whose only

lines in the movie, six in all, are lines from familiar commercials: "Don't leave home without them." Great fun.

Beetlejuice (the cartoon series)
Fox (1990), 24 min.
Animation   **T**

Another remake of a movie, turned into an animated series to grab the kids. (There are some interesting facets to this series, in the stories they sometimes choose to deliver. An example is of a dream adaptation of *The Wizard of Oz,* which becomes *The Wizard of Ooze,* with a skeleton/artist Tin Soldier, a Cowardly Lion with no eyes and a spider who becomes Toto.) It's a dream within a dream within a dream at the end, and there is some clever use of television techniques, moving from colour to black and white. The colours are fun, the animation good and the story interesting in an odd way. But the elements of Beetlejuice eating all the Munchkins and then belching loudly several times, the Witch having her makeup wash off to discover she has pimples, and the Oogleys who argue about who is most "oogley," take the show to a level of rudeness that is offensive. Not a favourite of ours.

Benji the Hunted
Disney Home Video (1987), 89 min.
Director: Joe Camp   **V**

Filmed in the breathtaking Pacific Northwest, this is the best of the Benji films. What is special about this film is that there is practically no dialogue. The film follows the adorable Benji, lost in the woods and in charge of a litter of cougar cubs. Perils abound, suspense and action follow this little band of creatures until they find safety. Harrowing and worrying for little ones.

Beyond the Stars
IVE (1989), 94 min.
Director: David Saperstein
Starring Christian Slater, Martin Sheen,
Olivia D'Abo and F. Murray Abraham   **V**

Eric dreams of being an astronaut, but his NASA-em-
ployed father is jealous of his friendship with ex-moon-
walker Paul Andrews, who has become progressively
more dysfunctional and embittered after his return to
Earth. Father and son work out their differences as Andrews discloses a secret to Eric about his discovery on
the moon, and Eric helps Andrews to begin to recover
emotionally. Despite the title, this is more a good relationship film than a sci-fi film (there are no sequences
of space flight, only some shots of Sheen on the moon).

Bill and Ted's Excellent Adventure
Orion Home Video (1989), 90 min.
Director: Stephen Herek
Starring Alex Winter, Keanu Reeves
and George Carlin   **V**

Bill and Ted, two California teenagers who aspire to
be rock stars, are definitely going to fail their high-
school history final unless a miracle happens. It comes
in the form of Rufus, a messenger in a time-travelling
phone booth, who tells them that in the future everyone worships them as gods because of their music. But
in order to bring this future about, it is imperative
that they pass their exam. With Rufus guiding them,
they go back in time and kidnap Socrates (So-Crates),
Joan of Arc (Noah's wife), Sigmund Freud (the Frude
Dude), Abe Lincoln, Genghis Khan (lured with a
Twinkie) and Napoleon. When they arrive in the
present, the school sees the best oral history presentation ever. This film is a fun, harmless romp with lots
of "historical jokes." Some coarse language.

The Black Stallion
MGM/UA (1979), 117 min.
Director: Carroll Ballard
Starring Kelly Reno, Teri Garr
and Mickey Rooney   **V**

A Francis Ford Coppola executive produced this visually beautiful film based on the novel by Walter Farley.
An Arabian stallion and a boy are shipwrecked and develop an almost telepathic relationship. Back in the
civilized world, Alec befriends a retired horse trainer
who helps him win a championship race. Mickey
Rooney was nominated for an Oscar for his supporting
role. See also the sequel, *The Black Stallion Returns*.

Born Free
RCA/Columbia (1966), 95 min.
Director: James Hill
Starring Virginia McKenna and Bill Travers   **V**

Based on the best-seller by Joy Adamson, this film
was photographed in the savannas of central Africa.
The true story of Elsa the lioness and her siblings and
the woman who raises her after the mother is accidentally killed. Two of the cubs are sent to zoos, but
George and Joy keep Elsa, knowing that eventually
they will have to set her free. It is not without pain,
dedication and mishaps that Elsa finally returns successfully to the wild. A fabulous film for the animal
lover, full of delightful shots of the three cubs' antics.
Winner of two Academy Awards, including Best Score.

The Boy From Andromeda
Atlantis/South Pacific Pictures (1991), 94 min.
Director: Wayne Tourell   **V**

A science fiction tale set in New Zealand. The story is
a little preachy and heavy in places, concerning war

and the environment, but exciting and suspenseful enough to hold interest. Lots of action scenes with computers versus human monsters, and good performances, especially from the kids, young teenagers playing characters who, of course, are much wiser than the adults.

The Boy Who Could Fly
Karl-Lorimar (1986), 108 min.
Director: Nick Castle
Starring Lucy Deakins, Jay Underwood,
Bonnie Bedelia and Fred Savage   **V**

"To dream is to love, to love is to soar, and to soar is to be healed." This is the underlying theme of the story of fourteen-year-old Millie, who has to move to a new neighbourhood and school after the protracted illness and eventual suicide of her father. There she meets Eric, a strange, silent boy who lives next door with his pathetically alcoholic uncle. Eric, evidently crushed by some undisclosed emotional hardship (the death of his mother is suggested), seems locked in fantasies about flight, but as the relationship between Millie and Eric grows, Millie discovers that they may be more than just fantasies, and that if one believes strongly enough, anything is possible. This film is a little too grounded in day-to-day life to really work as a complete fantasy.

The Boy Who Turned Yellow
Rank Film (1983), 54 min.
Director: Michael Powel   **V**

An interesting fantasy-adventure yarn about an English schoolboy, who loses his pet mouse in the Tower of London during a school trip. With the help of an extraterrestrial visitor, he not only finds his mouse, but also learns a great deal about the powers of electricity. Well acted, this is an attractive story with believable characters.

The Boy Who Wished for Christmas
Cambium / Delaney and Friends (1990), 24 min.
Director: Michael Fawkes
Animation / live action; starring Peter Fletcher;
featuring the music of Long John Baldry   **T**

Excellent animation, with live action at the beginning and end, takes the viewer into a fantasy world in which the Toymaster, an evil critter, has taken over the toyshop. Nicholas is a boy who has everything, and is sitting at his computer making up his Christmas list. The Toymaster is a computerized Jack-in-the-Box, who does a wonderful rap number that explains his role. Santa sings a fine song about how "They all wanted more." The story turns into an operetta. Nicholas destroys the Toymaster's system by giving up his bike. Santa is back in business at the end. The problem with this one is that it needed a more complicated story and would have been more fun had it been an hour long.

Bye, Bye, Red Riding Hood (Tales for All)
Astral Films (1984), 94 min.   **V**

This might sound like fun, but don't be fooled. It has a foreboding, frightening feel to it from the start. It's the story of a little girl, Fanny, whose parents have separated. The girl and her mother head off into a foreign country, where her mother works. They live in the woods, where the little girl meets a strange man, who turns out to be her father. There's a real wolf, and this strange man/father is dressed to represent the wolf. Both mother and daughter meet this man, and the mother seems not to be upset about Fanny meeting with him. Fanny also meets a young

adolescent boy who takes her off to the city. The
movie is convoluted for children, and has a disturbing sexual tone to it.

Call of the Wild
Vestron Video (1983), 67 min.
Director: Byrd Ehlmans
Animation   **V**

Set in 1899, and based on the Jack London novel, this
is the story of Buck, a dog who enjoyed four years of
pampered domestic life and then was stolen and sold
to join a gold prospector's dog team. Over the years
Buck suffers hardship and cruelty but triumphs over
all, changing from a household pet to a noble savage
beast. The animation is superb and the story gripping,
but the violence is horrendous, with vivid depictions
of devastating brutality of man and beast. Parental
discretion is advised. We do not recommend this for
viewers under ten.

Campfire Thrillers
Golden Home Video (1990), 30 min.
Director: Tom Deming
Animation / live action   **V**

A short compilation of three animated stories introduced by a live-action segment. One dark and eerie
night, some teenage campers seek out the storyteller
Tallow Glee. They find him in a forest grove, and magically he unfolds three (scary, or are they?) stories,
"The Hunter," "The Viper" and "The Sisters Sweet." A
good short video for Hallowe'en parties for children
aged six to nine.

The Cat From Outer Space
Walt Disney Productions (1983), 103 min.
Director: Norman Tokar

*Starring Ken Berry, Sandy Duncan, Harry
Morgan, McLean Stevenson and Roddy McDowall*   **V**

A preposterous but amusing fantasy about an
extraterrestrial cat named Jake, who leads the army,
a team of scientists, some gamblers and crooks on a
round of baffling escapades. A little overdone at times,
but some nice spoofs on military and scientific minds.
Typical Disney TV movie fun and frolics.

The Challengers
Lauron Productions (1991), 120 min.
Director: Eric Till
Starring Gema Zamprogna and Sarah Sawatsky   **T**

This made-for-TV-movie should be available to children on video. It's the kind of thing that kids will
return to, as they do to favourite books. The story of
young Mackie, whose father has died, and her relationships with the kids in a new town to which she and
her mother move, is lovingly told. Humour, some grief
and excellent presentations of the lives of boys and
girls, all make for a delightful movie for the entire
family. It also introduces some important issues to
talk about with your children aged eight to twelve.
Look for a series to be made out of this one.

A Child's Christmas in Wales
Atlantis Films (1987), 55 min.
Director: Don McBrearty
Starring Denholm Elliot   **V**

"I can't remember if it snowed for twelve days when
I was six, or six days when I was twelve," begins this
Dylan Thomas masterpiece, narrated by Denholm
Elliot as a grandfather telling his grandson a bedtime
story on Christmas Eve. This is beautifully spoken
and filmed, and satisfyingly full of Dylan Thomas

characters. This is an anytime treat for the whole family.

Clarence
Atlantis / North Star (1991), 24 min. each
Director: Eric Till
Starring Robert Carradine, Kate Trotter,
Louis DelGrande, Robert Fitzpatrick, Barbara
Hamilton, James Rainey, Nicholas Van Burek
and Jason McSkimming   **T**

The story opens in heaven in the midst of a discussion among the Guardian Angels, who don't want to let Clarence Oddbody, a bumbling angel, go down to earth because he messed up his last assignment. Back on Earth, Rachel, whose husband Jeremy has died and is one of the angels, is in the midst of some perilous business transactions. Jeremy wants Clarence to help her. He does, by going down and eating the contract, one of his many funny antics. A great family series.

The Computer Wore Tennis Shoes
Walt Disney Home Video (1969), 87 min.
Director: Robert Butler
Starring Kurt Russell, Cesar Romero
and Joe Flynn   **V**

A computer mishap turns mediocre college student Dexter Riley into a super-genius, but when Dexter starts revealing syndicate secrets, gamblers, gangsters and greedy college deans suddenly take an interest in him. Kurt Russell still holds appeal for today's youngsters, while Disney Studios' fast-paced slapstick humour moves the story line along well.

Cooking With Dad
TDF Pictures (1990), 30 min.

Director: R.D. Phippard
Starring Ronald Waddling, Celeste Hill
and Andrew Daniels   **V**

Here's a unique idea — a cooking show for kids! Only
this one could be called "Playing with Food." Dad and
his two children are natural and appealing. He tells
funny stories to accompany each dish. They make a
One-Eyed Tomato on a Cheese Raft and an Ugly
Apple. These recipes require the use of knives and the
stove, so parental guidance is required. The tape also
includes safety tips in the form of a quiz. Recipe cards
for four recipes are included.

Courage Mountain
RCA/Columbia (1989), 92 min.
Director: Christopher Leitch
Starring Charlie Sheen, Leslie Caron,
Jan Rubes and Juliette Caton   **V**

Whatever happened to Heidi and Peter after she
settled for a life with her grandfather? In this film you
find out (one version in any case). Heidi and four classmates are forced into an Italian orphanage run by the
evil Signor Bonelli during World War I. They escape
and make a daring climb over the Swiss Alps, but the
director of the orphanage is not far behind. Only Peter,
Heidi's childhood friend, is in a position to save them.
This is an exciting film with great ski sequences and
sometimes tense and worrying situations. The scenes
with Charlie Sheen seem to have been filmed later and
inserted into the original film.

The Court Jester
Paramount Home Video (1956), 101 min.
Directors: Norman Panama and Melvin Frank
Starring Danny Kaye, Glynis Johns,
Basil Rathbone and Angela Lansbury   **V**

Kaye plays a member of a Robin Hood-type band of rebels set on getting the real king (who is only a baby) to the throne. Disguised as a court jester, he infiltrates the castle and nearly causes more problems than solutions. The hilariously funny songs written by Kaye's wife Sylvia Fine include "You'll Never Outfox the Fox," with a great dance number that features Kaye and his little band of merry men. Glynis Johns as the captain of the rebel guard plays a refreshing role. A great family film with classically funny routines. Danny Kaye portrays a number of characters, but an especially amusing scene is one in which he impersonates an old man with a hearing problem. "The vessel with the pestle" and the sword fight with Basil Rathbone are the stuff of comedy legend. A must-see for every family.

A Cry in the Wild
MGM / UA (1990), 82 min.
Director: Mark Griffiths
Starring Jared Rushton, Ned Beatty   **V**
and Pamela Sue Martin

After surviving a plane crash in the wilderness, teenager Brian Robeson must learn to look after himself with only a few necessities he salvaged from the wreckage, including a hatchet his mother gave him. He braves the elements, a dive to the submerged plane (where he sights the drowned pilot), bears, a wolf and hunger, resorting eventually to eating bugs. This film is based on the Newbery Medal-winning book *Hatchet* by Gary Paulsen.

Winner of the Gold Medal — International Family Film Society; Gold Medal — Coalition to Save the Planet; Gold Medal — National Wildlife Association; Grand Champion — Mountain High Institute; Unanimous Choice — The Nature Prize; and Silver Medal — Houston International Film Festival.

Crystalstone
MCA (1987), 90 min.
Director: Antonio Pelaez
Starring Kamlesh Gupta, Laura Jane
Goodwin and Frank Grimes   **V**

Spain, 1908. On the death of their mother, two
young children, Pablo and Maria, live with their
hard-hearted aunt, who plans to keep only Maria
and send Pablo away to pick grapes in the south.
The children overhear the plans and run away,
embarking on a series of adventures that lead them
into a quest for a fabled talisman, the Crystalstone.
They run afoul of a sinister one-handed villain, and
eventually reunite with their long-lost father. Good
family viewing, but may be frightening for the very
young.

Curly Sue
Warner Brothers (1991), 105 min.
Director: John Hughes
Starring James Belushi, Kelly Lynch
and Alisan Porter   **V**

A rags-to-riches story with a con artist thrown in. Poor
man and daughter meet rich lawyer with snobby
boyfriend. Some good dramatic moments contrasting
the lives of the rich and poor in a large city in the win-
tertime, but very sloppy and sentimental. Reminds us
of the old-fashioned Shirley Temple movies complete
with happy ending. On a long winter's evening this
would be enjoyable for the family.

The Curse of the Viking Grave
Muddy River Films Ltd. (1989), 94 min.
Director: Michael Scott
Starring Cedric Smith, Nicholas Shield,
Evan Adams and Michele St. John   **V**

Based in part on a novel by Farley Mowat, this is the sequel to *Lost in the Barrens,* the further adventures of Jamie and his Indian friend Awasis. The problems of the white boy and the Indian boy are handled well. The story is complete with con men, villains and heroes, and even a touch of love interest at the end. Shot in the beautiful wilds of northern Manitoba, it is well performed by an all-Canadian cast and well produced. Suitable for children eight and older.

Davy Crockett and the River Pirates
Walt Disney Home Video (1956), 81 min.
Director: Norman Foster
Starring Fess Parker, Buddy Ebsen,
Kenneth Tobey and Jeff York   **V**

Originally a two-episode show on Disney's Sunday night television spot. Davy Crockett, the immortalized American hero, takes on Big Mike Fink in a keelboat race down the Mississippi River to New Orleans, the loser being required to "eat his hat." A group of bandits who disguise themselves as Indians complicate matters, but Davy comes through in the clinch, as always, and Big Mike dines on his own fedora.

The Dog Who Stopped the War
Roch Demers, Tales for All (1989), 90 min.
Director: Andre Melanson   **V**

Another in the fine, sometimes uneven series of Roch Demers's tales, this is a delightfully funny, touching story of a group of children in a small town over a Christmas holiday. They divide into teams and decide to have a war, which becomes a delightfully imaginative snow battle. The boy/girl theme is dealt with very well in this movie. It's a good script true to the language of nine- and ten-year-olds. There are beautiful snow forts, great snow fights, a wonderful barn and a lolloping St. Bernard named Cleo. The snow fort becomes more and more sophisticated as the story progresses. The armies grow as all the children in the town become involved. The last battle is truly epic, but this is where the movie falls down. Melanson has a wonderful sense of kids and their fun, but the script has him end the movie all too soon, as Cleo dies, buried under snow when the fort somehow explodes. The story ends with the burial of the dog — a great disappointment. One child's response: "Couldn't they have made a more peaceful ending?"

Down the Drain: 3-2-1 Contact Extra
CTW (1991), 30 min.
Director: Ozzie Alfonso   V

Host Stephanie Yu takes kids on a look into something we all take for granted: water. She shows us what happens to our water when it goes down the drain and what measures are being taken to clean it and return it for consumption. But she warns us that Nature cannot do the job fast enough to supply the world with adequate clean water, so suggestions are made as to how each individual can help. A thoroughly entertaining and informative tape.

Edward Scissorhands
Twentieth Century Fox (1988), 100 min.
Director: Tim Burton
Starring Johnny Depp and Vincent Price   V

This brilliant, Gothic yet modern fairy tale of a young man who has not been "finished" by his inventor, a scientist (Vincent Price), makes a most engaging movie for youngsters. It has much depth both in story and in film treatment, with brilliant fish-eye

camera lens shots, great colour and sound work and
the most wonderful creation of all, Edward Scis-
sorhands, first welcomed by the townspeople, who
see him as a novelty, then rejected when he does not
fit their pattern of acceptability. Well worth a watch
by the entire family together, as there is much to talk
about.

Eek the Cat
Warner (1992), 24 min.   **T**

Our cat hero goes through lots of biff-bam-pow and
the bad guy rats get the good guys all confused with
disguises and artful dodges. Eventually, with biff-
bam-whap, the good guys finally win out. And that
is about all this is about. Very violent. Not recommended.

The Electric Grandmother
LCA (1981), 50 min.
Director: Noel Black
Starring Maureen Stapleton, Edward Herrmann
and Robert MacNaughton   **V**

Based on the famous Ray Bradbury story "I Sing the
Body Electric," *The Electric Grandmother* takes place
in a world in the not-too-distant future. After the
untimely death of his wife, a man and his three children receive a made-to-order electric grandmother
from the Gothic Fantoccini company to take care of
them. She cooks their favourite meals to perfection,
pours the beverage of choice from her index finger
and generally runs a perfect household, recharging
her batteries in her rocker in the basement at night.
She stays with them until the children go off to
college, then returns to care for them in their old age.
The concept is a little bizarre. The film has a melan-
choly feeling about it, but it's beautifully done.

Encyclopedia Brown/Boy Detective: One Minute Mysteries
Hi-Tops Video (1988), 30 min.
Directors: David Scheerer and Savage
Steve Holland
Starring Scott Bremner   **V**

Well, five mysteries at five minutes each actually, with one minute per case of solving time. All the clues are there. Can you solve it with Encyclopedia in the time allotted? Based on the stories by Donald J. Sobol. Lots of fun.

Escape to Witch Mountain
Magic Lantern / Walt Disney Educational Media Company (1978), 27 min.
Starring Ray Milland, Donald Pleasence and Eddie Albert   **V**

A story about two young orphans with psychic powers. A rich old scoundrel, played by Ray Milland, tries to kidnap them in order to use their powers to make himself even richer. Their escape, and eventual destination, form the main action of this lively tale. Donald Pleasance is one of Milland's powerful henchmen, and Eddie Albert is the children's reluctant rescuer. The film is a bit cliché-ridden and stereotyped, especially in this shortened, television version, but on the whole it is well played and entertaining. You may want to get the full-length movie instead of this cut version, which we got from a library.

Ernest Goes to Camp
Walt Disney Home Video (1987), 92 min.
Director: John R. Cherry
Starring Jim Varney   **V**

Good-natured Ernest P. Worrell is promoted from Camp

Handyman to Camp Counsellor when a gang of juvenile
delinquents from the Midstate Boys' Detention Center
arrive at the camp. Amid the shenanigans, a big mining
company wants the camp's land, so Ernest teams up
with the boys to save the camp. As silly as this film is,
there are delightful slapstick moments, and Ernest has
a way of wearing down everyone's resistance.

E.T. — The Extra Terrestrial
MCA (1982), 115 min.
Director: Steven Spielberg
Starring Henry Thomas, Drew Barrymore,
Robert MacNaughton, Dee Wallace   **V**

One of the biggest box-office hits to be released on
video at a collectable price, *E.T.* caused a sales sensation seven years after its appearance in the theatres.
The film concerns the friendship between Elliott, a
young suburban boy, and a peace-loving little alien
accidentally stranded on Earth when his survey ship
is forced to take off without him. He evades capture
and finds refuge with Elliott, the middle child of a
divorcee, and a series of adventures ensues as E.T.
samples California life at close range, jury-rigs a
device with which to "phone home" and subsequently,
to Elliott's amazement and dismay, actually summons
his ship to rescue him. One of the most overwhelm-
ingly heartwarming stories on film, although at
nearly two hours it's a long one.

The Explorers
Paramount (1985), 109 min.
Director: Joe Dante
Starring Ethan Hawke, River Phoenix
and Jason Presson   **V**

Three adventurous young boys dream of space travel.
One receives mysterious inspiration for microchip

design through his dreams, the second has the know-how to build those circuits and the third has a dad with a junkyard. The boys take off on the time of their lives. In space, they meet the source of the design inspiration, some delightful aliens whose sole understanding of Earth comes from TV transmissions. Full of "in" jokes for the TV generation, and with an unpredictable ending, this film is good fun for the whole family. Some light profanity.

Fievel's American Tales
Universal (1992), 24 min. each
Director: Laurence Selig Jacobs
Animation   **T**

These tales are the animated adventures of a rather attractive little mouse and his family, along with a great variety of friends and foes in the Old West. There is some comic violence, but not the biff and bam of most Saturday a.m. shows. Each episode closes with a plug for reading. Quite good stories, worth a family look.

Fiddler on the Roof
MGM / UA (1971), 181 min.
Director: Norman Jewison
Starring Topol, Norman Crane, Leonard Frey
and Molly Picon   **V**

"If I Were a Rich Man," "Sunrise, Sunset," "To Life!" With beautiful songs and wonderful performances and production, this is a rich, moving and rewarding musical comedy experience for the whole family. Nine-year-olds just love it!

The Fisherman and His Wife
SVS (1989), 30 min.
Directors: Mark Sottnick and C.W. Rogers
Animation; narrated by Jodie Foster   **V**

Sometimes called *The Fisherman and the Fish,* this powerful, esoteric narrative tells the story of a desperately poor fisherman who lives in a miserable hovel by the sea, and who one day by chance snares a great flounder, which turns out to be a magic fish of limitless power. The fisherman is content with his life, but his domineering wife Isabel has her heart set on a larger dwelling, and sends him back to wish for a cottage. The wish is instantly granted, but the wife is not satisfied, and keeps sending her husband back, again and again, into an increasingly angry sea and with ever greater requests, until she finally demands to be like the Lord God Himself. The stark animation (composed entirely of silhouettes) and Foster's terse narration suit the grim tale perfectly, but the friendly little musical score seems utterly incongruous.

Flight of Dragons
CVL Video (1982), 98 min.
Directors: Arthur Rankin Jr. and Jules Bass
Animation; featuring the voices of John Ritter,
James Earl Jones and Henry Morgan   V

In the ancient Age of Magic, the evil Red Wizard Ommadon has devised a plan by which mankind will destroy itself, leaving him sole ruler of a devastated planet. A group of wise wizards realize that the only hope for saving Earth lies in a twentieth-century rationalist named Peter. The good wizards transport Peter back in time to the Age of Magic, where he is accidentally changed into a young dragon. Thus transformed, Peter must learn the art of being a dragon and lead a quest to destroy the Red Wizard and capture his Red Crown. The animation is above average for the Rankin–Bass studios, but the convoluted plot will likely leave some youngsters baffled, and the miscast and all-too-identifiable voice of Henry Morgan undermines an otherwise decent effort.

Flight of the Navigator
Walt Disney Home Video (1986), 90 min.
Director: Randal Kleiser
Starring Joey Cramer, Veronica Cartwright
and Howard Hesseman   **V**

After an accidental knock on the head, twelve-year-old
David wakes up and thinks everything is fine — but it is
eight years later. David is still twelve years old but now
his younger brother is his "older" brother. On investigation of his traumatic reappearance, it is discovered that
an alien spacecraft crashed at the same time. NASA discovers a link between the two and the fun begins. Special
effects are excellent in this fun-filled, delightful movie.

The 5,000 Fingers of Dr. T
RCA/Columbia (1953), 88 min.
Director: Roy Rowland
Starring Peter Lynd Hayes, Tommy Rettig
and Hans Conreid   **V**

This Dr. Seuss story vividly describes every child's
worst fear — the proverbial piano lesson. Poor young
Bart Collins has to suffer the tyrannical and slightly
maniacal piano teacher Dr. Terwilliker. The doctor's
"Happy Fingers Method of Piano Instruction" is anything but, and strikes terror into poor Bart. He has a
nightmare (complete with musical numbers using Dr.
Seuss lyrics) full of fanciful characters from his real
life. The images are both terrifying and funny (for
example, the largest keyboard you could ever imagine,
or Siamese twins on roller skates) and are set against
a surreal backdrop far ahead of its cinematic time. A
great movie for children.

F.R.O.G. (Friends of Research and Odd Gadgets)
OWL TV (1992), 30 min. each
Director: Greg Rist   **V/T**

A spinoff from the successful OWL TV series, the goal
of F.R.O.G. is "to bring science out of the textbook and
into the real world" by involving children in hands-
on projects. While the intentions are laudable, and
parts of the show informative, the overall production
leaves a great deal to be desired. The sound is bad,
and the result is that viewers lose interest because
the information becomes muddled. Scripts do not
lead kids into being able to carry out the activities.
Eight-year-olds tuned out quickly because, as they
said, the kids are talking to each other and not to the
audience.

George's Island
Astral Home Video (1989), 90 min.
Director: Paul Donovan
Starring Nathaniel Moreau, Sheila McCarthy,
Maury Chaykin and Ian Bannen   **V**

This winner of the 1989 Best Feature Film Award
from the Chicago International Festival of Children's
Films is a breath of fresh air. The story concerns ten-
year-old George Walters, who lives happily with his
wheelchair-bound, yarn-spinning, ex-seaman grandfather in a humble shack outside Halifax. When
George is placed with a pair of distinctly unpleasant
foster parents, his grandfather plans a rescue that he
puts into effect on Hallowe'en night. With Mr. Droon-
field, the social worker, and Miss Birdwood, his school
teacher, in hot pursuit, George and his grandfather
end up on George's Island where they encounter a
band of macabre yet hilarious ghosts.

Ghostwriter
PBS (1992), 60 min.   **V/T**

Jamal is given a computer by his sister who is going
off to college. The Ghostwriter communicates with

Jamal through his computer, sending messages that
help Jamal solve mysteries. The multicultural cast of
young people work well together, solving mysteries
through the written word. The only commercial is the
message "Do the word thing! Exercise your head!
Read!" by Nike. This engaging series draws its audience into the story, and invites viewers to participate.
A great show for kids six and up. The whole family will
enjoy it.

The Girl From Mars
Atlantis Films (1991), 90 min.
Director: Neill Fearnley
Starring Sarah Sawatsky, Eddie Albert,
Gary Day, Christian Hirt and Gwynyth Walsh   **V**

Eddie Albert is an astronomer friend of Deirdre, the
girl from Mars who has special powers. Living with an
Earth family, Deirdre eventually has to choose
whether to return to Mars or stay on Earth. This is a
mixed-up environmental sci-fi tale for kids that
becomes a crashing bore about halfway through. It's
very slow-moving and the dialogue is stilted. Not one
for the babysitter and your children — they'll be gone
from the movie in fifteen minutes.

The Girl From Tomorrow
Film Australia / CBC (1990), 24 min. each
Director: Dennis Kiely   **T**

An award-winning family adventure series about a
thirteen-year-old girl from the year 3000 who is
trapped in the Sydney of the 1990s. With excellent
production values and performances, the series combines lots of action with clever commentary on the
social and environmental issues of our time. Lots of
fun and lots to think about for children aged ten and
over.

Girl of the Limberlost
Public Media Video for Wonderworks (1989), 105 min.
Director: Burt Brinckerhoff
Starring Annette O'Toole, Joanna Cassidy
and Heather Fairfield   **V**

Set in 1908 against the backdrop of the destruction
of the Limberlost Forest by loggers, *Girl of the Limberlost* is the emotionally turbulent story of Elnora
Comstock, a talented young woman who longs to go
to high school and possibly even college. Her widowed
mother considers this nothing but "foolish dreams,"
and she is forced to earn the money for school books
by herself. Elnora manages with the aid and encouragement of Mrs. Porter, an emancipated writer and
photographer with whom she shares a deep love of
the Limberlost. But her hopes of continuing her
studies fade when the taxes on the farm fall due and
her mother demands that she stay home and help
bring in the harvest. How Elnora and her mother
come to terms with their differences and save their
farm is an inspiring story with an environmental
message that is even more important today than
when it was first written.

The Gold Bug
New World Video (1986), 45 min.
Director: Robert Fuest
Starring Robert Blossom, Geoffrey Holder
and Anthony Michael Hall   **V**

Off the coast of the Carolinas in 1866, a young boy
lands on Sullivan's Island in search of rare species of
insects to add to the collection his father left him when
he died. Instead, the youthful hero runs afoul of some
nefarious characters and gets drawn into adventures
and intrigue revolving around a hoard of treasure.
Excellent cinematography and performances make

this a gem. Based on Edgar Allan Poe's mystery story.
A few scenes might frighten younger children.

Golden Pennies
Australia Corp. TV/Central TV, UK/Radio Canada,
Montreal (1985), 25-min. episodes
Director: Oscar Whitbread   **V/T**

Set in 1854, in Australia, this series depicts the hard
times of a poor family digging for gold. There's the villainous merchant and various other local characters.
Each episode deals with one dangerous or exciting
adventure. A family-oriented soap. Not bad.

Goldie and Kids
Prism (1982), 90 min.
Director: Dwight Hemion
Starring Goldie Hawn and Barry Manilow   **V**

This educational video is an attempt to tell kids that
it is okay to talk to an adult and that it's okay to listen
to them. Goldie and Barry perform songs and skits
dealing with different issues such as sex, abortion,
marriage and music. The children with whom Goldie
speaks "spontaneously" are around ten to twelve
years old, but they seem remarkably self-assured —
dare we say "coached"? They give it away when you
see these children performing song and dance
numbers.

The Goonies
Warner Home Video (1985), 111 min.
Director: Richard Donner
Starring Sean Astin, Corey Feldman,
Kerri Green and Martha Plimpton   **V**

A group of misfit neighbourhood friends who call
themselves The Goonies spend their last Saturday

together because their parents don't have the money
to ward off a development project. The discovery of
a treasure map in one of the boys' attics leads them
on an adventure beyond their dreams. This is a high-
action, intense Steven Spielberg film with a relent-
lessly noisy soundtrack, but an exciting mix of
action, comedy, romance and pathos. Watch out for
the scene that appeals to every kid who takes piano
lessons.

Great Expectations
Paramount (1946), 118 min.
Director: David Lean
Starring John Mills, Bernard Miles, Alec
Guinness, Jean Simmons and Valerie Hobson   **V**

One of many fine screen adaptations of a Dickens
classic. Superb acting and settings carry young
viewers into the world of this fine story. It contains all
the things young people like: mystery, intrigue, villains and heroes, and a young person's struggle
against hardships in an adult-dominated world. Great
family viewing, and a good way to introduce young
people to the world of Dickens. Bring home the book
along with the video.

The Greenstone
Active Home Video (1987), 48 min.
Director: Kevin Irvine
Narrated by Orson Welles, with Joseph Corey   **V**

A strange but fascinating tale of a twelve-year-old
boy's adventures in a forest. In spite of his mother's
admonishing him to stay away from the woods, he is
drawn one day by a brilliant light and a strange
woman in white. In the forest he encounters several
weird, frightening and humorous characters. The
story is really an allegory, but may be enjoyed as pure

adventure and will appeal to most viewers ten and up. It's a little scary, perhaps, for the very young.

Gulliver's Travels
HTV (1939), 74 min.
Director: Dave Fleischer
Animation; featuring the voices of Lanny Ross
and Jessica Dragonette   **V**

A feature-length animated version of the first book of the Jonathan Swift epic. Gulliver is washed up on the shore of a strange island after a huge storm. The inhabitants (the Lilliputians), very tiny people, mistake him for a monster and imprison him. He soon becomes a valued citizen, however, by helping Lilliput conquer and eventually be reconciled with a hostile neighbour, Blefuscu; in turn, the two cultures help him to return home. The animation is at times breathtaking, and the story is classic to its period, filled with noble characters, adventurous situations and comic relief in the form of a goofy but well-meaning Lilliputian. Contains the award-winning song "It's a Hap, Hap, Happy Day."

Hang Your Hat on the Wind
Magic Lantern / Walt Disney Educational Media (1981), 48 min.
Director: Larry Lansburgh   **V**

The story of a little Navajo boy, a lost thoroughbred colt, a couple of bumbling crooks of the usual Disney type, a corny priest on a dirt bike, a wild bush pilot and a car chase. With beautifully photographed scenery and heartwarming plot, this is a typical Disney family hour, full of good deeds all the way through.

Hans Brinker
Warner Home Video (1979), 103 min.

Director: Robert Sheerer
Starring Eleanor Parker, Richard Basehart
and John Gregson   V

In the Holland of 1838, Hans's father, a mason, has been left crippled and catatonic by a terrible accident, leaving Hans and his mother and sister to scrape by as best they can. Central to the story is Hans's epic skate to Amsterdam to enlist the services of a famous surgeon to cure his father, and the great race that bestows upon the winner a set of valuable silver skates. Based on Mary Mapes Dodge's 1865 children's novel, this musical production is curiously listless despite the strong plot, and the songs seem superfluous.

Harry and the Hendersons
MCA (1987), 111 min.
Director: William Dear
Starring John Lithgow, Melinda Dillon,
Don Ameche and Lainie Kazan   V

A comic-strip artist who is fond of hunting wildlife gets a surprise when, returning from a family hunting trip, he accidentally hits a Sasquatch, or Bigfoot, with the car. Thinking it is dead, the Hendersons bring home the prize, only to find out he is quite alive, well and inquisitive. They realize that "Harry" must be returned to the wild but when word gets out of the find, it is not as easy as it seems. A great family film with a terrific ending.

Home Alone
20th Century Fox (1990), 105 min.
Director: Chris Columbus
Starring Macaulay Culkin, Joe Pesci
and Daniel Stern   V

Eight-year-old Kevin wishes his irritating family

would simply disappear, but he doesn't quite count on it actually happening. On the morning when the whole family is to leave for a Christmas holiday in Paris the alarm fails to go off and panic ensues; in the rush to make the airport on time Kevin is inadvertently left behind. Now he must defend the family home from burglars, which he does quite competently. A good "kids can do it" movie.

Home From Far
Atlantis Films (1983), 25 min.
Director: Bruce Pittman
Starring Fiona McGillivray, Simon Craig,
Diana Barrington and David Maier   **V**

A touching tale of an adolescent girl's struggle to accept a new foster brother after the death of her real brother in a car accident. The pace is slow at times, but on the whole this is sensitively played and directed. Fine family viewing.

Honey, I Blew Up the Kid
Walt Disney Productions (1992), 95 min.
Starring Rick Moranis, Marcia Strassman,
Lloyd Bridges, Robert Oliveri and John Shea   **V**

Not nearly as much fun as its predecessor (below). The joke of changing the kid's sizes wears thin very quickly. It took much too long to explode the kid. The effects are fun, at first, but the story sags very quickly and becomes, for adults at least, rather like watching a modern *King Kong*. A harmless movie that will probably amuse younger children, but not one of our favourites.

Honey, I Shrunk the Kids
Disney Home Video (1989), 101 min.
Director: Joe Johnston

Starring Rick Moranis, Matt Frewer,
Marcia Strassman and Thomas Brown   **V**

When an inventor accidentally reduces his children to
the size of a grain of rice and sweeps them into the
trash, they must struggle all the way home by cross-
ing their own backyard (now the trek of a lifetime)
fraught with dangers from their own lawnmower,
giant insects and torrents of water. Astounding state-
of-the-art effects support an excellent cast in a fast-
paced and thoroughly entertaining film. This video
also includes the amazing animated feature *Tummy
Trouble,* starring Roger Rabbit.

Hook
Tri-Star Productions (1991), 180 min.
Director: Steven Spielberg
Starring Dustin Hoffman, Robin Williams
and Maggie Smith   **V**

A review by an eight-year-old: "It was so-so. They tried
to make it too long. They stretched everything in the
story. There were wonderful scenes in it, like the war
in which they made people fall with marbles, and they
used blobs of paint and blobs of cream. But then they
ruined it. Ruffio, the leader of the lost boys, started a
sword fight. Hook ended up sticking a sword through
him. I didn't think he should have died because he was
the leader. When Tinker Bell grew big and wore the
exact same dress as his wife did, this was confusing."
It is indeed too long. Some great sets, and obviously a
lot of money spent here, but not a great movie for kids.

Hope and Glory
CBS Fox Productions (1987), 110 min.
Director: John Boorman   **V**

A superb story about a nine-year-old English boy

living with his mother, sister and aunts, through the
wartime bombing of London in 1940. All the pre-ado-
lescent problems, plus the trials of growing up in a
war-torn family atmosphere, are touchingly told with
a fine mixture of comedy and pathos. The performances are exemplary. Good family viewing for eight-
year-olds and up, but we caution that there are one or
two scenes of "growing-up, curiosity sex," though no
graphic descriptions or details.

Houdini
Paramount (1953), 106 min.
Director: George Marshall
Starring Tony Curtis, Janet Leigh
and Torin Thatcher   **V**

Not a factual account of the life of famous magician
Harry Houdini, but good enough to interest children
in a remarkable man's life. A good introduction for
young magic fans.

The Adventures of Huckleberry Finn
MGM / United Artists (1939), 127 min.
Starring Mickey Rooney   **V**

While it has the attraction of a young Mickey Rooney,
as well as several other interesting actors, the movie
is a disappointment and would bore children very
quickly. It starts out well, but there are too many long,
talky scenes.

The Adventures of Huckleberry Finn
Playhouse Home Video (1975), 74 min.
Director: Robert Totten
Starring Ron Howard and Antonio Fargas **V**

This 1975 remake stars a more grown-up Ron Howard
("Opie" from "The Andy Griffith Show") as the free-

wheeling Huck Finn. When Huck teams up with
runaway slave Jim, they raft down the Mississippi
River, getting into misadventures involving slave-
owners and con men. Howard's Huck is a little too
easygoing to be really mischievous, and seems a little
too old to be getting into the kinds of scrapes he does.
Not an entirely satisfactory version of this Twain
classic.

The Human Race Club: The Lean Mean Machine
Innervision Productions (1989), 30 min. each
Concept by Joy Berry   **V**

A tiny letter on the dust jacket: "Dear parents: Like
my self-help books for children, The Human Race Club
video series teaches living skills concepts in an entertaining format. I hope you and your children learn and
grow as you watch and discuss each tape. Sincerely,
Joy Berry." This is a series that begs to be watched by
parents with their children. It can be a great help, at
times when words are very difficult. Why not use television to help deal with strong emotions and uncom-
fortable feelings. With some fun music, very pleasant
animation, and good characterization, The Lean
Machine deals with anger, jealousy, and meanness in
a way that guides children to making decisions demo-
cratically, and understanding that "It's how you
handle the feelings that counts." A fine, most valuable
series both for home and the classroom, that deals
with issues such as self-esteem, the death of a friend,
the brother-sister clash, prejudice and discrimination,
and handling money.

The Odyssey
Waterstreet Productions / CBC (1991), 24 min. each
Director: Jorge Montesi
Starring Ashley Rogers, Illya Woloshyn
and Tony Sampson   **T**

This is an excellent series, beautifully directed by Jorge Montesi, with superior child acting, interesting sets, this is the unique story of Jay, who ends up in a coma after a struggle with a gang of boys in a tree-house, from which Jay falls and hits his head. Through his coma, we are taken into a "downworld" populated by young people trying to run their own society. The upworld is the real world of the hospital, Jay's mother, and the doctors. The movement back and forth between the two worlds is highly imaginative, and the links and counterpoints are superb. Look for this series as an example of television storytelling for children at its best.

The Johnstown Monster
International Telefilm (1979), 54 min.
Director: Olaf Pooley   **V**

An English family — brother, sister and father — are vacationing in a lake district in Ireland where, legend has it, a sea creature known as the Johnstown monster appears every leap year on Christmas Eve. The kids and dad make friends with an Irish family. Disappointed at not being able to see the legendary monster in the summertime, the kids decide to build one of their own, with surprising results. An excellent family show.

The Journey of Natty Gann
Disney Home Video (1985), 101 min.
Director: Jeremy Paul Kagan
Starring Meredith Salenger, Ray Wise,
John Cusack and Lainie Kazan   **V**

During the height of the Great Depression, Sol Gann leaves his young daughter Natty in the care of a hotel-keeper and heads to the northwestern United States to a logging camp, the only available job. He intends to send for Natty as soon as he is financially settled; however, Natty finds life with the abusive hotel-keeper unbearable and sets out west to find her father. During the course of her journey she makes two great friends, a wolf and a hard-bitten drifter named Harry, and after a series of adventures, she and her father are reunited.

K-9
Universal Pictures (1988), 108 min.
Director: Rod Daniel
Starring Bill Murray and Mel Harris   **V**

Begins with someone breaking into a car in which a couple are making love, then a helicopter blasts the car with machine-gun bullets. The story goes downhill from there. Not one we recommend for kids.

Kidzone: Kerrisdale V6B 1Z6
Knowledge Network (1992), 21 min. each
Director: Philip Spink   **V/T**

A send-up of "Beverly Hills, 90210," this good program uses the popular soap opera format to deal with issues of self-esteem, peer pressure and jealousy. Uses the familiar setting of school to present a number of situations children may find themselves in, and possible solutions.

The King and I
Twentieth Century Fox (1956), 133 min.
Director: Walter Lang
Starring Yul Brynner, Deborah Kerr,
Rita Moreno and Martin Benson   **V**

Good performances and Rodgers and Hammerstein music add up to pleasant entertainment for the whole family. There are several classic songs, including

"Hello, Young Lovers" and "Getting to Know You." Won several Oscars.

Labyrinth
Henson Associates, Inc., and Lucasfilm, Ltd. (1986), 101 min.
Director: Jim Henson
Starring David Bowie and Jennifer Connelly **V**

A teenage girl must rescue her baby brother from goblins, after she has wished him away and her wish is granted by the King of the Goblins, played ominously by David Bowie. She must journey through a treacherous maze to get to the castle of Jareth, the goblin king. A delightful fantasy adventure, with some great puppets and visual magic in the Henson tradition. A fine movie for children eight and up.

Ladyhawke
Warner Home Video (1985), 121 min.
Director: Richard Donner
Starring Michelle Pfeiffer, Rutger Hauer,
John Wood and Matthew Broderick **V**

In the dark and dreaded Middle Ages, two lovers, Isabeau and Navarre, are cursed by the jealous and corrupt Bishop of Aquila and transformed — she into a hawk by day and he into a black wolf by night. In these forms the lovers are always together but eternally apart, since they are both in human form only for the split second at the end of night and before the sun rises. After two years of wandering in this sorry state, Navarre believes a common thief named Phillipe "the Mouse" Gaston can help him wreak revenge on the bishop, his enemy. After witnessing many strange transformations, Phillipe becomes the lovers' go-between and is determined to help them break the curse. A visually stunning film full of adventure, romance and action.

Land Before Time
MCA (1989), 69 min.
Director: Don Bluth
Animation   **V**

Breathtaking animation, adorable characterization
and an inspirational story make this feature-length
animation a modern classic. After a great earthquake
leaves three toddler dinosaurs alone, they begin the
long trek to the Great Valley where, they are told, they
will find peace and happiness.

Lantern Hill
Kevin Sullivan Productions / Walt Disney / CBC
(1989), 96 min.
Director: Kevin Sullivan
Starring Zoe Caldwell, Marion Bennett,
Colleen Dewhurst and Sam Waterson   **V/T**

A story full of wonderful mystery, set in Prince
Edward Island and Toronto. After discovering that her
father is alive, contrary to what she had been led to
believe, twelve-year-old Jane Stuart is determined to
re-unite her separated parents. Jane's friends include
a young scullery maid, played by Sarah Polly, and a
ghost. The one problem with the movie is Sarah's
unconvincing and unnecessary Cockney accent. A tale
of love and loyalty, with fine performances from the
cast. Some of the ghost scenes may be frightening for
children seven and under.

Lassie Come Home
MGM (1943), 90 min.
Director: Fred M. Wilcox
Starring Roddy McDowall, Donald Crisp
and Elizabeth Taylor   **V**

Based on Eric Knight's novel, *Lassie Come Home*

introduced the canine heroine to the viewing public
for the first time. Joe (McDowall) is the son of a poor
but honourable man (Crisp), who is forced to sell
Lassie to a rich duke and his granddaughter Priscilla
(Taylor in her screen debut), who intend to use Lassie
as a show dog. Lassie refuses to remain sold, however,
and keeps escaping from her new masters, even when
the duke takes her to a show in Scotland. Lassie's
journey back to the boy she loves is an epic trek rem-
iniscent of Disney's *Incredible Journey*. This quality
film has charmed viewers of all ages for almost five
decades.

The Last Winter
Last Winter Productions / CBC (1990), 90 min.
Director: Aaron Kim-Johnston
Starring Joshua Murray, David Ferry
and Gerrard Parkes   **T**

A gem of Canadian television, made for family viewing
for ages seven and up. A tale of family, especially of
fathers and sons, and of children growing up, of boys
and girls together and of human relationships. The
settings are beautifully evocative of the magic of
Canadian changes of season, especially the magic of
Prairie winters. A bittersweet piece, told with humour
and a great deal of sensitivity.

Legend of Sleepy Hollow
Sony (1988), 30 min.
Director: Robert Van Nutt
Still animation; featuring the voice of Glenn Close **V**

The quintessential American ghost story, concerning
Ichabod Crane, the gangly, prickly, perpetually
hungry and superstitious schoolmaster who moves to
a small New England town, where he competes with
the burly local hero, Brom Bones, for the romantic

affections of the lovely (not to mention rich) Katrina Van Tassel. Oil paintings by Robert Van Nutt lend a wonderful rich flavour to the tale, and Academy award-winner Glenn Close reads with enthusiasm. One of a continuing series that match classic tales with narration by well-known actors, exquisite illustrations, and great music.

The Little Match Girl
Academy Entertainment (1987), 90 min.
Starring Twiggy and Roger Daltry   **V**

Based on the Hans Christian Andersen story. The young match girl is wonderful, and the production is smooth and easy enough to watch and listen to. The music, however, is mundane and predictable. It's a pleasant enough production, with the right kind of tear-jerking at times, a poor man's *Oliver!* made for Christmas TV viewing. Children under ten might be bored.

Little Monsters
MGM / UA (1989), 103 min.
Director: Richard Allen Greenberg
Starring Fred Savage, Howie Mandel
and Daniel Stern   **V**

When Brian's little brother begins complaining about monsters under his bed, Brian gallantly offers to trade rooms with him for the night, discovering to his amazement that there really *are* monsters. A smash hit with kids from nine to twelve, though some adults may find certain jokes on the crude side.

Little Women
MGM / UA Home Video (1949 / colourised 1976), 120 min.
Director: Mervin Le Roy

Starring June Allyson, Peter Lawford,
Janet Leigh, Elizabeth Taylor, Margaret O'Brien,
Mary Astor and Sir C. Aubrey Smith   **V**

Based on the novel by Louisa May Alcott, this is the
story of the March sisters, Jo, Beth, Amy and Meg,
who live with their mother in New England, while
their father is off fighting in the Civil War. To modern
eyes, it may seem overly sentimental and melodra-
matic, but is no more so than a modern soap opera, or
any romantic tale set in the nineteenth century. The
movie is well produced and acted, and portrays an
upper-middle-class life of family formal-dress house
parties, dances and balls, when the main ambition for
a mother of four attractive daughters was that they
become "beautiful, accomplished and good." Love tri-
angles, illness, tears and laughter, and portraits of
young people in another era make this enjoyable
family entertainment.

Look Who's Talking
Tri-Star Pictures (1989), 96 min.
Director: Amy Heckerling
Starring John Travolta, Kirstie Alley and
Olympia Dukakis, Abe Vagoda and Bruce Willis as
the voice of Mikey, the baby   **V**

The best part is the opening sex education sequence,
where we see sperm swimming up a vagina, searching
for the ovary, and finally, with one little guy bursting
through the side of the egg, the moment of conception.
From there, it's all downhill, with bad acting by most
principals. Some cute bits when the infants, even
prior to birth, are given voices, and we see the world
through their eyes. A great bit of crying to Janis Joplin
singing "Oh Baby." In all, a bit of fun, but it quickly
becomes silly and boring.

Look Who's Talking Too
Tri-Star Pictures (1990), 111 min.
Director: Amy Heckerling
Starring John Travolta, Kirstie Alley
and Olympia Dukakis   V

This one seemed like four hours. Again, we have the sex education sequence at the beginning. But first comes the preamble to the sperm/egg scene — Travolta and Alley in bed, with the line, "Have you got your diaphragm in?" The movie goes downhill from here, with a violent brother-in-law, and a lot of stuff that is not for kids. A bad movie.

Lost in the Barrens
Cineglobe (1990), 94 min.
Director: Michael Scott
Starring Nicholas Shields, Lee J. Campbell,
Graham Greene and Evan Adams   V

This fine Canadian film, based on the Farley Mowat novel set in 1935, tells the story of two teenagers, one white and one native. Jamie, an orphan from a car accident, is forced to leave the comfort and success of his life in a private school in Toronto to live with an uncle in northern Manitoba. From there he is taken on a hunting trip with a group of natives. He and the teenage native boy are thrown together in a terrifying and exotic wilderness adventure. The acting is excellent, the scenery magnificent, and the themes of two boys becoming men and two cultures coming together make this fine family viewing.

Lost in the Woods
Magic Lantern (1984), 23 min.
Director: Barry Casson   V

Eight-year-old Calvin, camping with his parents, is

intrigued by a deer and starts to follow it, getting
deeper and deeper into the woods, until he is lost.
"Calvin remembered the things they had talked
about. It is very important to keep warm. Once you get
cold, it's difficult to get warm again. And it's important to keep your head warm. And stay in one place.
An open one." This is from the simple, clear voice-over
narration we hear. The program conveys an important
lesson in a very effective way. It could be used at home
or in school. Great for young children. The good advice
is reviewed several times and reinforced at the end.

Lucas
CBS/Fox (1986), 100 min.
Director: David Seltzer
Starring Cory Haim, Charlie Sheen, Keri Green
and Winona Ryder   **V**

Lucas is a "runt," an accelerated 14-year-old student,
beginning junior high with a group of 16-year-olds. He
wants desperately to fit in, but his interest in insects
and classical music doesn't help him much. When he
finds a friend in a pretty cheerleader who is interested
in the captain of the football team, Lucas is determined to join the team and win her heart. Although
he nearly gets killed in the process, he learns a valuable lesson about friendship and being yourself. Has
one of the most touching endings of films in its genre.

The Man From Snowy River
CBS/Fox Home Video (1982), 115 min.
Director: George Miller
Starring Tom Berlinson, Sigrid Thornton
and Kirk Douglas   **V**

A visually stunning Australian film for horse buffs
about a handsome but strong-willed "mountain man"
who goes to work for a powerful cattleman and falls in

love with his equally strong-willed daughter. Rancher
and cattleman don't see eye to eye. Also see the sequel,
Return to Snowy River.

Many Voices
TVOntario (1991), 15 min. each
Director: Susan Murgatroyd   **V/T**

A nine-part series of open-ended dramas whose
purpose is to help young viewers, especially in grades
four to six, to learn about various cultural, religious
and racial groups, from the points of view of the
people in those groups. Each drama reflects the feelings and behaviour of people towards those who do
not fit the image of what many have come to feel is
"normal." Each program deals with a different focus
on stereotyping or prejudice, and reveals the struggle for self-discovery and pride, focusing on various
opportunities to fight against unfairness. On the
whole, the situations are interesting, and the series
probably works well in the classroom when accompanied by the teacher's guidebook, but the stories are
slow-moving, the performances forced and the dialogue unnatural.

Miracle at Moreaux
Magic Lantern's Christmas Collection / Atlantis
Films / Global / Telefilm / PBS (1985), 60 min.
Director: Paul Shapiro
Starring Loretta Swit, Robert Joy and Ken Pogue **V**

It's Christmas 1943, in Nazi-occupied France, near
the Spanish border. Three Jewish children, led by an
adult friend, are attempting to escape from France to
Spain. Loretta Swit plays a nun who runs a boarding
school near the border, Robert Joy is a Nazi officer
and Ken Pogue is a sergeant. After the leader of the
escapees is shot by the Nazis, the nun hides the three

children in her school. There is some tension and
suspense, as one of the students has Nazi parents,
and feels that the nun has put them all in danger by
hiding the Jews. Slow-moving at times, but on the
whole it's a good tale of compassion and courage
during a dark period of Western civilization. The
acting is uniformly good, and some of the children's
performances are exceptional. Although labelled as
part of a Christmas collection, it's good family
viewing for any time.

Molly's Pilgrim
Phoenix Films (1985), 24 min.
Director: Jeff Brown   **V**

Molly, a young Russian Jewish emigrant with warm,
loving parents, encounters insensitivity and intoler-
ance in her new American school. When the class is
given an assignment to create a doll based on the
Thanksgiving theme, Molly's mother makes a beautiful Russian doll which, of course, does not resemble
the picture Molly has of American Pilgrims. Molly's
mother points out that they are modern Pilgrims,
escaping a tyranny in a new land. Thanks to a patient,
understanding teacher, the class eventually comes to
appreciate Molly's plight. While the values and
virtues propounded in this film are stressed as American, the theme is universal, and the story is sensitively acted and directed. It received an Academy
Award for Best Live Action Short.

A Mom for Christmas
Walt Disney Productions (1990), 110 min.
Director: George Miller
Starring Olivia Newton-John, Doug Shehan
and Juliet Sorcey   **V**

From the novel *A Mom by Magic,* this insipid Disney

product tells of a little girl who doesn't have a mother
looking forlornly through a department store, when
she comes upon Philomena, a clerk with magic
powers, who grants her one free wish. Her one wish
for the holiday season is for a mom for Christmas. Her
wish is granted in the form of the coming-alive of a
store mannequin, played by Olivia Newton-John.
Their home is dominated by a computer and a fax
machine, indeed a modern household. Not much of
interest here; in fact, rather a bore.

The Moonspinners
Disney Home Video (1964), 118 min.
Director: James Neilson
Starring Hayley Mills, Peter McEnery,
Eli Wallach and Pola Negri   **V**

Based on the novel by Mary Stewart about a teenage
girl on vacation on the island of Crete with her aunt.
There she meets a handsome stranger and becomes
entangled in the theft of priceless jewels. A good
mystery film featuring a grown-up Hayley Mills. Nonviolent by today's standards.

Mr Majeika
TVS–England (1988), 25 min.
Director: Michael Kerrigan
Starring Stanley Baxter   **V/T**

A screwball comedy from Britain about a wizard who
is punished by his boss by being turned into a schoolmaster. His crime was that he turned his aunt into a
pheasant instead of a peacock, and she ended up as
Christmas dinner for the Queen. The situations and
the tricks are funny, and the school kids emerge as
real characters. There is even a song or two. Accents
may be a problem at first viewing.

My Friend Flicka
CBC Fox Home Video (1943), 89 min.
Director: Harold Shuster
Starring Roddy McDowall, Preston Foster
and Rita Johnson   **V**

A truly wonderful horse film about a young boy who desperately wants a horse of his own. His father can't seem to find a way to get close to his son. Following the mother's encouragement, he lets the boy choose from the ranch's herd. Much to his father's regret, Ken chooses a "loco" filly whom he names Flicka. When Flicka proves to be a handful, Ken's father teaches him how to win the filly's confidence and train her. The bond between boy and horse affects everyone. Based on the novel by Mary O'Hara.

My Girl
Columbia Pictures (1992), 102 min.
Director: Howard Zieff
Starring Macaulay Culkin, Anne Chomski,
Jamie Lee Curtis and Dan Ackroyd   **V**

Advertised as "an irresistible story of first love and loss," we found this a very bad, condescending treatment of death for children. Perhaps this is what happens when too many dollars meet serious emotions. A serious issue is trivialized and sentimentalized. The script is appalling, performances are uniformly bad and the ending, with Macaulay Culkin laid out dead in a casket, goes on forever. Not only do we not recommend this one, we strongly object to this poor treatment of a difficult issue.

My Side of the Mountain
Aims Media (1982), 38 min.
Director: James B. Clark

Starring Ted Eccles, Theodore Bikel
and Tudi Wiggins   **V**

The story of a young boy who wants to be a naturalist and is inspired by the writings of Thoreau. He leaves home with his pet racoon and runs away to the Laurentian Mountains, prepared to live off the land for a whole year. By the time the story is over, the boy has learned much about his environment, companionship and his own worth. An excellent story very nicely played. Good for seven- to fifteen-year-olds. Animal lovers will enjoy this film.

Mysterious Island
RCA/Columbia (1961), 101 min.
Director: Cy Endfield
Starring Michael Callan, Joan Greenwood,
Michael Craig and Herbert Lom   **V**

Three Confederate soldiers and two women are stranded on an island in the Pacific inhabited by strange, giant creatures. When they meet the enigmatic Captain Nemo, the perpetrator of these strange aberrations, they realize he is their only hope of escape before the island's volcano erupts. Ray Harryhausen's effects are still excellent. May spark young readers to tackle the book by Jules Verne.

The Mystery of the Million Dollar Hockey Puck
CIC Video (1975), 89 min.
Directors: Jean Lafleur and Peter Svatek
Starring Michael Macdonald, Angele Knight
and Jean-Louis Millette   **V**

Pierre, a promising young hockey player who adores the Montreal Canadiens, lives with his sister Catou and a number of other children in an orphanage in Northern

Quebec. Sent to the florists one day, he accidentally overhears a sinister plot: gangsters operating out of the back of the shop plan to smuggle a fortune in stolen diamonds into the United States inside one of the Canadiens' hockey pucks. Pierre is spotted, and while fleeing he drops his wallet. The gangsters identify him and the chase is on, climaxing in a Canadiens–Detroit Red Wings game in which the "million-dollar hockey puck" ends up on the ice in the action. (Features former celebrity announcer Danny Gallivan.)

National Velvet
MGM (1944), 125 min.
Director: Clarence Brown
Starring Elizabeth Taylor, Mickey Rooney,
Donald Crisp and Angela Lansbury   **V**

For children with a love of horses, this film still works. When a beautiful young girl wins a piebald horse in a raffle, she sets about realizing her dream of riding in the Grand National Steeplechase, with the help of a young hired hand who "knows horses." Warm family relationships, exciting horse racing sequences and good production values make this a classic.

Nature Connection
Film Images (1991), 24 min. each
Director: Allan Gibb
Hosted by David Suzuki   **T**

This thirteen-part series on environmental issues as seen through the eyes of young people, is far better in its intentions than in its execution. It is badly shot, stilted in its use of children and uses David Suzuki inappropriately. There is much too much talk from David and too many bored reaction shots of the kids. Too bad. Subjects such as the Carmanah forest, our very own rain forest, could have made for exciting, interesting shows. Instead, despite being aimed at children, the series cannot hold their interest.

Nature Watch Digest
TVOntario (1989), 15 min. each   **V/T**

Fifteen-minute programs segmented from "Nature Watch," a series co-produced by TVO and NHK in Japan. Well produced and informative, this is good solid information television at its best, for children and adults alike.

The Neverending Story
Warner Home Video (1984), 94 min.
Director: Wolfgang Peterson
Starring Noah Hathaway, Barrett Oliver,
Tami Stronach and Patricia Hayes   **V**

Bastien, a boy who loves books and is bullied by his classmates, finds that one book has the special power of drawing him into it. Inside the book, Bastien finds himself in the land of Fantasia, where The Nothing is a deadly despair that threatens to destroy the land by making people forget their dreams. He must help the young warrior, Atreyu, save the Empress of the land and allow Fantasia to live on in the hopes and dreams of the reader. This entertaining fantasy-adventure film is full of clever special effects. Children learn that you can be the hero of your own story.

The Neverending Story II
Warner Home Video (1991), 90 min.
Director: George Miller
Starring Jonathan Brandis, Kenny Morgan
and Clarissa Burt   **V**

Bastien returns to Fantasia in the sequel based on characters from Michael Ende's acclaimed novel. He rejoins Atreyu the young warrior, Falkor the Luck-dragon and the immense Rock Giant on a quest to save his imaginary world from the evil sorceress Xayide. Loaded with dazzling special effects and likely to be too intense for young children, this is an effective and exciting sequel.

Night Train to Kathmandu
Paramount Home Video (1988), 90 min.
Director: Robert Wiemer
Starring Mila Jovovich, Eddie Castrodad
and Pernell Roberts   **V**

Lily, a young girl, is unhappy when her parents, both archaeology professors, go on a year's sabbatical to Nepal. But on the last night aboard the train to Kath-mandu she meets a mysterious young vagabond, Johar, a prince of the Invisible City, which appears only once every hundred years for the space of a single moon. He has been sent to observe the progress of the outside world, but now his time is running short, and he desperately needs her to help him return over the mountains before the new moon. A little slow in the middle, but nevertheless a very popular film for children under twelve.

The Old Curiosity Shop
Ventron (1984), 30 min.
Animation   **V**

Ventron's "Charles Dickens Collection" presents animated versions of the author's masterpieces. In this one, a little girl named Nell and her grandfather are evicted from their curiosity shop and roam the streets of nineteenth-century London in search of a new home. Poor animation. Dreadful, irritating voices, a bad script and bad editing make this series a poor choice for young people.

Old Yeller
Walt Disney Home Video (1957), 83 min.
Director: Robert Stevenson
Starring Fess Parker, Dorothy McGuire,
Tommy Kirk and Chuck Connors   **V**

A real tear-jerker from the Disney studios. The story revolves around a "big, stray yellow dog" who befriends two boys and their mother in Texas during the 1860s. While their father is bringing in a herd of cattle, the dog proves to be a valuable protector. A wonderful family film, heavy on sentiment and guaranteed to wrench your heartstrings.

The Olden Days Coat
New World (1981), 30 min.
Director: Bruce Pittman
Starring Megan Follows, Doris Parr
and Kate Petrie   **V**

Based on the Margaret Laurence short story concerning a young girl, Sal, who is upset at being forced to spend a family Christmas at her grandmother's. However, everything changes when, while rooting around in her grandmother's attic on Christmas Eve, she is magically transported back in time and meets her grandmother as a young girl. They take a sleigh ride together and her grandmother accidentally loses a hand-carved and painted jewellery box, a gift from her own parents. Sal helps her recover it, returns to the present, and is given the same box from her grandmother on Christmas Day. A terrific Yuletide story about recognizing real value.

Oliver!
RCA/Columbia (1968), 153 min.
Director: Carol Reed
Starring Ron Moody, Oliver Reed and Mark Lester **V**

A fine musical based on Charles Dickens's *Oliver Twist*, expertly adapted from the Broadway hit. The production abounds with invigorating choreography and memorable songs by Lionel Bart, including "Consider Yourself One of Us" and "As Long as He Needs Me." A great way to introduce children to musical comedy and Charles Dickens at the same time.

Oliver Twist

Paramount (1948), 116 min.
Director: David Lean
Starring Alec Guinness, Robert Newton,
Francis L. Sullivan and Kay Walsh **V**

A faithful version of the classic Dickens story, with fine performance from Guinness and cast. This one has rated four stars from many critics over the years. Like *Scrooge* and *Great Expectations*, it serves as a fine introduction for young viewers eight and up to these classic novels. A fine use of television in the home.

OWL TV

OWL TV (1989–92), 30-min. episodes
Directors: various **V/T**

An interesting series of science magazine programs for seven-year-olds and up. While some of the children's interviews are stilted, the film footage from locations around the world is usually very good and informative. Each program contains four or five good sequences, ranging from a visit to a camel market in Morocco to the effects of acid rain in a urban setting, to the fascinating experiment in the children's eternal rain forest in Costa Rica. Each program includes a segment with the entertaining skeleton Bonapart and the well-known children's educator Dr. Zed. Soundly educational and slickly professional.

Paddle-to-the-Sea
NFB (1966), 28 min.
Director: Bill Mason   **V**

Holling C. Holling's children's story is beautifully interpreted in this Oscar-nominated short. In an Indian village nestled deep amongst the northern tributaries of Lake Superior, a young native boy whittles and paints a man in a canoe, and carves the inscription "I am Paddle-to-the-Sea. Please put me back in the water" under the hull. He then leaves the canoe in a frozen stream. With the spring thaw, Paddle-to-the-Sea begins an epic journey through the Great Lakes system. This extraordinary Canadian travelogue has charmed and educated generations of children.

The Parent Trap
Walt Disney Home Video (1961), 127 min.
Director: David Swift
Starring Hayley Mills, Maureen O'Hara
and Brian Keith   **V**

Tomboy Susan and sheltered Sharon are the twin daughters of estranged parents. Separated in infancy, they meet at a summer camp, and the cat is out of the bag. The reunited sisters vow to reconcile their mother and father, setting in motion a grand conspiracy to ruin their father's impending remarriage, and get their parents back together. With its infectious blend of slapstick comedy and lighthearted romance, *The Parent Trap* is one of Disney's most popular and enduring films.

The Peanut Butter Solution
New World Pictures and Roch Demers (1987), 91 min.
Director: Michael Rebbo
Starring Mathew Mackay and Siluk Saysonosy   **V**

Eleven-year-old Michael has a vivid imagination. While he is exploring an abandoned mansion he receives a shock that causes him to lose his hair. When some friendly ghosts pass on a magic solution to him, the "hair-raising" results lead to some wonderful, exciting adventures for Michael and his friends. This is a magical, exciting, sometimes scary story with an array of oddball characters. Young viewers may be frightened by some of the scenes in this movie, so preview it in advance.

The Phantom Tollbooth
MGM (1969), 90 min.
Director: Chuck Jones / David Monahan
Animation / live action; starring Butch Patrick,
featuring the voices of Hans Conreid and Mel Blanc   **V**

A young boy named Milo is in a perpetual state of boredom. One afternoon after school he finds an enormous package in his room that unfolds into the Phantom Tollbooth, the gateway to the (animated) Kingdom of Wisdom. There he has a number of exciting adventures, encounters a host of fascinating characters, finds that he has a gift to learn that he never suspected and gains a new respect for education. Based on Norton Juster's book.

The Point
Vestron Video (1985), 60 min.
Director: Fred Wolf
Animation; featuring the voice of Ringo Starr   **V**

Wonderful, whimsical animation and very bouncy, pleasing presentation of the music in this story about the land of Point, in which everything has a point, except Obleo, who is born without a point. A lovely tale that will entertain both children and adults who remember this musical story from the seventies. The dialogue is wonderfully funny in a low-key way. A well-told story, with a great point to it — a must for children seven and up and their parents.

The Ponies of Miklaengi
Phoenix Films (1978), 25 min.
Directors: Thomas Hurwitz and Gary Templeton   **V**

Filmed on location in Iceland, this is the story of two days in the life of a farm family — mother, father, grandmother, brother and sister. There is a search for lost sheep, a minor earthquake and the birth of a foal. Slow-moving at times, but realistic, with beautiful scenery and wonderful low-key performances. A good story for eight- to ten-year-olds who love animals. Opens with a wonderful scene of wild ponies running across the horizon.

Popeye
Paramount Home Video (1980), 114 min.
Director: Robert Altman
Starring Robin Williams, Shelley Duvall,
Ray Walston and Paul Dooley   **V**

Not well received at the box office, this is one of those films that did much better on video. The casting is superb. Robin Williams is excellent as the mumbling sailor Popeye and Shelley Duvall is ideal as Olive Oyl. The songs by Harry Nilsson are so unusual that somehow the terrible singing voices of Duvall and Williams bring just the right amount of humour and charm. Parents can enjoy the wit of Popeye and his Pappy's understated mumblings.

The Priest Know-All/The Grief of Pi Kari
Walt Disney Home Video/Stories and Fables (1981 and 1984), 25 min.

Director: Sebastian Robinson
Live action with narration   **V**

The first story is of a lazy young man who masquer-
ades as a priest and worms his way into the court of
an unsuspecting king and queen. A light-hearted,
amusing tale, nicely acted.

The second story is of a strange Maori legend of a
village chief whose life is consumed by the spirit of a
woman whose skull he finds and buries. A beautiful
exotic setting, very slow-moving but fascinating. A
gentle, quiet story, though some children might find it
too slow.

The Prince and the Pauper

Walt Disney Educational Media Productions
(1978), 28 min.   **V**

This live-action Disney version of the famous Mark
Twain story is perhaps not as good as the longer
British version produced in the late seventies and
seen on TVOntario. It is, however, well played and, in
keeping with the Disney tradition, lavishly produced.
Would serve as a good introduction, for young people,
to the Twain story.

The Princess and the Pea

Fairie Tale Theatre (1983), 60 min.
Director: Tony Bill
Starring Liza Minnelli, Tom Conti
and Beatrice Straight   **V**

A good cast wasted on a silly script. Another episode
in a series that tries to be comic and semi-sophisti-
cated for an adult audience and forgets about the kids.
Teens may get a laugh or two, but younger children
are confused or bored. This series is found in most
libraries, so we discussed it with several librarians.

Some episodes are fine, while others are not suitable
for children. Parents would be well advised to check
with librarians, or, better still, preview the episode
before viewing with youngsters.

Rags to Riches
New World (1986), 96 min.
Director: Bruce Seth Green
Starring Joseph Bologna and Douglas Seale   **V**

Nick Folatini, an ambitious sixties millionaire, adopts
six orphan girls from a rundown orphanage to boost his
public image. The girls promptly disrupt his life, and
things are touch and go for a while, but in the end the
tough, self-made, image-conscious Nick grows to love
the girls just as if he had wanted them in the first place.
A good little film, which spun off into a series, interspersed with lively, familiar rock-and-roll classics.

The Railway Children
HBO (1972), 102 min.
Director: Lionel Jefferies
Starring Jenny Agutter, William Mervyn
and Dinah Sheridan   **V**

A thoroughly enchanting adaptation of E. Nesbit's
touching tale of a mother and three children who are
forced to move out to the country after their father is
falsely arrested and imprisoned. They develop a rather
special relationship with a train that travels daily past
their home, and especially with an old gentleman who
rides in it. Various adventures occur, usually associ-
ated in some way with the train, and in the end their
father is restored to them. Not to be missed.

The Railway Dragon
f.h.e. (1989), 30 min.
Directors: Hilary Philips and Gerald Tripp

Animation; featuring the voices of Barry Morse,
Tracey Moore and Leslie Nielsen **V**

The story of young Emily who befriends the centuries-
old dragon that lives in the old railway tunnel.
Together, they embark on an exciting adventure, but
ultimately they learn that there is no place for
dragons in our modern world. Although no one else
believes Emily's stories about her dragon friend, she
discovers that it doesn't matter, because "things are,
if they are true in our hearts." A reasonably well-
animated production.

Raw Toonage
Disney Animation Studios (1992), 24 min. each **T**

In this series, various Disney characters introduce and
host each half-hour show, which opens with a cartoon
doctor explaining away some of the violence (he puts
characters back together) and ends with him cleaning
up the set. Each half-hour contains three short cartoons often modelled on stereotyped TV shows or
movies such as "Doggie Schnowzer, M.D.A." and "Dr.
Morgensten, Monster Maker." Lots of slapstick and
sight gags. A bit much for under eight, even though the
cartoon doctor tries to remedy things at the end.

Really Rosie
Weston Woods (1976), 26 min.
Director: Maurice Sendak **V**

A beautifully animated musical tale about Rosie, the
inner-city neighbourhood "star" who wants to produce
and direct her own movie called "What Happened to
Chicken Soup?" Each of her friends auditions for the
movie by performing songs about such things as the
alphabet, counting and caring. Rosie does the last big
production number called "Chicken Soup." Rosie's

voice is that of pop singer and composer Carole King,
who wrote the score for the show. Good, lively fun.
Songs like "I Don't Care" and "Chicken Soup" are
superb.

Red Riding Hood and the Well-Fed Wolf
Churchill Films (1987), 15 min.   **V**

A health video stressing good eating and exercise
habits, it is also an entertaining satire on the well-
known fairy tale and a takeoff of TV interview and
adventure shows. There's a wonderful interview with
the wolf — how he likes living in the woods, the fact
that he doesn't get enough exercise and eats junk food.
A good health lesson. This program will appeal to pre-
teens and many parents.

Ring of Bright Water
Fox Video (1969), 107 min.
Director: Jack Couffer
Starring Bill Travers and Virginia McKenna   **V**

After a chance encounter with an energetic tame otter,
Graham Merrill moves from the bustle of London to a
small cottage in the outer reaches of Scotland. There,
he mystifies the local villagers with his strange ways
and falls in love with the local doctor, a beautiful and
feisty woman who appreciates animals as much as he
does. This by turns hilarious and touching true family
drama is based on the book of the same name by Gavin
Maxwell and features fine performances by Bill
Travers and Virginia McKenna, the same couple who
starred in the film *Born Free*.

The Road to Avonlea
Sullivan Productions (1989–92), 48 min. each
Directors: various
Starring Sarah Polly and Jackie Burroughs   **T**

This series has probably done more to bring families together over Sunday dinner than anything else in the past twenty years. In our family, dinner is at 6:00 p.m., and timing is geared so we can sit down with dessert in front of the television just as the opening credits are coming on. We all settle in and enjoy the lovely warmth of each story. Our two seven-year-olds laugh and cry with the children of Avonlea, and I must say I've shed many a tear myself. The scripts are well crafted, the programs lovingly produced. There is always such a feeling of richness as we watch and become a part of this world.

Robin Hood: Prince of Thieves
Warner Brothers (1991), 144 min.
Director: Kevin Reynolds
Starring Kevin Costner, Morgan Freeman
and Christian Slater   **V**

This movie was promoted as *the* gift for a child. Well, it's not. It is one of the worst versions of the famous legend that we have seen. Kevin Costner has neither the accent nor the sense of the energy of Robin of Locksley. The saving grace is the characterization of the Sheriff of Nottingham, but this is not a characterization for children. There are frightening scenes in the film, such as the opening in a squalid prison, in which a man is about to have his hand chopped off. Watch this one before you decide to give it as a present.

Robin Hood and the Sorcerer
CBS/Fox (1986), 115 min.
Director: Ian Sharp
Starring Michael Praed   **V**

The beginning of this one sets the scene, with a lot of killing. We watch one character being shot with ten arrows, in true Sam Peckinpah style. The pace is much too slow, the costumes silly, with helmets that have nose pieces that make the actors look idiotic. The jacket calls it an "intense, lavish and gritty production." It is none of these. Badly directed, full of empty sound and fury, with a dreadful script, this is one to avoid.

The Adventures of Robin Hood
Warner Home Video (1938), 102 min.
Directors: Michael Curtiz and William Keighley
Starring Errol Flynn, Olivia de Havilland,
Basil Rathbone and Claude Rains **V**

Errol Flynn plays an energetic, handsome and charismatic Sir Robin of Locksley in this big-budget film. Olivia de Havilland brings both femininity and feistiness to the role of Maid Marian. Even with all the later versions of the famous legend now on video, this film still has a lot going for it. Claude Rains plays a dignified but sinister Prince John and Basil Rathbone is the perfect foil as Sir Guy of Gisbourne. Elegant and classic, but with more than enough swashbuckling to keep today's action fans interested.

Robinson Crusoe
Rank / Bass Productions / USA Tomorrow Productions (1972), 30 min.
Animation **V**

An animated adaptation of Daniel Defoe's novel in the series "Festival of Family Classics." This production has some merit, apart from schmaltzy music and Disneyland opening credits. The story moves along well and can serve as a good introduction or review of this tale for young viewers and their families.

The Rotten Truth
Children's Television Workshop (1990), 30 min.

Director: Ozzie Alfonso
Hosted by Stephanie Yu   **V**

This episode of the popular television program "3-2-1
Contact" deals with the rotten subject of garbage —
how it's produced and how it's disposed of. Full of fascinating, eye-opening information, this is a video from
which both parents and children can learn. Charmingly hosted by Stephanie Yu.

Russkies
Lorimar Home Video (1987), 100 min.
Director: Rick Rosenthal
Starring Whip Hubley and Peter Billingsly   **V**

While playing military games, three Floridian boys
find an injured Russian sailor, who has been washed
ashore after accidentally falling off his ship during a
storm. The boys have a conflict: they have been
taught that the Russians are the enemy, but Misha
seems like a regular nice guy, and when their parents
don't initially believe their captive exists, the boys
agonize over whether or not to turn him in to the
authorities. Finally, they elect to help him, and the
action heats up. A warmhearted film about the power
of real friendship to overcome cultural differences.

Scrooge (also listed as "A Christmas Carol")
UI (1951), 86 min.
Director: Brian Desmond Hunt
Starring Alistair Sim   **V**

A fantasy based on Charles Dickens's *A Christmas
Carol*. Sure, we know you've seen it many times. But
this is still the best version. Now it's colourized (and
we are of two minds about this, but the kids love it).
And we love it still. Sim brings wonderful touches of
pathos and humour to the role, and there is the great

supporting cast of British actors and the fine production from an era when British film making set an example for the world. This is a family treat.

Dickens wrote this story in the fall of 1843, completing it in time for Christmas. It was a very difficult period in his own life, and a time when the Christmas festive season and spirit seemed to be in decline in England. The acceptance and success of the story turned life around for Dickens, and many others. The Alistair Sim film is a wonderful way to introduce young children to a great storyteller.

The Sea Gypsies
Warner Home Video (1978), 102 min.
Director: Stewart Raffill
Starring Robert Logan, Heather Rattray
and Mikki Jamison-Olsen   **V**

The tale of a family that sets out to circumnavigate the world and is shipwrecked off the coast of Alaska. After enduring a wilderness life, including encounters with a territorial Kodiak bear, they realize that they have no hope of surviving the approaching winter, and that they must build a ship to save themselves. An exciting and worthwhile film.

The Secret Garden
Playhouse Home Video (1984), 107 min.
Starring Sarah Hollis Andrews, David Patterson
and John Woodnutt   **V**

An outstanding BBC production of the Frances Hodgson Burnett book about overprivileged Mary Lennox, an orphan who is sent from luxury in India to live with her negligent uncle on the moors of England. There she discovers her recently deceased aunt's secret garden, a special place that changes her profoundly for the better. She also befriends her invalid cousin, showing surprising

strength in squashing his self-pity. This moving classic
is especially appealing for the literary child.

The Secret Life of Walter Mitty
Embassy Home Video (1947), 110 min.
Director: Norman Z. McLeod
Starring Danny Kaye, Virginia Mayo
and Boris Karloff   **V**

Based on the story by James Thurber, this is a charming telling of the tale about Walter, a mild-mannered
man whose dream world is more exciting than his real
life, until he becomes the target of a real gang of jewel
thieves who believe he has the loot. Danny Kaye is
delightful in this silly story.

The Secrets of the Titanic
Vestron Home Video (1986), 60 min.
Director: Nicholas Noxon
Narrated by Martin Sheen   **V**

One of the most popular with children in the National
Geographic series, this superior production is fascinating from the start. First, the brief history and
design of the monster ocean liner are described, after
which the camera follows the innovative expedition
headed by Robert Ballard, and chronicles the ups and
downs of the great search, climaxing in the dramatic
discovery of the wreck through the use of astonishing
robotic inventions. Bearing in mind that there were
absolutely no guarantees of success when the filming
started, this extraordinary journal is proof that real
life can rival the greatest of adventures.

Shipwrecked
Disney Home Video (1991), 93 min.
Director: Nils Gaup
Starring Gabriel Byrne and Stian Smestad

Based on the book *Haakon Haakonsen* by O.V. Falck-Yttr about a young boy in 1859 who takes his father's place and goes to sea in order to earn money to save the family homestead. While the ship is on its way to Calcutta via Australia, villain John Merrick impersonates an officer to gain entry onto the ship. When a storm wrecks the boat, Haakon finds a treasure and evidence of Merrick's treachery. When he is reunited with his friends (Jens, a shipmate, and Mary, a stowaway), they scuttle the bad guys, escape with the treasure and return home to pay the family debts. This is a truly amazing adventure film, nonviolent by today's standards but still exciting. It even contains model male/female interaction.

The Simpsons
Fox Broadcasting (1991), 24 min. each
Director: Jim Reardon
Animation   **T**

It's difficult to decide whether this series is for adults or children. We think it spans both audiences, and is successful for both. Two episodes stand out as examples of its success — and of its importance. The first is when Marge discovers that the violent actions of little Lisa have been induced by the television programs that her child is watching. Marge takes on the broadcasting giants, and brings them to their knees with her campaign to end television violence. The second is an episode in which neighbour Ned Flanders starts a "Leftorium," stocking everything for lefthanded people. Homer wins a wishbone-breaking session with Ned and secretly wishes that Ned's store will fail. Ned, who has staked everything on his new venture, almost loses all because Homer will not help him by spreading the word to all the lefties he knows. In the end Homer does indeed help and Ned is successful. Important themes in both these shows are treated with fine

animation, excellent scripts and, as we said, there is
something for everyone. However, some episodes, one
of which we discussed earlier in this book, do not offer
such positive role models. A preview may be wise.

Sister Act
Touchstone Pictures (1992), 108 min.
Director: Emile Ardolino
Starring Whoopi Goldberg, Maggie Smith,
Harvey Keitel and Bill Nunn   **V**

A very funny, fast-moving story with some great
music. Two nuns interviewed at the movie thought it
was great, very funny and with a tasteful handling of
the Catholic religious elements. The theatre audience
applauded the super, up-tempo rock versions of religious hymns, blended with such oldies as "I Will
Follow Him" and "My Guy," which becomes "My God."
Whoopi is superb in this story of a bar singer who,
having witnessed a gangland killing, is hidden in a
convent, disguised as a nun, where she takes over the
choir. Especially funny if you know something about
Catholicism.

Snow Spider
HTV— Wales (1988), four 25-min. episodes
Director: Pennant Roberts   **T**

Based on a book by Jenny Nimms (Welsh children's
author), this is a story of a nine-year-old boy who lives
with his parents on a farm in a remote area of Wales.
The tales revolve around the disappearance of an
older sister when the boy is five, and his longing for
her return, or for some solution to the mystery. The
boy discovers a magic "snow spider" spell that he
hopes he can use to bring her back. The production is
excellent, with some fine acting. The tale will fasci-
nate adults as well as children.

Space Camp
Vestron Home Video (1986), 115 min.
Director: Harry Winer
Starring Kate Capshaw, Lea Thompson,
Kelly Preston, Tate Donovan and Tom Skerret   **V**

Filmed on location at the U.S. Space Camp in Huntsville, Alabama, this authenticity is the only good thing going for this weak and pretentious film. We review it to warn parents who might take it out of the library thinking it will be a good space education film for their children. A group of teenagers attends the summer camp designed to teach them the operations of the NASA Space Program. By accident they are launched into space. The ecstatic looks on their faces as they reach orbit tells all. This is a ridiculous, far-fetched story.

The Space Watch Club
Rudy, Inc. Home Video (1991), 24-min. episodes
Director: Douglas Kiefer   **V**

This series centres around young people in a clubhouse and their computer, which takes them on various adventures into the world of space science. Each episode has special guests such as astronauts and scientists. Excellent documentary footage and a good review halfway through each program. Great for children eight to twelve.

Star Trek: The Next Generation
Gene Roddenberry Productions (1990), 47 min. each
Directors: various
Starring Patrick Stewart, Levar Burton   **T**

This new generation of one of our most popular sci-fi series that has lasted several decades is a modern fairy tale for children and adults. Consider one episode in which the beautiful Betazoid Deanna Troi mysteriously becomes pregnant, gives birth, thirty-six hours from conception to a baby who grows into a four-year-old within a few days, and to age eight in a few more. There is a power problem on board the *Enterprise* as all this happens, which is resolved only when the child, appearing to die, transforms itself into a light source and magically disappears. We discover that this was a being who, when passing the *Enterprise* in space, became curious about human beings and decided to become one in order to find out more about them. No great dangers, no cataclysmic happenings, no violence, only the intrigue of a story well told that gives one the feeling of being read to in a warm bed by one's parents. Fine sets, interesting, well-scripted characters and some beguiling stories.

Street Cents
CBC (ongoing), 29 min. each
Director: Henry Sarwer-Foner   **T**

This series rates a special review because of its consistent improvement in quality, and its importance to young people. We've watched most of the fall 1991 programs; the Christmas show was one of the best. It is well shot, the pace is excellent, the three young hosts work well, there is a lot of good humour and fun, along with valuable information about Christmas shopping, pictures with Santa, credit cards and other items of interest and value. There is an excellent review, by kids, of *Miracle on 34th Street*, a test of various kinds of turkey dinners, an item about the Salvation Army and some good fun with a bogus company, Buyco, to illustrate the worst of corporate commercialism. Good scripts, fine directing and lots of energy add up to a great series for kids. It's on every Saturday morning. If CBC is persuaded of the importance of this program, we might hope to see it in a time slot that makes sense for this kind of kids' program, like 7:00 p.m. perhaps.

Street Cents: Stay in School
CBC Halifax (1992), 29 min.
Director: Henry Sarwer-Foner   **T**

One of the most serious subjects this series has tackled in its three-year history. A lively plot involves one of the hosts who decides to quit school. A scene in Saskatchewan involving native youth is particularly strong and innovative. This is a good model of entertainment and education in a kids' show. Watch for the series on CBC. It's a valuable consumer show for young people.

Tadpole and the Whale
Cinema Plus (1987), 91 min.
Director: Dominique Ricard
Starring Fanny Lauzier, Denis Forest
and Marina Orsini   **V**

Daphne (nicknamed Tadpole) is an otherwise normal young girl who possesses one amazing talent: through extremely acute hearing she can communicate with whales. This is one of the most extraordinary and topical of Roch Demers's "Tales For All," and despite its almost mystical plot it seems to hold a particular fascination for the very young.

Take Off: Dreams
Friday Street Productions (1991), 25 min.
Director: Hilary Jones-Farrow   **V/T**

This series is aimed at children aged six to eleven to entertain and encourage creative and divergent thinking. This episode offers a fascinating treatment of the world of dreams, a world that fascinates youngsters. The television techniques are interesting. The program launches the "Take Off" kids into their own dreams, where they learn about brain waves, dream inventions, nightmares and world peace. Intelligent, fascinating and entertaining.

Tarzan the Ape Man
MGM / UA (1932), 99 min.
Director: W.S. Van Dyke
Starring Johnny Weissmuller,
Maureen O'Sullivan and Neil Hamilton   **V**

Edgar Rice Burroughs's hero as Hollywood sees him. Weissmuller went from Olympic swimming champion to star with this black and white vehicle. Die-hard Tarzan fans will defend this version to the death. Terribly dated but lots of fun.

They Shall Have Music
MGM (1939), 101 min.
Director: Archi Mayo
Starring Yasha Hiefetz, Joel McRae,
Walter Brennan, Marjorie Main, Peter Hall   **V**

A fine, old movie in which Yasha Hiefetz tries to act. But this is beside the point. The simple plot has a group of poor kids convincing him to play a benefit concert to save Walter Brennan's music school, which is in the slums and serves these poor kids. Brennan is great, as is Joel McRae. Excellent music, some astounding shots of Hiefetz playing, and a strong focus on learning and loving music makes this a great one for kids who are interested in music.

Tommy Tricker and the Stamp Traveller
Roch Demers Productions (1988), 95 min.
Director: Michael Rubbo
Animation / live action   **V**

A boy travels to faraway lands by chanting rhymes
that make him small enough to fit on postage stamps.
This live-action and animation tale is slow-moving at
the beginning, and marred a little by some overacting
by the adults, but it is an imaginative and suspenseful story, beautifully animated. There are fascinating
scenes of life in Montreal, China and Australia, seen
from a kid's point of view. Good family viewing for children aged eight and up.

The Transformers
Davenport Productions (1984), 15 min.   **V**

We review this one because it is a series that seems
to turn up in many video stores as commonly accepted
fare for children. The animation is atrocious, the
voices and sound effects dreadful and the story lines
nothing more than crude shoot-'em-up stuff. It's hard
to distinguish, with these programs, who are the good
guys and who the bad. They all sound like wrestlers
from the *WWF.* Avoid this series when you see it.

The Moon Stallion
BBC (1985), 95 min.
Director: Dorothea Brooking
Starring Sarah Sutton, David Haig
and James Green   **V**

While accompanying her father on an archaeological dig
in northern England, blind young Diana Purwell encounters the Moon Stallion, a magnificent wild white
horse with whom she shares a strange, almost psychic
relationship. This horse, the servant of the lunar god-
dess Diana, is being hunted down by Professor Purwell's
patron, Sir George Mortenhurze, who seeks to exploit its
tremendous power. The Moon Stallion engages Diana in
a dangerous and mysterious adventure with mytholog-
ical repercussions. An engaging and literate offering.

The Quest
MCA (1986), 93 min.
Director: Brian Trenchard-Smith
Starring Henry Thomas, Tony Barry,
Rachel Friend and Tamsin West   **V**

In Australia, fourteen-year-old Cody and his friend
Wendy come across an unmapped inland lake apparently inhabited by a "Donkegin," a monster out of an
old Aboriginal folk legend. In order to prove his
manhood, Cody must uncover the mystery. His inquis-
itiveness gets him into danger when he is trapped
under the water, and it takes Wendy's intelligence to
solve the mystery behind "Donkegin" and save Cody.

The Three Worlds of Gulliver
RCA / Columbia (1960), 100 min.
Director: Jack Sher
Starring Kerwin Matthews and Jo Morrow   **V**

A fanciful version of the Jonathan Swift novel with
special effects by the master, Ray Harryhausen. Gulliver visits the land of Lilliput, where he is a giant,
and Brobdingnag, where he is tiny. Youngsters will
have a hard time believing these places are only
fantasy.

Toby McTeague
Charter Entertainment (1987), 94 min.
Director: Jean-Claude Lord
Starring Winston Rekert, Yannick Bisson
and Stephanie Morganstern   **V**

In the remote northern town of Silver Creek, accessible only by air, Tom McTeague is the regional dog-
team racing champion four years running, an award
desperately coveted by the richest man in the community, Edison Crowe. When Tom is injured prior to

the championships and their lead dog goes down, things look bleak. But Tom's fifteen-year-old son Toby forgoes his irresponsible ways, earns Tom's trust and, with the loan of a powerful lupine lead dog from a friendly native chief, Toby wins the day. A rousing, come-from-behind, underdog-wins tale.

Treasure Island
Disney Home Video (1950), 96 min.
Director: Byron Haskin
Starring Bobby Driscoll, Robert Newton
and Basil Sydney   **V**

This brilliant adaptation of the time-honoured Stevenson yarn immortalized Newton as the quintessential Long John Silver. Jim Hawkins, the son of a tavern mistress, comes by chance into possession of a map that reveals the location of the immense treasure of the legendary pirate Flint. Local gentlemen outfit a ship to sail to Treasure Island, but unwittingly hire a crew composed almost entirely of the late Flint's former shipmates, led by the one-legged galley cook Long John Silver. Then follows, predictably, murder, treachery, savage combat and the strange tale of the unique friendship that develops between a not-entirely-ruthless pirate and a courageous cabin boy. The violence is tame by today's standards. Represents a perfect example of exciting action contained within the boundaries of good taste.

Treasure Island
Malofilm (1990), 94 min.
Director: Fraser C. Heston
Starring Christian Bale, Charlton Heston,
Christopher Lee and Oliver Reed   **V**

This latest big-budget remake is rather less restrained than the Disney version, but is a tribute to the former movie and to MGM's original in 1934. Heston carries off the difficult job of playing Silver, Bale is a fine Hawkins and the story is faithfully followed. Toss in Oliver Reed as the best Billy Bones ever, and you have a decent production that just might get young people interested in reading the book.

20,000 Leagues Under the Sea
Walt Disney Home Video (1954), 127 min.
Director: Richard Fleischer
Starring Kirk Douglas, James Mason
and Peter Lorre   **V**

A Jules Verne fantasy-adventure in the great Disney tradition. What once were exciting action sequences have some trouble holding up today, especially the famous giant squid battle scene. Kids today are somewhat more sophisticated in their knowledge of film, and demand much more.

With teeth gritted, Kirk Douglas acts his heart out as a shipwrecked survivor held involuntarily on board the submarine *Nautilus,* and James Mason makes a wonderful Captain Nemo. Films like this often give children a "kick-start" towards reading the books on which the films are based. Winner of two Academy Awards in 1954 — Best Special Effects and Best Art Direction/Set Decoration.

Vincent and Me
Cinema Plus (1990), 99 min.
Director: Michael Rubbo   **V**

When thirteen-year-old Jo wins a scholarship to art school, she hopes to paint as well as her idol Van Gogh. But when an art dealer sells one of her drawings as "an authentic work of the young Van Gogh," she knows she must use her special psychic connection with the long-dead artist to stop the fraud. The eleventh film in the "Tales for All" series produced by Quebecois filmmaker Roch Demers, and one of the best.

War Games
CBS/Fox (1983), 110 min.
Director: John Badham
Starring Matthew Broderick, Dabney Coleman,
Ally Sheedy and David Warner   **V**

Broderick plays a brilliant, lazy high-school student who solves the problem of poor grades by breaking into the school computer and altering his marks at the source. He's also into computer games, and on one hacking escapade he inadvertently encounters "Joshua," an enigmatic entity linked to an array of defence programs. "Joshua" represents an irresistible challenge. After brain-racking research, he solves the riddle, gets inside and challenges the computer to a game of "Thermonuclear War." But to the computer, which in fact controls the entire strategic nuclear force of the United States, it's no game. So begins the countdown to Armageddon, and a wild and brilliant action film races to a tremendous climax. Great fun, with a stern warning.

Where the Red Fern Grows
Doty-Dayton Productions (1974), 90 min.
Director: Norman Tokar
Starring James Whitmore and Beverly Garland   **V**

The heart of this gentle film is a boy's love for two hunting dogs in 1930s Oklahoma and the events that lead to his growing up. A particular favourite with children who know the story from the book, the film still has its appeal, especially to educators.

White Fang
Walt Disney Productions (1991), 109 min.
Starring Robert Wood and Pedro Sanchez **V**

This movie, based on the novel by Jack London, is well
filmed, with much pretty geography and interesting
sets of the Klondike, and holds a young audience well.
There's a lot of excitement to this story of a young man
and a young wolf/dog, both of them growing up in their
respective elements, both orphaned, both full of
courage. The scriptwriter handles the animal adventures better than the human ones. At times it becomes
tedious, as we wander across the landscape waiting for
things to happen. The writer cannot decide whether it's
a story about a wolf/dog or a young man, and for this
reason it wanders. And some of the intimate scenes between the young man and the young wolf happen much
too quickly, and lack credibility. Scenes of organized
dog fights, and of a frozen corpse, might frighten
younger children. This is one to watch with your kids.

White Lies
Atlantis Films (1984), 25 min.
Director: Don McBrearty **V**

An interesting story that examines some of the pres-
sures on teenage friendships. Two girls, very good
friends, are trying out for the basketball team. They
vow that if one doesn't make the team, the other will
not participate either, but in the event this promise
becomes strained. Worth watching for the discussion
it can promote amongst pre-teens and teens.

Who Has Seen the Wind?
Astral Video (1977), 100 min.
Director: Allan King
Starring Brian Painchaud, Gordon Pinsent
and Jose Ferrer **V**

Based on the W.O. Mitchell book. Life in rural Saskatchewan during the Depression is especially difficult for young Brian, forced to endure punishment from an unusually strict teacher. He is sent to live at his uncle's farm when his father falls ill. When his father dies, Brian is unable to show any sorrow. It is only while experiencing the force of a Prairie storm that he is able to let go. A wonderful coming-of-age film set against the stark Prairie skyline.

Wild Hearts Can't Be Broken
Walt Disney Productions (1990), 81 min.   **V**

A plodding, badly acted and vacuous story of a girl from the southern United States during the Depression leaving her home, finding work in a riding show, in which she learns to leap from a tower on a horse, becomes blinded in a jump in which she kept her eyes open too long as she and the horse hit the water. The treatment of blindness is absurd, the resolution much too easy, even for children. Some funny and exciting parts about horse riding. Not one we recommend.

The Wild Pony
Vestron Video (1983), 87 min.
Director: Kevin Sullivan
Starring Marilyn Lightstone, Art Hindle,
Josh Byrne and Kelsey McLeod   **V**

This excellent Canadian production tells the story of a family divided. Twelve-year-old Christopher can't bear his new stepfather, and finds an outlet for his resentment in his desire for an apparently unbreakable pony owned by another man. In his efforts to reconcile himself to his stepson, the stepfather buys it for him over the protests of his mother. The spirited animal causes more than its share of trouble, but when it falls gravely ill the family unites in their desire to save it.

Wild West C.O.W.-Boys of Moo Mesa
Green Grass Productions (1992), 24-min. each
Director: Mitch Aur   **T**

A cartoon western, supposedly set in outer space, where all the police are cows. The theme is law and order, or, as they keep saying, "We're keeping evil on its toes." The usual stock characters, complete with singing cowboy heroes, evil politicians such as the sheriff and mayor, and even a cute cow barmaid. Comic violence. Lots of fun. Improbable happenings and all the stuff kids expect in cartoons, but not upsetting in the least.

Willy Wonka and the Chocolate Factory
Warner Home Video (1971), 100 min.
Director: Mel Stuart
Starring Gene Wilder, Jack Albertson
and Peter Ostrum   **V**

Roald Dahl's novel *Charlie and the Chocolate Factory* is adapted in musical form in this favourite children's film. Gene Wilder is suitably zany as the mastermind behind the amazing Chocolate Factory. In order to find a suitable successor for his candy business, Wonka hides five Golden Tickets in his candy bars. These tickets entitle five children to a grand tour of the Wonka Chocolate Factory. The rude and disrespectful behaviour of four of the children is rewarded in kind, while the fifth, a poor but honest and caring boy named Charlie, wins the prize. All in all, great fun.

The Wonderful World of the Brothers Grimm
MGM / UA (1962), 128 min.
Director: George Pal
Starring Laurence Harvey, Claire Bloom,
Karl Boehm   **V**

A romanticized account of the famous storytellers.
Wilhelm and Jacob Grimm are hired by a local noble-
man to chronicle his family history, but Wilhelm
prefers more fantastic subjects: fairies, elves, giants
and dragons, so he travels the roads of his homeland
with his reluctant brother gathering folklore for a
book. These tales are enacted by a host of period stars,
and the film is still satisfying, even thirty years later.

The Wonders of Earth and Space
NFB (1966–81), 61 min.
Directors: various   **V**

Six brilliant National Film Board independent short
films make up this video, all more or less concerned
with geological and cosmological themes. "64 Million
Years Ago" concerns North American dinosaurs; "Evolution" takes a lighthearted look at Darwin's theories;
"Boomsville" traces technological evolution from the
sixteenth century to the present; "What on Earth!" is
a twisted look at life on earth from a Martian viewpoint. "Cosmic Zoom" is a breathtaking journey from
the infinitely small to the infinitely vast, and "Satellites of the Sun" takes us on a tour of the solar system.

The Yearling
MGM (1946), 134 min.
Director: Clarence Brown
Starring Gregory Peck, Jane Wyman
and Claude Jarman   **V**

Marjorie Kinnan Rawlings's touching story of a young
boy's love for a pet fawn and the tragic circumstances
that surround them. A visually beautiful and gentle
film. Superb performances make this an excellent
film, although for today's children it is slow-moving
and requires attentiveness. Those children able to
sustain the effort are in for an experience. Won

Academy Awards for Cinematography, Art Direction
and newcomer Claude Jarman.

Young Detectives on Wheels
MCA Home Video (1987), 107 min.
Director: Wayne Tourell
Starring Josie Vendramin, Neha Belton
and Don Selwyn   **V**

Financial difficulties force Susan Mitchell's family to
move from their comfortable life in Australia's
outback to a new and unpleasant home in the city.
Things go from bad to worse when, on the first day in
their new home, Susan's father is arrested for the
theft of a three-million-dollar collection of emeralds.
When Susan finds the emeralds, she sets out to prove
her father's innocence, and with the help of a local
gang of BMX bike-riding kids who befriend her, she
begins the dangerous task of luring the true thief out
of hiding. Uniformly excellent.

Young Einstein
Warner Home Video (1988), 90 min.
Director: Yahoo Serious
Starring Yahoo Serious, Odile de Clezio
and John Howard   **V**

As the opening credits indicate, this is a Serious film.
Albert Einstein is the twenty-year-old son of an apple
farmer in the rugged heart of turn-of-the-century Tas-
mania. Albert enjoys contemplating the universe, for-
mulating complex scientific principles and working on
his new musical style — rock and roll. During the
course of his experiments he succeeds in splitting a
Tasmanian beer atom and, armed with his new
formula $E=MC^2$, sets off for the mainland patent
office. There he encounters, in rapid succession, his
true love Marie Curie, all the corruption of the big city

and devious evil men intent on stealing his formula to
mass-produce carbonated alcoholic beverages.
Delightful, skilfully crafted surreal comedy suitable
for just about anyone.

Young Sherlock Holmes
Paramount Home Video (1985), 109 min.
Director: Barry Levinson
Starring Nicholas Rowe, Sophie Ward
and Alan Cox   **V**

A Steven Spielberg production full of fun, high-power
effects and fantasy about the great detective Sherlock
Holmes as a young man. We meet Watson, a school
chum, and references are made to events that will
take place in Holmes's adult life. Wonderfully cast and
set in Victorian times, this film is a fabulous mystery-
adventure film. A good introduction for youngsters to
the great Conan Doyle detective.

Yours, Mine and Ours
MGM / UA (1968), 111 min.
Director: Melville Shavelson
Starring Lucille Ball, Henry Fonda
and Van Johnson   **V**

A timely film based on the true story of the Beardsley
family of Northern California. When an army widow
who has eight children marries a naval officer/widower
with ten children, the term "large" family takes on a
new meaning. Getting along and practically taking
care of this brood are an adventure in itself. A great
family film with real, honest-to-goodness values.

Ages 12+

African Journey
Filmworks (1990), 30 min. each
Director: George Bloomfield
Starring Jason Blicker, Allan Jordan, Pedzisai
Sithole, Eldinah Tshatedi and Jesese Mungoshi **V/T**

Filmed on location in Zimbabwe, this is the story of
Luke Novak, a normal, fun-loving kid whose life has
been torn apart by the divorce of his parents. His
father, a mining engineer who works in East Africa,
has Luke come to stay with him in Africa, where many
things about Luke's life begin to change through his
friendships with young Africans. This is a world of
beauty fraught with intrigue, romance, and sometimes danger. The six episodes take young people into
an inspiring experience of Africa. Available through
TVOntario, this is another series that belongs on
course outlines as core curriculum material.

Borderline High
YTV (1992), 60 min.
Director: Richard Mortimer
Starring Alanis **V/T**

As one student wrote in a review of this program, *Borderline High* "is an informative, shocking docudrama
on high school dropouts" that left her "horrified."
Overall, this is an excellent production, with an
attractive, likeable teenage host and fast-paced treatment of a very important topic. This is one that
parents will have to point out to teenagers, but
teenagers will stay with it once they begin to watch.

286

Again from the teenage reviewer: "One of the most important reasons I liked *Borderline High* was because the statistics were so astonishing. I know that this will prevent me from becoming one of those statistics."

California Dreams
Warner (1992), 24-min. episodes
Director: Don Barnhardt **T**

A story of a young teenage music group trying to make it in California. This one is full of one-liners supported by a laugh track and hoots and hollers from an unseen audience. The cast is made up of cute kids from appropriate mixed races, with a plot of boys-versus-girls-really-want-boys-and-the-girls-are-smarter, plus trying to make it in the music field. Each episode has a moral about subjects such as honesty or cheating. Some good performances. Pretty harmless.

Chemical Solutions
Lauron Productions / Elan Productions / TVOntario (1990), 15 min. each
Director: Geoff Bowie **V/T**

The guidebook to this series, available from TV-Ontario, describes the series as "six . . . open-ended dramas that are intended to stimulate discussion about substance abuse among students in the senior grades." They will certainly do this, because they are for the most part well shot, well acted and intelligently directed. From a very realistic treatment of alcohol abuse by young people to a surrealistic drama, "Dark Comedy," a brilliant treatment of cocaine amongst the well-to-do, this series presents the issues simply, but does not preach. There's much to talk about, and parents would do well to use this as a jumping-off point to an understanding of substance abuse and, perhaps, to better communication with their children.

Cool World
Paramount Pictures (1992), 102 min.
Director: Ralph Bakshi
Starring Kim Bassinger, Gabriel Byrne
and Brad Pitt
Animation / live action   **V**

The opening song, "Play With Me," sets the almost soft-porn tone of this film that is definitely not for kids. Parents who look at the poster with their children outside movie houses, and are being pressured by their kids because of the TV advertising, be warned. It is not even a very good movie for adults. The only interesting aspect is Bakshi's combination of animation and live action.

Degrassi Talks
Playing With Time (1991), 24 min. each
Director: Kit Hood
Starring the young people of the
Degrassi Company   **V/T**

One of Canadian television's most creative efforts to address the needs of young people. The documentary format is not one that usually appeals to kids. However, Kit Hood and Linda Schuyler have put cameras and sound equipment into the hands of the kids of Degrassi, and have sent them out to talk to teenagers across Canada about the issues that matter in their lives and in the lives of all young people: substance abuse, safe sex, depression and so on. The interviews are sensitive but probing, and what constantly emerges is a moving portrait of young people talking to other young people. All of the programs are produced with class and dignity, and without sensa-

tionalism. Rarely have we seen television programs
that speak with such power and eloquence to young
people. This series is a must for adults to watch with
their children or on their own, in order to gain some
insight into the world of their teenage children.

Diary of a Teenage Smoker
Atlantis Films (1991), 25 min.
Director: Kai Skogland   **V/T**

Using a combination of dramatic and documentary
techniques in a dynamic, interesting way, and without
being preachy, this film encourages young women to
understand why they smoke, and why they shouldn't.
Worth the time of a young person who may be about
to take up smoking. Parents should know about it for
when this problem arises.

Ferris Bueller's Day Off
Paramount Home Video (1986), 103 min.
Director: John Hughes
Starring Matthew Broderick, Jefferey Jones,
Alan Ruck and Mia Sara   **V**

Every teen's fantasy, putting the big one over on the
parents and school. Ferris fakes an illness and takes
the day off school with two of his friends. The plot
hinges on the battle between Ferris and the Dean of
Students, and there are some mildly amusing adventures along the way. Good performances all round, but
as usual in this kind of film, the parents and teachers
are stock, completely two-dimensional characters,
who are completely flummoxed by the young people.
And all of them live in rich, sunny upper-class white
America.

Hamlet
Avcel Productions (1975), 40 min.   **V**

A live-action, much-truncated version of Shakespeare from the "Classic Books on Video" series. Dreadful and to be avoided at all costs. The acting is laughable and the production ludicrous. Gives credit for the use of someone's condominium for the setting, which gives you some idea of the production quality. The costumes are leftovers from someone's Hallowe'en party, and what little verse there is is badly spoken, often out of textual order and mixed with colloquial speech. A narrator tries to link the whole mess together and several times we are asked to stop the tape and answer questions printed on the screen. We assume this was meant to be some kind of student or educational exercise. Teenage viewers will be bored or driven to laughter, and young children will be completely confused. If you're going to introduce your family to "Hamlet," for the same price as this video you can get the 1948 Olivier version (also cut down, but beautifully played by a cast of classically trained English actors). Another alternative is the popular Mel Gibson/Glenn Close 1989 version.

The Hit List
YTV (1992), 48 min.
Director: Rick Watts
Starring Tarzan Dan   **T**

According to *Starweek*, Canada's Swingin'est DJ "rolls through the week's Top 30 hits, and rocks with the hottest videos and special guest stars." Tarzan Dan has a lot of radio pizzaz that he brings to the TV screen. Good style and lots of fun that works well for the audience at which this series is aimed — about age thirteen plus.

Jack and The Dentist's Daughter
Davenport Films (1984), 50 min.   **V**

An awful piece set in the Depression, with a white preacher, a white boss and black workers. All the clichés are here. The stuff of Amos 'n' Andy. Stay away.

Junior High Ethics
Access Alberta (1989), 15 min. each
Director: Darold Black   **V/T**

This six-part series, produced primarily for use in the classroom, is an upbeat collection of programs about everyday moral and ethical situations that young people, ten to fifteen years old, constantly face. Good rap numbers, an engaging cast of young actors and fast-moving scripts with interesting, sometimes funny, always incisive situations hold the young audience of this series. Topics range from "Winning and Losing" to an excellent two-part treatment of religion and values presented from a broad, multicultural perspective. A valuable, well-produced series for use either in school or at home.

A League of Their Own
Columbia Pictures (1992), 102 min.
Director: Penny Marshall
Starring Geena Davis, Madonna, Tom Hanks
and Lori Petty   **V**

A fine baseball movie for the whole family, this is a must especially for girls who love baseball. Excellent baseball action in a story of the development of the All-American Girls' Professional Baseball League, who briefly played major league baseball when all the boys went off to World War II. Fine acting by all, good direction and an interesting script make this an amusing, moving story that tells of the problems of women, but doesn't preach. Some problematic language.

Lethal Innocence
PBS American Playhouse (1991), 118 min.
Starring Blair Brown, Brenda Frick
and Theresa Wright   **T**

A marvellous story of courage and devotion based on
actual events. A family in Vermont adopts two Cam-
bodian refugee boys at the end of the Vietnam War,
and faces the problems and challenges of family relationships and political realities in the United States
and the Third World. Features superb production and
outstanding performances, especially by the children.
Some of the flashback scenes may be too violent for
very young viewers, so viewer discretion is advised,
but this is excellent family viewing for ten-year-olds
and up.

Maniac Mansion
Atlantis, YTV/Family Channel (1992), 25-min.
episodes
Director: Perry Rosemond
Starring Eugene Levy, Colin Fox   **T**

One episode, a parody of *The Princess Bride*, smacks
of inside jokes, a weak script and many double enten-
dres that just don't work. We question the reasons for
producing this series. As well, we question whether
the series will attract the audience that YTV and
Family seek. A disaster.

Melrose Place
Fox Television (1992), 60-min. episodes
Director: Howard Deutch
Starring Doug Savant, Grant Show, Andrew Shue,
Courtney Thorne-Smith and Vanessa Williams   **T**

Here are two reviews by grade twelve students that
say all that needs to be said:

"In my opinion, the network could have thought of a more interesting show to fill this time spot: perhaps 'How to Chew Gum in Ten Easy Steps' would have been a better idea with more substance."

"Congratulations, television! What was once impossible has now been achieved! I have just finished watching the longest commercial in history: 'Melrose Place.' The only problem is, what are they trying to sell? Perhaps the fabled lives of eight young, good-looking, mostly white (only one of them is black) people living in Hollywood. Despite all the heavy problems each one faces (poor babies!) there are still enough smiles and bikini shots to make me think this is a Miller ad."

Northwood
CBC/Soapbox Productions (1990), 24-min. each
Director: Neill Fearnley   **T**

From a trial run of six programs in early 1991, this series has developed an interesting style of its own in dealing with the lives of older teens, and some younger ones as well. One episode treats sixteen-year-old Karen, trying to kick hard drugs, another young woman coping with date rape, a serious couple, Jason and Maria, dealing with their ongoing relationship, and different aspects of the young lives of various others. We meet entire families in this series, and see the interaction between parents and children, and the effects of parental action on children. The direction is crisp. The feel is natural and intimate. We recommend this series to parents of older teens, as it offers a means of looking objectively at young people of this age.

The Orphan Train
Prism Entertainment (1979), 144 min.
Director: William A. Graham

Starring Glenn Close, Kevin Dobson
and Jill Eikenberry   **V**

We found this one in the children's section of a video
outlet, but it's definitely an adult, or at least older
teen movie with some very troubling material. It's
New York City in 1854, when over 10,000 abandoned
children were living on the streets of the city. Out of
this desperate situation was born the orphan train.
This is a fictionalized account based on historical
fact. But the opening scenes, in which poor children
trap rats to sell them to be killed by dogs in betting
houses (whichever dog kills the most rats wins), and
a scene in which a young man is hanged for assault-
ing a police officer, make this movie most definitely
not for children.

Press Gang
Richmond Films—UK (1991), 24-min. each
Director: Bob Spiers   **V**

This twelve-part series centres around an English secondary school and a mixed bag of teens who publish
the *Junior Gazette* by working on it before and after
school. The kids and teachers are rather stereotyped,
but much more interesting than the bunch in the
American *Saved by the Bell*. Interesting enough, but
the accents are very heavy and might be a problem.
Worth viewing an episode or two.

Pump Up the Volume
RCA / New Line Cinema (1990), 105 min.
Director: Alan Moyle
Starring Mark Hunter   **V**

The story of a shy teenager by day who becomes a
loquacious underground radio DJ, broadcasting from
his basement, by night. He enthralls his young listen-

ers with monologues on sex, love and rock and roll, and eventually exposes a corrupt school principal. Viewer discretion advised, as there is coarse language and delicate subject matter. But there are splendid performances and it's a teenage rebel movie that should be seen by parents.

A Question of Justice
TVOntario (1990), 30 min. each
Producer: Shelley Smith **V/T**

This series examines the basic components of the Canadian legal system through dramatizations and/or actual court cases. A young host interjects with questions for discussion, and students and lawyers comment on the cases presented.

The issues covered and the points discussed are of interest and importance to teenagers as well as to parents. One program deals with the arrest of a young woman accused of theft from her employer, and follows her through the experience of the trial and her frustrations in attempting to understand the justice system. Other topics treat break-and-enter and impaired driving charges, equality rights, children in divorce proceedings, and the Canadian Charter of Rights and Freedoms.

Road Movies
Why Not Productions / CBC (1992), 24-min. each
Hosted by Michelle Moffat **T**

This series of on-location items about Canada and Canadians is shot by young people. While it's a good idea, it doesn't work as prime time television. There is little focus, and a lot of very amateurish shooting, with the result being not too much of anything. The stories are often so fragmented that they are meaningless.

Saved by the Bell
Warner (1992), 24-min. episodes
Director: Don Barnhardt   **V**

High school situation comedy, set at Bayside High with
a studio audience and laugh track. Trivial problems
(getting parking spots, going to the fall prom, etc.)
abound. Atrocious acting and clichéd characters, especially the teachers. Several actors are too old for their
parts. Something less than an inspiring half-hour.

School's Out
Playing With Time (1991), 86 min.
Starring the Degrassi Street Company   **V/T**

A powerful, hard-hitting finale to the excellent
"Degrassi High." The story of the final summer of this
class is full of fun, pain, anger and everything that
goes to make up the life of a young person graduating
from high school. Joey and Caitlin break up. Tessa is
pregnant through her affair with Joey, and has an
abortion. Simon and Alexis have a fairy-tale teenage
wedding. Snake moves apart from his group of
buddies into a totally different world from them.
Wheels, who has taken to drinking too much, ends up
in jail after a car accident that kills a young child and
severely injures Lucy. All of this amidst the hubbub of
a teenage summer of work and parties at various
homes and cottages — lots of beer, some marijuana, a
lot of sex, but all in a credible and questioning context.
The direction is very strong, the script, by Yan Moore,
is the best in the series, and the visual texture is
superb. There's much to talk about and much of value
for young people.

Stand and Deliver
Warner Home Video (1988), 103 min.
Director: Ramon Menendez

Starring Edward James Olmos,
Lou Diamond Phillips and Andy Garcia   **V**

A true story of teacher Jaime Escalante, who took an
underachieving class in East Los Angeles (not even
expected to pass basic arithmetic) and cajoled, bullied
and inspired them into achieving record high scores in
the state's Advance Placement Calculus Exams. The
feat was so unexpected that the students were accused
of cheating and had to take the test again. This is an
extremely touching and inspiring film about a teacher
still working in East Los Angeles today. A film for
everyone with a math phobia and for every teacher
who needs inspiration.

streetNOISE
YTV (1989 –), 30 min. each
Director: Dave Beatty   **V/T**

A fine example of what television can do so well: fast
pace, quick cutting, creating montages of images.
Good questions, strong visuals and fine music all work
together to create an innovative, much-needed
program for teens about issues that concern teens.
The combination of items that are fun and funny with
others that are hard hitting — for example, one of the
strongest treatments of alcohol abuse we have seen —
make this an interesting series for the teen audience.
The style is not every adult's cup of tea, but this is a
street video for kids.

Tough To Be Young
Artray Productions / YTV (1991), 24-min. each
Director: Henry Irizawa   **T**

This series dramatizes real life therapy sessions with
teenagers and Dr. Don Dutton, in which real problems
of teenagers are presented. May serve as a catalyst for

dispassionate family discussions of problems of young
people. There is much courage in the dealing with difficult issues. Sometimes somewhat contrived, but well
worth a view. This is also a series that could be used
well in the classroom.

Where the Spirit Lives
Filmworks (1989), 120 min.
Director: Bruce Pittman
Starring Michelle St. John, Anne-Marie
MacDonald, Cynthia Debassige, Ron White,
David Hemblen   **V/T**

The time is 1937, the setting a small Indian village,
from which children are lured to be flown off to residential schools, where the rest of the story takes place.
For many years in Canada, young native children
were forcibly removed from their culture and homes
and incarcerated in so-called religious schools. The
tragic brutality and inhumanity of these schools is
clearly and powerfully delineated in this story of the
lives and, sometimes, deaths of young native children.
Although this is not a film for younger children, it is
a fine piece of art that belongs in the education of children ten years old and older. As well as a full-length
movie, it has also been produced as a six-part series,
available to schools through TVOntario. This is the
kind of material that should be on history, Native
Studies and Multicultural Studies courses.

The Witches
Lorimar Home Video (1990), 92 min.
Director: Nicolas Roeg
Starring Anjelica Huston, Rowan Atkinson,
Bill Paterson and Brenda Blethyn   **V**

On the night that nine-year-old Luke is chilled by his
grandmother's spooky tales of child-hating witches,

his parents are killed in a tragic car accident. Luke remains with his grandmother, who moves to England, and the pair live happily enough, until a vacation at a seaside resort coincides with an international witches' convention. Luke overhears a dastardly plot to turn every child in Britain into a mouse, is caught by the evil crones, and becomes one of their first victims. Nonetheless, he escapes as a mouse and uses his small size and quick wits to win the day. This Jim Henson production of Roald Dahl's tale of murderous magic features dazzling special effects. Care must be taken with this film, however. Some children can be quite frightened by the witches and the fact that they are so threatening to young children.

Acknowledgments

The authors wish to thank the following people for their generous and valuable assistance:

Children and teachers in schools
Etobicoke Board of Education: Brenda Ansara and the students of Bloordale Middle School; Gillian Al-Jbouri and the students of Islington Middle School; Barrie Duncan; students and teachers of Kipling C.I. North York Board of Education: Jane Campbell and the students of Fenside P.S.; Mark Kennedy and the students of Arbour Glen P.S.; Carina Van Heyst and the students of Dunlace P.S.; Lynda Pogue, Consultant; Nina Silver and the students of Emery Collegiate; Rick Shepherd, Consultant. Peel Board of Education: Sherrill Ledingham and the students of Sir John A. Macdonald Sr. P.S.; Barbara Cole and the students of Bramalea S.S. Halton Board of Education: Gerry Smith, Principal, River Oaks P.S. York Region Board of Education: Susan Gaby-Trotz, Margaret Lowe and the students of Pine Grove Public School.

Public libraries

Etobicoke Public Library: Cathy Richardson, Co-ordinator of Visual Services and the staffs of the Children's Departments of Richview and Brentwood Public Libraries. Toronto Public Library: Ted Karkut, Assistant Head, A.V. Department. York Region Public Library: The staff of the Kleinburg Public Library. Vancouver Public Library: Terri Clarke, Director of Youth Department, Vancouver P.L.

Video Stores

A very special thanks to Fiona Zippan and Douglas Atkinson at Kids' Video, Toronto; and the management and staffs of the following: Academy Movie Rentals, Toronto; Blockbuster Video, Woodbridge, Ont.; Budget Video, Weston, Ont.; All Star Video, Etobicoke, Ont.; Maple Video, Maple, Ont.; Rogers Video, Etobicoke, Ont.; Royal York Video, Etobicoke; Kleinburg Market Video Rentals; Moyer's, The Teachers' Store.

TV Networks, production houses and distributors

Family Channel: Barbara Baillie; Alison Clayton. YTV: Dale Taylor, Merv Stone and the staff of YTV. TVOntario: Barbara Martin, Lu Cormier, Rechilde Volpatti, Marion Bacon, Anita Pintulis, Ruth Vernon, Jeremy Pollock, Jed McKay, Antonia Reilly. Knowledge Network, B.C.: Caroline Young. Staffs of the Departments of Education of New Brunswick, Nova Scotia, Prince Edward Island, and Newfoundland. Access Alberta: Jean Campbell. Saskmedia, Saskatchewan: Bill Jones; Elizabeth Lowry; SaskEd: Delee Cameron. CBC: Angela Bruce. Also Cinar Productions, Montreal; Lauron Productions, Toronto; Magic Lantern, Oakville, Ont.; Atlantis Productions, Toronto; Playing With Time Productions, Toronto; Filmworks, Toronto; OWL Productions, Toronto; Rudy Inc. Productions, Toronto; Nelvana Productions Toronto.

And the following wonderful individuals: Clive Van-
derBurgh, Clive Endersby, Heather Conkie, Carolann
Reynolds (Challenge Media Productions, Inc.),
Andrew Cochran (Andrew Cochran Associates), Ted
Regan (Regan Productions), Linda Schuyler, Dr.
Arlette Lefebvre (Staff Psychiatrist, Hospital for Sick
Children), Peter Dalglish (Street Kids International),
Robert Roy, Alan Mirabelli, Kees Vanderheyden,
Margie Golick, Bob Leitch, Lorne Mitchell and Nancy
Reynolds.

And a special thanks to David Schatzky, former Executive Director of the Children's Broadcast Institute.
And to our editor, David Kilgour, for his most helpful,
incisive criticism.

Bibliography

Allen, R.C., editor. **Channels of Discourse: Television and Contemporary Criticism.** Chapel Hill, N.C.: University of North Carolina Press, 1987.

Arlen, Michael J. **Thirty Seconds.** Markham, Ontario: Penguin Books, 1988.

Berger, A.A., editor. **Television In Society.** New Brunswick, N.J.: Transaction, 1987.

Berger, J., et al. **Ways Of Seeing.** London: British Broadcasting Corporation, 1972.

Davies, Dr. Maire Messenger. **Television Is Good For Your Kids.** Highbury, London: Hilary Shipman Limited, 1989.

Ewen, S. **All Consuming Images: The Politics Of Style in Contemporary Culture.** New York: Basic Books, 1988.

Fiske, John. **Television Culture.** New York: Methuen, 1987.

Gitlin, Todd. **Inside Prime Time.** New York: Pantheon, 1985.

Gitlin, Todd, editor. **Watching Television.** New York: Pantheon, 1986.

Gunter, B., and J.L. McAleer. **Children And Television, The One Eyed Monster?** London and New York: Routledge, 1990.

Hodge, Bob, and David Tripp. **Children And Television.** Stanford, California: Stanford University Press, 1986.

Landsberg, Michele. **Michele Landsberg's Guide To Children's Books.** Toronto: Penguin Books, 1985.

Lesser, Gerald S. **Children And Television: Lessons From Sesame Street.** New York: Random House, 1974.

Liebert, R.M., and J. Sprafkin. **The Early Window: Effects Of Television On Children And Youth.** Toronto: Pergamon Press, 1988.

Livingstone, Sonia M. **Making Sense Of Television: The Psychology Of Audience Participation.** Toronto: Pergamon Press, 1990.

Luke, Carmen, **Television And Your Children: A Guide For Concerned Parents.** Toronto: Kagan and Woo, 1988.

Meyrowitz, Joshua. **No Sense Of Place: The Impact Of Electronic Media On Social Behaviour.** New York: Oxford University Press, 1985.

Miller, Mark Crispin. **Boxed In: The Culture of TV.** Evanston, Illinois: Northwestern University Press, 1988.

Moodie, Kate. **Growing Up On Television.** New York: Times Books, 1977.

Moog, C. **"Are They Selling Her Lips": Advertising And Identity.** New York: William Morrow, 1990.

Nelson, J. **The Perfect Machine: TV In The Nuclear Age.** Toronto: Between the Lines, 1987.

Nelson, J. **Sultans Of Sleeze: Public Relations And The Media.** Toronto: Between the Lines, 1989.

Palmer, Edward L. **Television And America's Children: A Crisis Of Neglect.** New York: Oxford University Press, 1988.

Postman, Neil. **The Disappearance Of Childhood.** New York: Dell, 1982.

Postman, Neil. **Amusing Ourselves To Death: Public Discourse In The Age Of Show Business.** New York: Viking, 1985.

Powers, Ron. **The Beast, The Eunuch, And The Glass-Eyed Child.** San Diego: Harcourt Brace Jovanovich, 1990.

Rainsberry, Fred B. **A History Of Children's Television In English Canada, 1952–1986.** Metuchen, N.J., and London: The Scarecrow Press, 1988.

Rapping, Elayne. **The Looking Glass World Of Non-Fiction Television.** Boston: South End Press, 1987.

Rogers, Fred, and Barry Head. **Mister Rogers Talks With Parents.** New York: Berkley Books, 1983.

Rutherford, Paul. **When Television Was Young: Prime-time Canada 1952–1967.** Toronto: University of Toronto Press, 1990.

Salutin, Rick. **Living In A Dark Age.** HarperCollins, Toronto, 1992.

Singer, Dorothy G., Jerome L. Singer and Diana M. Zuckerman. **The Parent's Guide: Using TV to Your Child's Advantage.** Reston, Va.: Acropolis Books, 1990.

Stewart, Sandy. **From Coast To Coast: A History Of Broadcasting In Canada.** Toronto: Gage, 1975.

Stewart, Sandy. **Here's Looking At Us: A Personal History Of Television In Canada.** Montreal: CBC Enterprises, 1986.

Settel, Irving, and William Laas. **A Pictorial History Of Television.** New York: Grosset & Dunlap, 1969.

Taylor, Ella. **Prime-Time Families: Television Culture In Post-War America.** Berkley: University of California Press, 1989.

Trelease, Jim. **The Read-Aloud Handbook.** Markham, Ontario: Penguin Books, 1982.

Winn, Marie. **Unplugging The Plug-In Drug.** Markham, Ontario: Penguin Books, 1987.

Wolfe, Morris. **Jolts: The TV Wasteland And The Canadian Oasis.** Toronto: James Lorimer, 1985.

Research Documents

Sharon, Donna: Project Co-ordinator. **Educational Television In English Language Schools In Ontario: Teacher Survey, 1989–1990.** Toronto: TVOntario, 1990.

Caron, Andre H., Sylvie C. Croteau and Elizabeth Van Every. **Children's Television In Canada And Europe: An Analysis Of Canadian Children's Programming And Preferences. Examples Of Children's Television Programming In Europe.** Montreal, Quebec: Centre for Youth and Media Studies, University of Montreal, 1991.

Periodicals

Adbusters Quarterly. The Journal of the Mental Environment.
Available by subscription from:
The Media Foundation
1243 West 7th Ave.
Vancouver, B.C.
V6H 1B7

Media & Values: A Quarterly Resource For Media Awareness.
"Children and Television: Growing Up in a Media World." Fall 1990/Winter 1991, Numbers 52 and 53.
Available by subscription from:
Centre for Media and Values
85 St. Clair Ave. East
Room 500
Toronto, Ontario M4T 1M8

Newsweek, Inc. "Special Edition: Education: A Consumer's Handbook." Fall/Winter 1990. New York: The Washington Post Company, 1990.

Index